Colloquial
Spanish of
Latin America

The Colloquial Series

Series adviser: Gary King

The following languages are available in the Colloquial series:

Albanian
Amharic
Arabic (Levantine)
Arabic of Egypt
Arabic of the Gulf and Saudi
   Arabia
Basque
Bulgarian
* Cambodian
* Cantonese
* Chinese
Croatian and Serbian
Czech
Danish
Dutch
Estonian
Finnish
French
German
Greek
Gujarati
Hindi
Hungarian
Indonesian
Italian
Japanese

Korean
Latvian
Lithuanian
Malay
Mongolian
Norwegian
Panjabi
Persian
Polish
Portuguese
Portuguese of Brazil
Romanian
* Russian
Slovak
Slovene
Somali
* Spanish
Spanish of Latin America
Swedish
* Thai
Turkish
Ukrainian
* Vietnamese
* Welsh

Accompanying cassette(s) (* and CDs) are available for the above titles. They can be ordered separately through your bookseller or send payment with order to Routledge Ltd, ITPS, Cheriton House, North Way, Andover, Hants SP10 5BE, or to Routledge Inc., 29 West 35th Street, New York, NY 10001, USA.

COLLOQUIAL CD-ROMs
Multimedia Language Courses

Available in: Chinese, French, Portuguese and Spanish
Forthcoming: German

Colloquial
Spanish of
Latin
America

Roberto Rodríguez-Saona

Lecturer in Spanish, Trinity and All Saints
College of the University of Leeds

London and New York

First published 1994
by Routledge
11 New Fetter Lane, London EC4P 4EE

Simultaneously published in the USA and Canada
by Routledge
29 West 35th Street, New York, NY 10001

Reprinted 1995, 1996, 1998 (twice), 1999, 2000

Routledge is an imprint of the Taylor & Francis Group

© 1994 Roberto Rodríguez-Saona

Typeset in Times Ten by Florencetype Ltd, Kewstoke, Avon
Printed and bound in Great Britain by
Clays Ltd, St Ives plc

British Library Cataloguing in Publication Data
A catalogue record for this book is available from the British
Library

Library of Congress Cataloguing in Publication Data
A catalog record for this book is available from the Library of
Congress

ISBN 0–415–08952–2 (book)
ISBN 0–415–08953–0 (cassettes)
ISBN 0–415–08954–9 (book and cassettes course)

To Hazel and Emma

Contents

Introduction

Spanish in Latin America developed independently of, but at the same time in parallel to, that in Spain. There are lexical and some grammatical differences between the two main varieties of the language, but they share the same basic structure. Within Latin America regional accents have developed due to a number of factors, which include the influence of the language of Southern Spain and the Canaries, the language of the indigenous people of Latin America, African languages brought by the slaves and in recent times, American English. However, by acquiring the basic functions, notions and grammar of Spanish the learner should be able to communicate effectively in situations likely to be encountered as a visitor to one of the Spanish-speaking countries of Latin America. The aim of this book is to help you achieve this level of fluency.

This book is intended for learners with little or no knowledge of Spanish. The language in the book includes the kind of Spanish used in everyday life by native speakers in Latin America, especially in oral communication. In some Language Points sections an explanation is given regarding the use of an alternative form in Peninsular Spanish, i.e. that used in Spain. In the glossary at the back of the book you will find additional words with different uses in Latin America and in Spain.

In each chapter – with the exception of the last one, which is a revision chapter – the language presented to the learner is focused on some specific functions, notions and grammar points. These concepts are explained in the Language Points section which usually appears after a dialogue. At the beginning of each chapter you will find a list of the main objectives expected to be achieved by the learner. The book deals with a number of situations in which you are likely to use Spanish, e.g. using the phone, booking a hotel room, eating in a restaurant, routine at work, etc. There are also a number of functions that will be learned in each chapter, e.g.

greeting people, apologizing, telling the time, expressing likes and dislikes, describing objects, and others.

The Language Points are illustrated in examples that follow each explanation. It is essential to read these examples carefully before proceeding to the exercises. It is advisable that you write all answers to the exercises in a notebook to keep a systematic record of your progress.

There is a variety of exercises; some require completion of a sentence with a word, others involve rewriting sentences in different words, changing the word order or matching questions with answers, etc. With the exception of open exercises, i.e. those in which there is more than one possible answer, you will find answers to the exercises at the end of the book. It is advisable to consult these answers only after you have provided your own.

The glossary at the end of the book lists, in alphabetical order, all the vocabulary introduced throughout the chapters. In some cases it provides a comparison between current terminology in Latin America which is different from that used in everyday Peninsular Spanish.

The Grammar section at the end of the book gives a brief description of the main points of the Spanish language. It is not intended to be a comprehensive grammar but a quick, essential reference section.

The recorded material for this book is optional, but you are advised to have access to it in order to improve your listening and understanding skills.

The author would like to thank Katia Valdeos Ardiles, Carolina Alegre Bellasai, Lena Gazey, Juliet Wood, Penny Levene and Genista Horsley for their help in the preparation of this book.

Pronunciation

The following section on pronunciation is intended as a guide, comparing the sounds of Spanish to the closest equivalent in English. You would also find it useful to listen to the recorded material which accompanies this book.

Vowels

Vowels in Spanish are clearer than in English, and all are considered of the same quality, that is, they are pronounced whether they are stressed or unstressed. There are five vowels in Spanish:

a	similar to the **a** in 'father', but shorter	**casa**
e	similar to the first **e** in 'elephant'	**elegir**
i	similar to the **i** in 'clean', but shorter	**mirar**
o	similar to the **o** in 'cot', but shorter	**moto**
u	similar to the **oo** in 'boot'	**cuna**

Consonants

b	similar to the English **b** but less explosive	**baño, ambos**
c	preceding **e** or **i** it is pronounced like the s in 'simple'	**ceder, hacer**
	preceding **a**, **o** or **u**, it is pronounced like the **c** in 'cat'	**carga, coro**
ch	like the **ch** in 'chair'	**chico, rancho**
d	in initial position it is pronounced like the English **d** but not aspirated. The tip of the tongue is placed lower than in the production of the English **d**. When it is not in initial position it is practically imperceptible to English speakers	**dar, cada**
f	like the English **f**	**feria, garrafa**
g	preceding **a**, **o**, **u**, like the **g** in 'god'	**ganar, gol**
	preceding **e** or **i**, like the **h** in 'hen'	**general, ágil**
h	silent	**hacer, ahora** — now
j	like the **h** in 'hen'	boss — **jefe, caja** — box-wicket
k	like the English **k**	**kilo, káiser**
l	like the **l** in 'live'	**libro, papel** — paper
ll	like the **y** in 'young', but a bit stronger; in Argentina and Uruguay it is pronounced like the **s** in the English word 'vision'	**llamar, pollo** — chicken
m	like the English **m**, but with the lips not firmly closed when it is not in initial position	sea **mar, América**
n	like the English **n**	nothing **nada, pena** pity
ñ	like the **n** in 'onion'	**caña, niño**
p	like the English **p** but not aspirated	**papa, tapa**
q	like the unaspirated English **k**; found only in the groups **que** and **qui** in a word	**quince, porque** — because
r	more rolled than in English; in initial position it is trilled twice	**rosa, ramo**
	between vowels it is rolled once	**coro, pero** — but

rr	strongly trilled	**carro, perro**
s	like the **s** in 'sample'	**santa, suero**
t	less aspirated than in English; the tip of the tongue is placed against the back of the upper front teeth	**tomar, gato**
v	the same as the sound **b** described above	**vaca, cueva**
w	like the English **w**; only found in a few words of foreign origin	**whisky, Walter**
x	softer than the English **x**	**éxito, sexto**
y	the same as the sound **ll** described above	**mayo, yo**
z	the same as the sound **s** described above	**zona, zapato**

1 Saludos

Greetings

By the end of this chapter you should be able to:

- Use some greetings
- Use numbers up to 100
- Make simple enquiries
- Use personal pronouns (I, you, etc.)
- Use some verbs in the present tense indicative
  (e.g. I live in Mexico)

En la agencia de viajes ▫▫

Miguel is trying to find out the travel agent's fax number over the phone. He talks to a member of the staff called Cecilia

CECILIA: Aló, buenos días. Agencia de Viajes El Sol.
MIGUEL: Buenos días, señorita. ¿Tienen fax?
CECILIA: Sí, señor.
MIGUEL: ¿Qué número es?
CECILIA: Es el dos, noventa y dos, treinta y cinco, setenta y seis, noventa y ocho (292–357698).
MIGUEL: Gracias.
CECILIA: De nada.

CECILIA: *Hello, good morning. El Sol Travel Agent.*
MIGUEL: *Good morning. Do you have a fax?*
CECILIA: *Yes, sir.*
MIGUEL: *What's the number, please?*
CECILIA: *It's 292–357698.*
MIGUEL: *Thank you.*
CECILIA: *That's all right.*

Language points

Números de teléfono 🔳

When reading aloud telephone or fax numbers it is usual in Spanish to say them in pairs: e.g. 356791, **treinta y cinco**, **sesenta y siete**, **noventa y uno**; 031–705466, **cero**, **treinta y uno**, **setenta**, **cincuenta y cuatro**, **sesenta y seis**.

Por favor

The use of **por favor** 'please' in requests is not as common in Spanish as it is in English.

De nada/No hay de qué / A usted

When somebody thanks you, apart from the usual response **De nada**, you can use the expression **No hay de qué**, although it sounds slightly more formal. Both mean 'You're welcome'.

Números 🔳

As in English, a number precedes the noun it refers to:

dos boletos	two tickets
diez alumnos	ten students

Uno becomes **un** before a masculine noun and **una** before a feminine noun (see Chapter 3 for information on masculine and feminine nouns):

un diccionario	one dictionary
una lección	one lesson

0 cero

1	**uno**	11	**once**
2	**dos**	12	**doce**
3	**tres**	13	**trece**
4	**cuatro**	14	**catorce**
5	**cinco**	15	**quince**

6	seis	16	**dieciseis**
7	**siete**	17	**diecisiete**
8	**ocho**	18	**dieciocho**
9	**nueve**	19	**diecinueve**
10	**diez**	20	**veinte**

¡Más números!

Note: in Spanish, an exclamation mark is used at the beginning as well as at the end of a sentence. The same rule applies to question marks.

21	**veintiuno**	60	**sesenta**
22	**veintidos**	63	**sesenta y tres**
25	**veinticinco**	70	**setenta**
30	**treinta**	77	**setenta y siete**
36	**treinta y seis**	80	**ochenta**
40	**cuarenta**	88	**ochenta y ocho**
49	**cuarenta y nueve**	90	**noventa**
50	**cincuenta**	91	**noventa y uno**
52	**cincuenta y dos**	100	**cien**

101 ciento uno
1000 ~~A~~ mil

Exercise 1

Arrange these numbers in order of value and write next to the word or phrase the corresponding figure.

(a) **cien**
(b) **noventa y tres**
(c) **uno**
(d) **treinta y cuatro**
(e) **trece**
(f) **veintisiete**
(g) **quince**
(h) **doce**
(i) **noventa y cuatro**
(j) **siete**
(k) **sesenta y dos**
(l) **setenta y nueve**

Exercise 2

Write the Spanish word for the answer to these operations.

(a) $16 + 9 =$
(b) $17 \times 4 =$
(c) $91 - 15 =$
(d) $39 \div 3 =$
(e) $27 + 17 =$

Exercise 3

These are the dates of birth of some people. How old are they?
Write the Spanish words for the answers. (Note: **años** = years.)

Carlos	27/07/80	_____	**años**
Luisa	19/03/77	_____	**años**
Milagros	02/12/45	_____	**años**
Carolina	25/05/73	_____	**años**
Esteban	28/07/02	_____	**años**

Language points

Saludos

These are the phrases most frequently used to greet somebody:

Hola	Hello
Buenos días	Good morning
Buenas tardes	Good afternoon
Buenas noches	Good evening; Good night

During the evening/night **Buenas noches** is used to say 'Hello' or
'Goodbye'.

Sometimes in informal spoken language to greet somebody,
Buenas replaces the phrases **Buenos días, Buenas tardes, Buenas
noches**.

Despedidas

Saying goodbye

Chao/Chau	Goodbye (informal)
Adiós	Goodbye (more formal)
Hasta luego	See you later (slightly formal)
Nos vemos	See you (informal)

In Latin America the most common way of saying goodbye is **chao**
or **chau**, while in Spain it is **adiós**.

Exercise 4

Write in your notebook what you would say to greet somebody in Spanish at these times:

(a) 9.00 a.m.   (d) 10.00 p.m.
(b) 1.00 p.m.   (e) 11.30 a.m.
(c) 6.00 p.m.

Language points

The infinitive

The infinitive is the form of a verb given in a dictionary. It is also the form that you will find in the glossary at the back of this book. According to the ending of the infinitive there are three types of verbs in Spanish:

verbs ending in -ar	also called verbs of the first conjugation
verbs ending in -er	also called verbs of the second conjugation
verbs ending in -ir	also called verbs of the third conjugation

Examples:

-ar	comprar	to buy
	trabajar	to work
	estudiar	to study
-er	comer	to eat
	vender	to sell
	comprender	to understand
-ir	vivir	to live
	escribir	to write
	subir	to go up

The present tense indicative

The present tense indicative is used with actions which are habitual or timeless.

Examples:

habitual

Siempre voy en tren.	I always go by train.
Teresa no trabaja los sábados.	Teresa does not work on Saturdays.

timeless

Mi gato come mucho queso.	My cat eats a lot of cheese.
Martha es peruana.	Martha is Peruvian.

Subject pronouns

Usually, it is not necessary to use the words for 'I', 'you', 'he', etc. to indicate who performs the action. For example, **tengo** means 'I have'. You do not need to include **yo** 'I'.

Pronouns may be used to emphasize the subject of a verb or to avoid ambiguity. For example:

Yo trabajo en Lima, María no.	I work in Lima, María doesn't.

There are two ways of addressing a second person in Spanish.
Tú for friends, relations, people of the same age group as you, your classmates. **Usted** for people you do not know, somebody you have just met, somebody much older than you, your superior. **Usted** is abbreviated as **Ud**. In the plural **ustedes**, abbreviated as **Uds.**, is used for both formal and informal situations.

yo	I	**nosotros**	we
tú	you (informal)	**ustedes**	you (formal and informal)
usted	you (formal)	**ellos**	they (masculine)
él	he	**ellas**	they (feminine)
ella	she		

Unlike Peninsular Spanish, Latin American Spanish does not use the **vosotros** form of a verb for the informal second person plural. Compare these sentences:

Vosotros trabajáis en Guatemala. (Spain)	You (pl.) work in Guatemala.
Ustedes trabajan en Guatemala. (Latin America)	

¿Habéis visto a Juan? (Spain)   Have you seen Juan?
¿Han visto a Juan? (Latin America)

¿A qué hora os vais? (Spain)   What time do you leave?
¿A qué hora se van? (Latin America)

Regular verbs

Most Spanish verbs are regular. They follow a certain pattern or rule when changing their endings, depending on which person performs the action. Here are three examples of regular verbs: **trabajar**, **comer** and **escribir**.

trabajo	I work
trabajas	you work (informal)
trabaja	you work (formal); he/she works
trabajamos	we work
trabajan	you work (formal and informal)
trabajan	they work
como	I eat
comes	you eat (informal)
come	you eat (formal); he/she eats
comemos	we eat
comen	you eat (formal and informal)
comen	they eat
escribo	I write
escribes	you write (informal)
escribe	you write (formal); he/she writes
escribimos	we write
escriben	you write (formal and informal)
escriben	they write

Irregular verbs

Some verbs do not follow the pattern or rule of regular verbs. For that reason they are called *irregular*. Here is one example: **tener**.

tengo	I have
tienes	you have (informal)
tiene	you have (formal); he/she/it has
tenemos	we have
tienen	you have
tienen	they have

See Chapter 2 for more irregular verbs.

Forming questions

Both regular and irregular verbs form questions by adding question marks to affirmative and negative statements. When speaking you sound as if you are asking a question. Unlike English, you do not need an auxiliary word like 'do'.

Trabajan mucho.	They work hard.
¿Trabajan mucho?	Do they work hard?
No tienes tiempo.	You don't have time.
¿No tienes tiempo?	Don't you have time?

As in English, questions can begin with a question word (who, what, etc.) as shown below:

qué (what)	**¿Qué tienes ahí?**	What have you got there?
quién (who)	**¿Quién tiene uno?**	Who has one?
cuál (which)	**¿Cuál tienes?**	Which one have you got?
cómo (how)	**¿Cómo es?**	What is it like?
cuándo (when)	**¿Cuándo es?**	When is it?
dónde (where)	**¿Dónde está?**	Where is it?

cuánto (how much)

Exercise 5

Give the Spanish equivalent for these expressions:

1 Arturo has a car.
2 Lupe works in Mexico.
3 The travel agency has a fax.
4 Do you work?

Exercise 6

Complete the sentences with the correct form of **tener**.

1 **Yo _____ el asiento 7D y María _____ el 7C.**
2 **(Nosotros) _____ problemas en el hotel.**
3 **¿Ustedes _____ un periódico?**
4 **La impresora no _____ papel.**
5 **Silvia y Luisa _____ clase.**

asiento	seat
impresora	printer
papel	paper
clase	lesson, class

¿Cambia dólares? 🔘🔘

While reading the dialogue below, see if you can find answers to these questions:

> How much money does Amalia want to change?
> Does she have traveler's checks to change?

AMALIA:	Buenas tardes.
JAVIER:	Buenas tardes. ¿Qué desea?
AMALIA:	¿Cambia dólares?
JAVIER:	Sí, señora. ¿Billetes o cheques de viajero?
AMALIA:	Billetes.
JAVIER:	¿Cuántos dólares?
AMALIA:	Doscientos cuarenta.
JAVIER:	Un momento, por favor. Acá tiene. Doscientos cuarenta dólares en moneda nacional.
AMALIA:	Gracias.
JAVIER:	A usted.

AMALIA:	*Good afternoon.*
JAVIER:	*Good afternoon. Can I help you?*
AMALIA:	*Do you change dollars?*
JAVIER:	*Yes, madam. Notes or traveler's checks?*
AMALIA:	*Notes.*
JAVIER:	*How many dollars?*
AMALIA:	*Two hundred and forty.*
JAVIER:	*One moment, please. Here you are. Two hundred and forty dollars in local currency.*

AMALIA: *Thanks.*
JAVIER: *Thank you.*

Language points

¿Qué desea?

The polite expression **¿Qué desea?** 'Can I help you?' is usually used by assistants in shops to greet you as a potential customer.

¿Cuánto?/¿Cuántos?

To find out amounts you use **¿cuánto?** 'how much' and **¿cuántos?** 'how many' – masculine – or **¿cuánta?** and **¿cuántas?** – feminine.

¿Cúanta plata tienes?	How much money do you have?
¿Cuántos empleados trabajan acá?	How many employees work here?

Addressing people

Señor is the usual polite expression to address a man, **joven** if it is a young man, **señora** for a lady and **señorita** for a young lady. In the case of children, **niño** is for a boy and **niña** for a girl.

Acá tiene/Aquí tiene

Acá tiene/Aquí tiene 'Here you are' is an expression said when you hand over something to another person, e.g. money to the taxi driver, passport to the immigration officer, etc. **Acá tienes/Aquí tienes** is used when addressing somebody informally.

Reading 🔲

While reading the passage below, see if you can find answers to these questions:

Is Spanish the only language in Latin America?
Are any indigenous languages spoken?

Idiomas de Latinoamérica

La mayoría de la población de Latinoamérica habla castellano. En Brasil hablan portugués y en algunos países del Caribe, inglés o francés. Los indígenas del Perú y Bolivia hablan quechua y aymara.

idiomas	languages	**quechua**	indigenous language spoken in the Andes
mayoría	majority		
población	population		
habla	speaks	**aymara**	indigenous language spoken in Peru and Bolivia
castellano	Spanish		
portugués	Portuguese		
inglés	English		
francés	French		
indígenas	indigenous people		

2 Salgo a las seis

I leave at six

By the end of this chapter you should be able to:

- Use some irregular verbs in the present tense
- Identify and use colors
- Use numbers over 100
- Ask and give information about times
- Make negative statements using **no**

¿A qué hora sales?

MARINA: ¿A qué hora sales?
GABRIEL: Salgo a las seis. A esa hora podemos discutir el plan para mañana.
MARINA: Muy bien. Yo vengo a la cafetería de abajo a las seis y cuarto.
GABRIEL: Muy bien. Hasta más tarde.

MARINA: *What time do you leave?*
GABRIEL: *I leave at six. Then we can discuss our plan for tomorrow.*
MARINA: *Fine. I'll come to the cafe downstairs at a quarter past six.*
GABRIEL: *Fine. See you later.*

Language points

The Present tense indicative of irregular verbs

Apart from the verb **tener** studied in Chapter 1, there are other irregular verbs. The irregularity of these verbs is sometimes only in the first person singular (the 'I' form), sometimes in several forms. The following are the most commonly used irregular verbs in the present tense.

decir to say

digo	**decimos**
dices	**dicen**
dice	**dicen**

Example:

Rosario dice la verdad. Rosario tells the truth.

hacer to do, to make

hago	**hacemos**
haces	**hacen**
hace	**hacen**

Examples:

¿Qué haces los sábados? What do you do on Saturdays?
Quiero hacer una torta. I want to make a cake.

ir to go

voy	**vamos**
vas	**van**
va	**van**

Example:

¿Vas al colegio? Do you go to school?

salir to leave, to go out

salgo	**salimos**
sales	**salen**
sale	**salen**

Example:

Salgo de casa a las seis. I leave home at six.

venir to come

vengo	**venimos**
vienes	**vienen**
viene	**vienen**

Example:

¿A qué hora viene Eduardo? What time is Eduardo coming?

Negative statements

The particle **no** is always used before a verb to make a negative statement:

Gabriela no trabaja.　　　Gabriela doesn't work.
Hugo no habla inglés.　　Hugo doesn't speak English.

Exercise 1

Complete the sentences below with the correct present indicative form of the verb in brackets.

1 **Delia (venir) temprano al trabajo.** *early*
2 **¿A qué hora sales de la reunión?**
　(Yo) (salir) a las siete.
3 **Víctor no (ir) a clases de noche.**
4 **Oscar no (hacer) sus tareas.** *homework*
5 **Nosotros (decir) lo mismo.** *same*

Language points

¿Qué hora es?

¿Qué hora es? is the question to ask the time. Sometimes the plural version **¿Qué horas son?** is used, especially in spoken Spanish in Latin America. In Spain, only **¿Qué hora es?** is used.

las doce

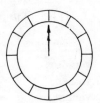

la una

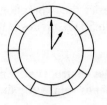

las cuatro y media

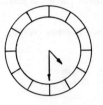

las tres y cuarto

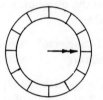

las ocho y veinte

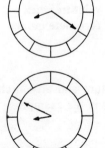

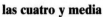
για
diez para las nueve

un cuarto para las doce

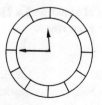

Note: in Latin America the expression **para** is used to indicate minutes 'to the hour'. In Spain, **menos** is used.

Examples:

> **Son veinte para las cuatro.** (Lat. Am.)   It's twenty to four.
> **Son las cuatro menos veinte.** (Spain)

> **La cita es a un cuarto para las once.**   The appointment is at a
> (Lat. Am.)   quarter to eleven.
> **La cita es a las once menos cuarto.** (Spain)

¿A qué hora? ⬛

¿A qué hora . . . ? is the question you ask to find out at what time something takes place.

> **¿A qué hora es el concierto?**   At what time is the concert?
> **¿A qué hora terminas?**   At what time do you finish?

As in British English, Spanish speakers sometimes use the 24-hour clock for departures and arrivals of trains, flights, etc.

12.05	**las doce cero cinco**
17.52	**las diecisiete cincuenta y dos**
23.10	**las veintitrés diez**
07.15	**las cero siete quince**

Exercise 2

Look at the departure and arrival chart below and then ask and answer questions as in the example.

Example:

> **¿A qué hora sale el avión a Miami?**
> **Sale a las once.**
> **¿A qué hora llega el avión de La Habana?**
> **Llega a las quince cero cinco.**

Salidas		Llegadas	
Miami	11.00	La Habana	15.05
Caracas	13.45	Madrid	11.45
Lima	09.20	Santiago	11.50
Quito	06.00	México D.F.	10.20

sale	it leaves	**salida**	departure
llega	it arrives	**llegada**	arrival

En la tienda 📼

While reading the dialogue below, see if you can find answers to these questions:

Does Pablo ask for a particular color of shirt?
Does he buy the shirt?

Pablo sees a shirt he likes in a shop in Lima.

PABLO: Buenas tardes, ¿tiene esta camisa para caballero en talla 15?
EMPLEADA: Sí, tengo en blanco, azul, verde o marrón.
PABLO: ¿Cuánto cuesta?
EMPLEADA: 35 soles.
PABLO: ¡Muy cara!
EMPLEADA: Pero . . . muy fina.

PABLO: *Good afternoon, have you got this shirt in size 15?*
ASSISTANT: *Yes, I have it in white, blue, green or brown.*
PABLO: *How much is it?*
ASSISTANT: *35 soles.*
PABLO: *That's very expensive!*
ASSISTANT: *But . . . it is very good quality.*

Language points

¿Cuánto cuesta?

¿Cuánto cuesta? is used to find out the price of an item. If it is more than one item, you use **¿Cuánto cuestan?**

¿Cuánto cuestan las blusas?   How much are the blouses?

¿Cuánto es? is the expression used to find out how much it all adds up to at the end.

Muy

Muy is used to intensify the meaning of the adjective which follows. Here are some examples:

muy inteligente	very intelligent
muy interesante	very interesting
muy bonita/o	very nice
muy barata/o	very cheap

Colores 〔◯◯〕

blanco	white	**verde**	green
negro	black	**amarillo**	yellow
rojo	red	**marrón**	brown
azul	blue		

Examples:

blusa blanca	white blouse
auto verde	green car

Exercise 3

The following products are reduced. What is their new selling price? Give the answers in full, in Spanish.

artículo	precio normal	descuento	precio de venta
Camisas	40.00	10%	
Blusas	35.00	20%	
Abrigos	99.00	5%	
Pañuelos	6.00	10%	
Pantalones	48.00	20%	
Camisetas	12.00	10%	

(handwritten margin notes: shirt, coat, hankerchief, Pants, T-shirt)

Exercise 4 〔◯◯〕

Arrange the following words in three groups under the headings **Hombres** (items usually only for men), **Mujeres** (items usually only for women) and **Ambos** (items worn by either sex).

camisa	**suéter/chompa**
zapatos	**blusa**
corbata	**calzoncillo**
medias	**pañuelo**
vestido	**aretes**
falda	**lápiz labial**

Hay un problema 📼

While reading the dialogue below, see if you can find answers to these questions:

Is the problem something to do with the room itself?
Can the problem be solved at once?

Mr Carter explains to the receptionist at the hotel where he is staying that something is not working

SR CARTER: Disculpe. Hay un problema. El televisor no funciona.
RECEPCIONISTA: ¿Qué número de habitación?
SR CARTER: Cuarenta y uno.
RECEPCIONISTA: Bien. Vamos.
(*They go in the room, and the receptionist tests the TV.*)
Un momento, por favor.
(*He leaves the room and comes back after a few minutes with another TV set.*)
Acá tiene. Otro televisor.
SR CARTER: A ver . . . ¡Funciona! Gracias.
RECEPCIONISTA: De nada.

MR CARTER: *Excuse me. There is a problem. The TV doesn't work.*
RECEPTIONIST: *Which room number is it?*
MR CARTER: *Forty-one.*
RECEPTIONIST: *Right. Let's go.*
One moment, please.
Here you are. Another TV set.
MR CARTER: *Let me see. It works! Thank you.*
RECEPTIONIST: *You're welcome.*

Language points

Disculpe

Disculpe 'Excuse me' is one way of catching other people's attention (formal). There is also the form **disculpa** (informal).

Hay

Hay indicates existence or presence. The same word is used in singular or plural, in question or statement.

| hay | there is | ¿hay? | is there? |
| hay | there are | ¿hay? | are there? |

Examples:

Hay un problema en el hotel. There is a problem at the hotel.
¿Hay clases de castellano? Are there Spanish lessons?

No funciona

To explain that something is not working, you use the expression **no funciona**. In the dialogue above, the television doesn't work. Here are more examples:

El teléfono no funciona. The phone is not working.
La máquina no funciona. The machine does not work.
*El computador no funciona. The computer is not working.

* To refer to a computer some Latin American countries use the feminine noun **computadora**, e.g. Peru, and others prefer the masculine **computador**, e.g. Mexico.

Exercise 5

You cannot say **no funciona** when something goes wrong for all things listed below. But for some, you can. Which ones?

1 **la máquina de escribir** ✓
2 **el pasaporte** ✗
3 **la motocicleta** ✓

4 **el carro** ✓
5 **el diccionario** ✗

Language point

¡Y más números! 📼

200	**doscientos**	2,000	**dos mil**
300	**trescientos**	10,000	**diez mil**
400	**cuatrocientos**	50,000	**cincuenta mil**
500	**quinientos**	100,000	**cien mil**
600	**seiscientos**	500,000	**quinientos mil**
700	**setecientos**	1,000,000	**un millón**
800	**ochocientos**		
900	**novecientos**		
1,000	**mil**		

Exercise 6

You have to pay a bill for 2,425 soles. You are paying by cheque. Rewrite the cheque in your notebook including the amount in words.

```
┌─────────────────────────────────────────────────┐
│   BANCO COMERCIAL      . . . . . . . . . . . . .  │
│                                                   │
│  Páguese a _____ │
│  la suma de ___dos mil, cuatrocientos_____ │
│  _____vienticinco soles,_____ │
│                                                   │
│                              . . . . . . . .      │
│                                  Firma            │
└─────────────────────────────────────────────────┘
```

páguese a	payable to	**firma**	signature
la suma	the amount, the sum	**fecha**	date

Reading 🔊

While reading the passage below, see if you can find answers to these questions:

Where does Carmen want to travel?
Does she buy a ticket?

En la Agencia de Viajes

Carmen tiene un carro amarillo muy bonito. El carro cuesta veintiocho mil quinientos (28,500) soles. Carmen visita la agencia de viajes El Sol. El viaje a Canadá cuesta mucho y ella no tiene suficiente dinero. ¡Qué pena!

carro	car	**dinero**	money
viaje	trip	**qué pena**	what a pity
suficiente	enough		

3 Reserva en el hotel

Reserving a hotel room

By the end of this chapter you should be able to:

- Reserve a room at a hotel
- Ask and give information about dates
- Write a short letter
- Use definite and indefinite articles
- Introduce yourself

Reservando una habitación 🔲

While reading the dialogue below, see if you can find answers to these questions:

When is Mr Carter starting his stay at the hotel?
How many nights will he be staying?

RECEPCIONISTA:	¡Aló! Buenas tardes. Hotel Excelsior.
SR CARTER:	Buenas tardes. ¿Tiene una habitación libre a partir de mañana?
RECEPCIONISTA:	¿Individual o doble?
SR CARTER:	Individual.
RECEPCIONISTA:	¿Para cuántas noches?
SR CARTER:	Para cinco noches.
RECEPCIONISTA:	Un momento, por favor.
	Aló. Sí, tenemos una habitación individual libre. 90 dólares por noche.
SR CARTER:	Está bien. Mi nombre es Carter.
RECEPCIONISTA:	Bueno, Sr. Carter. Hasta mañana.
SR CARTER:	Hasta mañana.

RECEPTIONIST:	*Hello. Good afternoon. Hotel Excelsior.*

MR CARTER:	*Good afternoon. Do you have a room available from tomorrow?*
RECEPTIONIST:	*Single or double?*
MR CARTER:	*Single.*
RECEPTIONIST:	*How many nights?*
MR CARTER:	*Five nights.*
RECEPTIONIST:	*Just one moment, please.*
	Hello. Yes, we have one single room free. It is 90 dollars per night.
MR CARTER:	*That's all right. My name is Carter.*
RECEPTIONIST:	*Right, Mr Carter. See you tomorrow.*
MR CARTER:	*See you tomorrow.*

Language points

Aló

When somebody answers the phone, the usual expression is **Aló**. It is also used when you want to resume a conversation after a brief pause. In Mexico, **Bueno** is used instead.

Me llamo . . .

Me llamo . . . 'I am called . . .' is one way of telling somebody else what your name is.

> **Me llamo Esteban.**
> **Me llamo Juan García.**

Another way to introduce yourself is to use **Mi nombre es**, followed by your name.

> **Mi nombre es Guillermo.**
> **Mi nombre es Jorge Castañeda.**

¿Cómo te llamas?

You say **¿Cómo te llamas?** to ask somebody else what his or her name is, addressing that person informally. **¿Cómo se llama?** or **¿Cómo se llama usted?** is the formal question.

Another way of asking a name is **¿Cuál es tu nombre?** (informal) or **¿Cuál es su nombre?** (formal).

Masculine and feminine nouns

Spanish nouns are either masculine or feminine. Usually nouns ending in -**o** are masculine and those ending in -**a** are feminine. This rule is for guidance only, since there are exceptions. It is advisable to try to learn the gender as you learn the noun. The glossary at the end of the book will help you.

Examples:

libro (m.)	book
vuelo (m.)	flight
revista (f.)	magazine
impresora (f.)	printer
estudiante (m. & f.)	student
papel (m.)	paper

The definite article

El/la

The words **el** and **la** correspond to the English 'the'. The definite article **el** is used before masculine singular nouns and the definite article **la** is used before feminine singular nouns:

el colegio	the school
la niña	the girl

The majority of nouns ending in -**nte** keep the same form for masculine and feminine.

el estudiante	the student (m.)
la estudiante	the student (f.)

Nouns ending in a consonant are usually masculine.

el actor	the actor
el campeón	the champion

Los/las

The definite article **los** is used before masculine plural nouns and the definite article **las** is used before feminine plural nouns. There has to be agreement between article and noun in both gender and number.

los colegios	the schools
los libros	the books
las mañanas	the mornings
las motocicletas	the motorcycles

Exercise 1

Which definite article should be before these nouns?

1	**documentos**	6	**profesor**
2	**casa**	7	**bailarina**
3	**carro**	8	**representante**
4	**alumnos**	9	**amigos**
5	**adolescente**	10	**papel**

The indefinite article

The words **un** and **una** correspond to the English 'a/an'. **Un** is used before a masculine noun and **una** is used before a feminine noun.

un libro	a book
una pregunta	a question
un animal	an animal

In English the indefinite article appears in a sentence before a noun indicating profession or occupation. In Spanish this is not the case.

Elena es secretaria.	Elena is a secretary.
Jorge es arquitecto.	Jorge is an architect.

Exercise 2

Match the symbol with the word or words:

1 **céntrico** (a)

2 **estacionamiento** (b)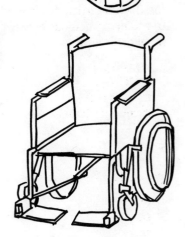

3 **acceso para minusválidos** (c)

4 **servicio médico** (d)

5 **televisión en la habitación** (e)

6 **aire acondicionado**   (f)

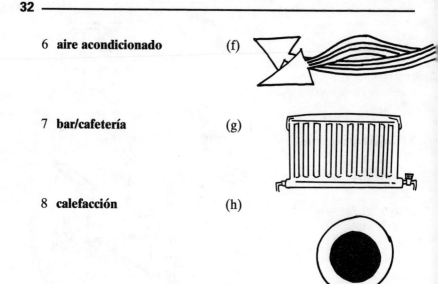

7 **bar/cafetería**   (g)

8 **calefacción**   (h)

Exercise 3

Write down the facilities mentioned in the previous exercise in order of priority when you choose a hotel.

In your opinion,

What is most important for a disabled person?
What is most important for a business person?
What is most important for a family on holiday?

Exercise 4

You want to reserve a room in a hotel. You like quiet places. At the moment it is very hot in the city you are going to. You sort out your travel money in advance and you like to have all your meals in nice little cafés and local restaurants. Which of the following facilities are advantages (**ventajas**) and which are disadvantages (**desventajas**) in your case? Write them down in two separate lists.

céntrico
piscina
calefacción central
aire acondicionado
caja fuerte individual

desayuno incluido
cambio de moneda
restaurante
teléfono en la habitación

Language points

Días de la semana ●●

Days of the week

domingo	Sunday	**jueves**	Thursday
lunes	Monday	**viernes**	Friday
martes	Tuesday	**sábado**	Saturday
miércoles	Wednesday		

In Spanish it is not necessary to write the days of the week beginning with a capital letter, except at the start of a sentence.

El sábado llega mi hermana. My sister arrives on Saturday.
Domingos: de 10 a 5. Sundays: from 10 to 5.

Exercise 5

Explain what you plan to do each day based on the page of a diary below. (The abbreviated form of each day in Spanish is given in brackets.)

Example:

¿Qué piensas hacer el lunes?
Mis planes para el lunes ... comprar los boletos de avión y comprar una maleta nueva.

Lunes	(Lun)	**Comprar los boletos de avión**
		Comprar una maleta nueva
Martes	(Mar)	**Leer la guía turística**
Miércoles	(Mié)	**Buscar información**
Jueves	(Jue)	**Estudiar el informe**
Viernes	(Vie)	**Preparar documentos**
		Hacer las maletas

Sábado	(Sáb)	Llegar al aeropuerto a las 2.30
		Comprar una novela
Domingo	(Dom)	Descansar

comprar	to buy	informe	report
boleto de avión	flight ticket	preparar	to prepare
maleta	suitcase	llegar	to arrive
nuevo, nueva	new	novela	novel
guía turística	tourist guide	descansar	to rest
buscar	to look for		

¡Hasta mañana!

Hasta, meaning 'until', is used to form expressions of farewell like the following:

Hasta mañana	Until/See you tomorrow
Hasta el sábado	Until/See you Saturday
Hasta la próxima clase	Until/See you next lesson
Hasta luego	Until/See you later

Exercise 6

How could you say goodbye using **hasta** in the following circumstances?

1 Your next lesson is on Monday.
2 You will see this person this coming Saturday.
3 You will meet again on Sunday.
4 You will see each other on Tuesday.
5 Your next meeting is tomorrow.

Meses del año

Months of the year

enero	julio
febrero	agosto
marzo	septiembre
abril	octubre
mayo	noviembre
junio	diciembre

Exercise 7

Say and write in Spanish the date of the following events.

Example:

New Year's Eve   **31 de diciembre**

1 Christmas
2 Your birthday
3 New Year
4 Today
5 Your mother's birthday

Exercise 8

Answer these questions about the fax below.

1 What type of room does Mrs Stewart want?
2 Which day of the week will she leave the hotel?

TELEFAX

Dirigido a: Sr. A. Sánchez   Fax No 010 xx 14 298765
            HOTEL EXCELSIOR

Estimado señor:
Le ruego reservar una habitación individual con baño para 5 noches a partir del domingo próximo.

Atentamente

Helen Stewart

---

le ruego	would you please	**próximo**	next
a partir de	as from	**dirigido a**	for the attention of

Language points

Starting a letter

In Spanish, a colon appears after the salutation in written corre-
spondence. In English a comma is used. Here are some examples:

Estimada señora:	Dear Madam,	(formal, no name used)
Querido Esteban:	Dear Esteban,	(informal, first name used)
Distinguido señor:	Dear Sir,	(formal, no name used)
Querido señor Milla:	Dear Mr Milla,	(formal, followed by surname)

Ending a letter

A straightforward way of finishing a formal letter in Spanish is by
using one of the following expressions:

Muy atentamente	Yours faithfully
Le saluda atentamente	Yours sincerely

If it is a more informal letter, it can be finished with:

Saludos	Regards
Con cariño	Love

Exercise 9

Write a fax to reserve a room at Hotel Embajador. You want a
double room for three nights from next Saturday, with bathroom
and telephone in the room. The person in charge is Sra Urrutia.

Reading

Ecuador

While reading the passage below, see if you can find answers to
these questions:

What type of terrain predominates in Ecuador?
Which racial groups are in the majority in Ecuador?

La mitad del territorio de Ecuador es zona de selva. Una tercera parte es zona de montañas y el resto lo forman la costa y las Islas Galápagos. Los mestizos y los indígenas forman el ochenta por ciento de la población (40% cada grupo) y los blancos y negros forman el otro veinte por ciento. La capital es Quito y otra ciudad muy importante es Guayaquil. Quito está a unos tres mil metros de altura. Guayaquil es un puerto.

mitad	half	**población**	population
selva	jungle	**otro**	other, another
el resto	the rest	**ciudad**	city
mestizos	mixed-race people	**puerto**	port

4 ¿Dónde está?

Where is it?

By the end of this chapter you should be able to:

- Enquire about location
- Describe people and objects
- Talk about nationality
- Use the verbs **ser** and **estar** (to be)

Rentar un carro

While reading the dialogue below, see if you can find answers to these questions:

Does Karen find the car she wants?
Does she want the car for that same day?

Karen Stewart wants to rent a car.

ANA: ¿En qué puedo servirle?
KAREN: Quisiera rentar un carro.
ANA: Aquí tiene la lista de modelos.
KAREN: ¿Hay un Citroen libre para mañana?
ANA: Citroen no hay, pero tenemos un Renault.
KAREN: ¿Es económico?
ANA: Sí, es económico y cómodo.
KAREN: Muy bien. ¿A qué hora mañana?
ANA: A partir de las siete y media de la mañana.

ANA: *How can I help you?*
KAREN: *I would like to hire a car.*
ANA: *Here you are. The list of models.*
KAREN: *Is there a Citroen free for tomorrow?*

ANA: *There isn't a Citroen, but we have a Renault.*
KAREN: *Is it economical?*
ANA: *Yes, it's economical and comfortable.*
KAREN: *Fine. At what time tomorrow?*
ANA: *From half past seven in the morning.*

Exercise 1

¿Cómo es tu carro?

Describe your car (or the car you would like to have, if you do not have one at the moment) choosing features from the list below. Start your answer like this:

Mi carro es ...

potente	**cómodo**	**chico**
deportivo	**incómodo**	**antiguo**
ecológico	**grande**	**económico**
nuevo	**mediano**	

potente	powerful	**grande**	large
deportivo	sporty	**mediano**	medium
ecológico	ecological, 'green'	**chico**	small
cómodo	comfortable	**antiguo**	old
incómodo	uncomfortable	**económico**	economical

Congreso empresarial 🔊

Three people attending a business conference introduce themselves to each other at the bar during a break

HELEN: Me llamo Helen Stewart. Soy consultora de negocios. ¿Es usted consultor, también?
PETER: No, soy representante de ventas. Mi nombre es Peter Harris.
LUPE: Yo me llamo Lupe Arenas. Soy agente de viajes.

HELEN: *I'm Helen Stewart. I'm a business consultant. Are you a consultant as well?*
PETER: *No. I'm a sales representative. My name is Peter Harris.*
LUPE: *I'm Lupe Arenas. I'm a travel agent.*

Language point

Ser

One equivalent of 'to be' is **ser**. The other, **estar**, is explained later on in this chapter. The difference between the two is not easily learned by an English speaker.

Ser is used to explain the nature of people or objects and also to identify them.

Ramón es respetuoso.	Ramón is respectful.
¿Eres socialista?	Are you a socialist?
Bogotá es la capital de Colombia.	Bogotá is the capital of Colombia.
Es un libro de castellano.	It is a Spanish book.

To describe your occupation or profession you use **soy**, as in **soy consultora** 'I am a consultant', **soy representante** 'I am a representative'.

To describe somebody else's occupation or profession you say **es**, as in **Lorena es profesora** 'Lorena is a teacher'. For the second person (formal) you also use **es**, as in **¿Es usted consultor?** 'Are you a consultant?'.

In the case of the second person (informal) you use **eres**. For example: **¿Eres turista?** 'Are you a tourist?', **Eres estudiante. Yo también** 'You are a student. Me, too'.

These are all the forms:

soy	I am
eres	you are (informal)
es	You are (formal), he/she/it is
somos	we are
son	you are (formal and informal)
son	they are

Exercise 2

Match the unfinished sentence with the correct word in the column on the right.

1 **Edward Kennedy es** _____   (a) **lago**
2 **Gabriel García Márquez es** _____   (b) **capital**

3 **Managua es una** _____   (c) **río**
4 **El Amazonas es un** _____   (d) **escritor**
5 **El Titicaca es un** _____   (e) **político**

Soy mexicano

In the following short dialogue three people talk about their nationalities

PERSONA 1: Soy inglesa. ¿Usted es inglés también?
PERSONA 2: No, soy mexicano. Mi padre es inglés.
PERSONA 3: Yo soy nicaragüense.

PERSON 1: _I am English. Are you English too?_
PERSON 2: _No, I am Mexican. My father is English._
PERSON 3: _I am Nicaraguan._

Language point
Nationality

Soy, es, eres can be used to describe nationality for people. **Es** can be used for things as well. For example:

Pablo es panameño.	Pablo is Panamanian.
Todos somos latinoamericanos.	We are all Latin Americans.
El ron es cubano.	The rum is Cuban.
El producto es canadiense.	The product is Canadian.

Some more examples in the plural:

Marta y yo somos estadounidenses.	Marta and I are Americans.
Manuel y Esteban son salvadoreños.	Manuel and Esteban are Salvadorians.
Los carros son europeos.	The cars are European.
Ustedes son estudiantes.	You are students.

Exercise 3

Complete the sentences with the correct form of the verb **ser**.

Examples:

(Nosotros) ____ **estudiantes**
Somos estudiantes.

Mario _____ inteligente
Mario es inteligente.

1 **(Yo)** _____ **profesor.**
2 **Elena y Sara** _____ **amigas.**
3 **(Nosotros)** _____ **colombianos.**
4 **Caracas** _____ **la capital de Venezuela.**
5 **El Espectador y El Comercio** _____ **periódicos.**

Exercise 4

Can you match each country and its nationality?

1	**Perú**	(a)	**canadiense**
2	**México**	(b)	**salvadoreño**
3	**Brasil**	(c)	**hondureño**
4	**El Salvador**	(d)	**inglés**
5	**Guatemala**	(e)	**argentino**
6	**Jamaica**	(f)	**peruano**
7	**Inglaterra**	(g)	**guatemalteco**
8	**Puerto Rico**	(h)	**chileno**
9	**Argentina**	(i)	**jamaiquino**
10	**Honduras**	(j)	**puertorriqueño**
11	**Estados Unidos**	(k)	**brasileño**
12	**Panamá**	(l)	**mexicano**
13	**Chile**	(m)	**paraguayo**
14	**Paraguay**	(n)	**estadounidense**
15	**Canadá**	(o)	**panameño**

¿Dónde está el carro?

Mr Carter goes to pick up the car he has hired

SR CARTER: Buenos días. Soy el Sr Carter y . . .
JULIÁN: Ah, sí. Es un Renault, ¿verdad?
SR CARTER: Sí. ¿Dónde se recoge el carro?
JULIÁN: Enfrente, en el garaje. Acá tiene las llaves.
(*Mr Carter asks Paulina, the attendant, at the garage*)
SR CARTER: Disculpe, ¿dónde está el Renault?
PAULINA: El Renault está allá a la derecha.
SR CARTER: Gracias.
PAULINA: De nada.

MR CARTER:	*Good morning. I am Mr Carter and . . .*
JULIÁN:	*Ah, yes. It's a Renault, isn't it?*
MR CARTER:	*Yes. Where do you pick up the car?*
JULIÁN:	*Opposite, at the garage. Here you are. The keys.*
MR CARTER:	*Excuse me, where is the Renault?*
PAULINA:	*The Renault is over there on the right.*
MR CARTER:	*Thank you.*
PAULINA:	*You're welcome.*

Language point

Estar

Estar also means 'to be' (see **ser**, earlier in this chapter, for the other use of 'to be'). **Estar** is used to describe location or a temporary state.

Examples of description of a state with **estar**:

Está enfermo.	He is ill.
Estoy triste.	I am sad.
Estamos seguros de eso.	We are sure about that.

Examples indicating location with **estar**:

El carro está a la derecha.	The car is on the right.
Guadalajara está en México.	Guadalajara is in Mexico.
Atlanta está en los Estados Unidos.	Atlanta is in the United States.
El hotel está en el centro.	The hotel is in the center of town.

Exercise 5

Complete the sentences with the correct form of **ser** or **estar**.

1 **El restaurante _____ en la calle principal.**
2 **_____ estudiante (yo).**
3 **María _____ molesta.**
4 **_____ en la casa de mi hermana (nosotros).**
5 **Estela y Lucrecia _____ pintoras.**
6 **Guadalajara _____ en México.**
7 **El autor del libro _____ peruano.**
8 **El banco _____ cerca.**
9 **_____ vendedores (Nosotros).**
10 **No _____ en su casa (ella).**

Prepositions of place

en

al lado de

enfrente de

sobre

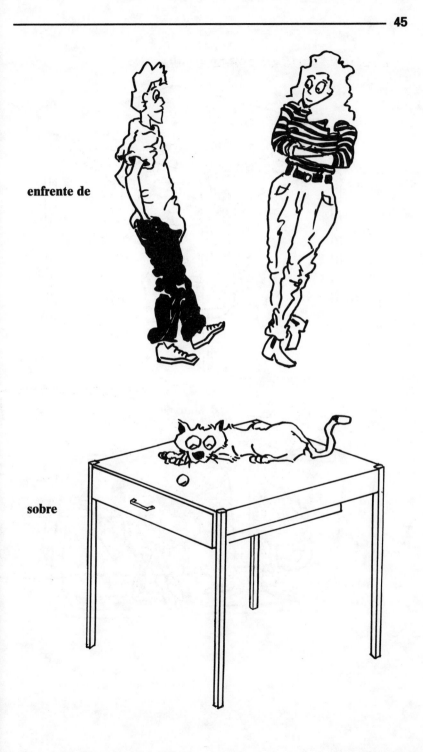

abajo de/debajo de

delante de

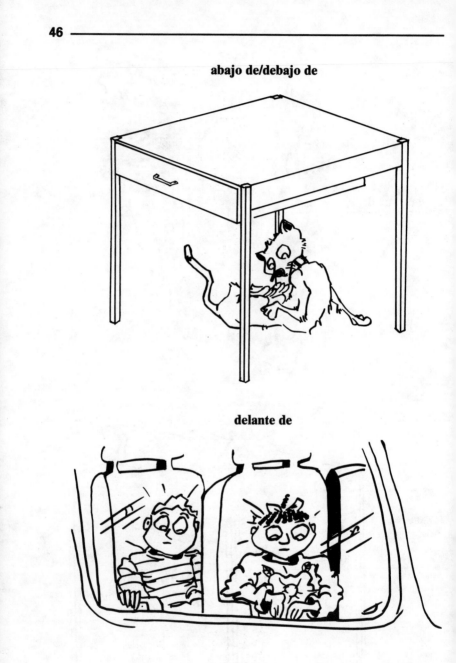

atrás de/detrás de

entre

Exercise 6

A LA IZQUIERDA
←

A LA DERECHA
→

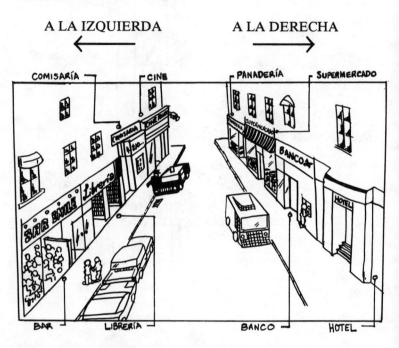

(a) Ask and/or answer questions based on the street plan above.

Example:

> **¿Dónde está el bar?**
> **El bar está a la izquierda.**

Continue: **¿Dónde está el hotel?**, etc.

(b) Look again at the street plan and ask and/or answer questions, as in the following example.

> **¿Dónde está el bar?**
> **El bar está a la izquierda, enfrente del hotel.**

Now continue asking and/or answering questions about the hotel, supermarket, etc.

(c) Look once again at the street plan and ask and/or answer questions, as in the following example:

> **¿Dónde está el bar?**
> **El bar está a la izquierda, enfrente del hotel, al lado de la librería.**

Juan está *enfrente de* **Luis**

Juan está *al lado de* **Lucía.**

Continue asking and answering questions about the hotel, super-market, etc., giving as much information as possible.

Exercise 7

Complete the sentence on the left with one (or more) expression(s) from the column on the right.

1 **Viajar es** _____	(a) **agradable(s)**
2 **La comida latinoamericana es** _____	(b) **interesante(s)**
3 **La Ciudad de México es** _____	(c) **variada(s)**
4 **Comer fruta es** _____	(d) **saludable(s)**
5 **Los animales domésticos son** _____	(e) **grande(s)**
6 **La política es** _____	(f) **complicado (/a)(s)**
7 **Las reuniones de negocios son** _____	(g) **necesario (/a)(s)**
8 **Los problemas ecológicos son** _____	(h) **urgente(s)**

Language point

Pero

As in English, **pero** ('but') is used to contrast two ideas or state-ments without contradicting the first one.

Hablo francés, pero sólo un poco.	I speak French, but only a little.
No tengo auto, pero no me importa.	I haven't got a car, but I don't mind.

Note: For more on **pero**, see Chapter 19.

Reading

Costa Rica

Costa Rica es uno de los países latinoamericanos con menos población. Cuenta con unos tres millones de habitantes. El ochenta por ciento de los habitantes de Costa Rica son de raza blanca y el diecisiete por ciento son mestizos. El resto son de raza negra e indígena. San José es su capital. En su zona metropolitana se encuentra medio millón de habitantes. Costa Rica es un país que no tiene ejército. Es un país exportador de café.

raza	race
ejército	army
indígena	indigenous

Exercise 8

Based on the passage above, say if the following statements are **verdadero** (true) or **falso** (false).

1 **Costa Rica no tiene ejército.**
2 **La mayoría de la población es de raza mestiza.**
3 **Es uno de los países más poblados.**
4 **El café es un producto importante para su economía.**
5 **San José es su capital.**

5 El clima y los viajes

Weather and travel

By the end of this chapter you should be able to:

- Comment about the weather
- Talk about transport
- Express frequency
- Refer to the parts of the day

¿Como está el clima? 📼

While reading the dialogue below, see if you can find answers to these questions:

Is it a sunny place?
Does it rain much?

Mr Carter is talking to one of the local women in the resort where he is spending his holiday

SR CARTER:	¿Hace calor aquí?
SRA LOPEZ:	Generalmente sí, pero la temperatura es agradable.
SR CARTER:	¿Cuál es la temperatura media?
SRA LOPEZ:	En enero es de 28 grados centígrados.
SR CARTER:	¿Y hace mucho sol?
SRA LOPEZ:	Sí, normalmente ocho horas diarias.
SR CARTER:	¿Llueve también?
SRA LOPEZ:	Muy poco.

MR CARTER:	*Is it hot here?*
SRA LOPEZ:	*Usually it is, but the average temperature is pleasant.*
MR CARTER:	*What is the average temperature?*
SRA LOPEZ:	*In January it is 28 degrees centigrade.*

MR CARTER: *And is it very sunny?*
SRA LOPEZ: *Yes, usually the sun shines eight hours a day.*
MR CARTER: *Does it rain too?*
SRA LOPEZ: *Very little.*

Language points

Hace

The word **hace** is used to form some expressions which refer to the weather. (For another use of **hace** see Chapter 12.)

hace calor   it's hot

hace frío it's cold

hace viento
it's windy

hace sol   it's sunny

The four expressions above can be used to describe the usual climatic conditions, e.g. **En enero hace calor en Lima** (January is hot in Lima.), or to refer to what the weather is like at the time of speaking, e.g. **Hoy no hace sol** (It's not sunny today.).

In the following cases a different expression is needed:

está lloviendo	it's raining
llueve	it rains
está nevando	it's snowing
nieva	it snows

Poco/mucho

When you use **poco** and **mucho** as adjectives, they agree in number and gender with the noun they refer to.

Hay pocos estudiantes.	There are few students.
Llueve poco en enero.	It doesn't rain much in January.
Tengo poca información.	I have little information.
No hay muchas mujeres en este grupo.	There aren't many women in this group.
Hace mucho calor	It is very hot
Tiene mucha suerte.	He is very lucky.

Expressions of frequency

generalmente	generally
normalmente	normally

Examples:

Normalmente salimos a las siete.	Normally we leave at seven.
Generalmente hace calor en diciembre.	Generally it is hot in December.

siempre	always
nunca	never

Examples:

Siempre vamos al mercado los sábados.	We always go to the market on Saturdays.
Nunca viajamos al extranjero.	We never travel abroad.

a veces	sometimes

muchas veces *many times*

Examples:

A veces vamos al cine.	Sometimes we go to the cinema.
A veces juego fútbol.	Sometimes I play football.

Daily, weekly, etc.

These expressions have the same meaning in English, but some are used as an adjective – to indicate the characteristic of a noun - or as an adverb – to indicate the manner in which it is done.

diario (/a)	daily	**diariamente**
semanal	weekly	**semanalmente**
mensual	monthly	**mensualmente**
trimestral	quarterly	**trimestralmente**
semestral	six-monthly	**semestralmente**
anual	yearly	**anualmente**

Es una publicación diaria.	It is a daily publication.
Se publica diariamente.	It is published daily.
Es una visita semanal al club.	It is a weekly visit to the club.

Voy al club semanalmente.	I go to the club weekly.
Este es un pago mensual.	This is a monthly payment.
Escribo a esos amigos mensualmente.	I write to those friends monthly.

Exercise 1

Classify the following activities according to their frequency in your life, e.g. **diario**, **mensual**, etc.

1 **desayuno**
2 **vacaciones**
3 **cuenta del teléfono**
4 **sueldo**
5 **compras en el supermercado**

desayuno	breakfast
vacaciones	holiday
cuenta del teléfono	telephone bill
sueldo	salary
compras	shopping
supermercado	supermarket

Cada

It is also possible to form expressions of frequency using the word **cada**:

cada día	each day
cada semana	each week
cada mes	each month
cada tres meses	every three months
cada año	every year

Vez/veces

These words are used to form expressions of frequency such as 'once', 'twice', etc.

una vez	once
dos veces	twice
tres veces	three times
a veces	sometimes

Por

The word **por** can also express frequency:

Desayuno en el tren dos veces por semana.	I have breakfast on the train twice a week.
Limpian las ventanas dos veces por mes.	The windows are cleaned twice a month.

Exercise 2

Complete the phrases with a suitable expression of frequency.

1 **Limpio el carro** _____
2 **Escucho la radio** _____
3 **Compro leche** _____
4 **Voy a Latinoamérica** _____
5 **Voy de vacaciones** _____

Exercise 3

Complete the phrases with something that you do with the frequency suggested.

1 _____ **una vez por semana.**
2 _____ **anualmente.**
3 _____ **a veces.**
4 _____ **diariamente.**
5 _____ **cada domingo.**

Exercise 4

Answer the following survey:

In your own town or city, what happens to the weather in January?

1	**Hace calor**	sí	no	poco	mucho	a veces
2	**Hace frío**	sí	no	poco	mucho	a veces
3	**Hace viento**	sí	no	poco	mucho	a veces
4	**Llueve**	sí	no	poco	mucho	a veces
5	**Nieva**	sí	no	poco	mucho	a veces
6	**Hace sol**	sí	no	poco	mucho	a veces

A Cancún 📼

Sr Ruiz wants to make a reservation to fly to Cancún in Mexico the next morning. Unfortunately that flight is full

Sr Ruiz:	Quisiera reservar un pasaje para Cancún.
Empleada:	¿En qué vuelo?
Sr Ruiz:	Mañana por la mañana.
Empleada:	Por la mañana está completo, pero hay espacio en el vuelo de la tarde, a las 14:20.
Sr Ruiz:	Muy bien. Por la tarde.
Empleada:	¿Fumador o no fumador?
Sr Ruiz:	No fumador.
Empleada:	¿Pasillo o ventanilla?
Sr. Ruiz:	Ventanilla.

Mr Ruiz:	*I would like to book a seat to Cancún.*
Assistant:	*When is it for?*
Mr Ruiz:	*Tomorrow morning.*
Assistant:	*The one in the morning is full, but there is room on the 14:20 afternoon flight.*
Mr Ruiz:	*That's fine. In the afternoon then.*
Assistant:	*Smoking or no smoking?*
Mr Ruiz:	*No smoking.*
Assistant:	*Aisle or window?*
Mr Ruiz:	*Window.*

Language point

Quisiera 📼

Quisiera is used to express what you would like. It is usually followed by a verb in the infinitive.

Quisiera hablar con el Sr Fuentes.	I would like to talk to Mr Fuentes.
¿Quisiera hablar con él en privado?	Would you like to talk to him in private?
Quisiera un boleto para el vuelo de las diez.	I would like a ticket for the ten o'clock flight.
Quisiéramos una habitación doble.	We would like a double room.

Here are all the forms:

quisiera	**quisiéramos**
quisieras	**quisieran**
quisiera	**quisieran**

Exercise 5

Give Spanish equivalents for the following:

1 I would like to buy a newspaper.
2 We would like to visit the museum.
3 We would like two single rooms.
4 I would like a new book.
5 I would like to go to Uruguay.

Language point

Parts of the day

To explain which part of the day you refer to, these expressions are used:

por la mañana/en la mañana	in the morning
por la tarde/en la tarde	in the afternoon
por la noche/en la noche	in the evening/at night
al mediodía	at noon
a la medianoche	at midnight
en la madrugada	in the early hours

Note: in Latin America **por** and **en** are used with parts of the day. In Spain usually **por** is the only form used.

Exercise 6

Write the expression indicating the part of the day for each of these times:
(a) 10.00 a.m.
(b) 2.30 a.m.
(c) 7.45 p.m.
(d) 2.30 p.m.
(e) 11.15 p.m.

Exercise 7

Write out things that are usually done in the morning, in the afternoon and in the evening/at night. Write the usual time when most people do it or when you do it. Below there are some suggestions of activities.

Example:

POR LA MAÑANA
desayunar: 7.30 a.m.

POR LA TARDE
almorzar: 1.30 p.m.

POR LA MAÑANA	POR LA TARDE	POR LA NOCHE
————	————	————
————	————	————
————	————	————

tomar un café	to have a coffee	**ver televisión**	to watch television
pasear	to go for a walk	**escuchar música**	to listen to music
comprar el	to buy the	**volver a casa**	to return home
periódico	newspaper	**almorzar**	to have lunch
ir a trabajar	to go to work		

Viajar en el metro 🔲

Miguel wants to go to Emilio's house in Mexico City later the same day. Emilio suggests the Metro (subway) as the quickest way to get there

MIGUEL: ¿Dónde está tu casa, entonces?
EMILIO: Está en Panteones. Acá tienes la dirección exacta.
MIGUEL: ¿Cómo voy hasta allá?
EMILIO: Lo mejor es ir en Metro. La estación Revolución está cerca de aquí. Tomas la línea a Cuatro Caminos y te bajas en Panteones.
MIGUEL: ¿Es caro?
EMILIO: No, es barato y rápido.

MIGUEL: *Where is your house, then?*
EMILIO: *It's in Panteones. Here is the exact address.*
MIGUEL: *How do I get there?*

EMILIO: *The best way is by subway. The Revolución station is nearby. You get on the Cuatro Caminos line and get off at Panteones.*

MIGUEL: *Is it expensive?*

EMILIO: *No, it's cheap and fast.*

Language point

¿Cómo?

This is the question word used to ask the way you do things.

¿Cómo voy hasta allá?	How do I get there?
¿Cómo funciona esta máquina?	How does this machine work?

In informal speech, **¿Cómo?** is also the expression used when you do not hear what somebody has just said and you want that person to repeat the message.

A: **Mario está en casa.**
B: **¿Cómo?**
A: **Digo que Mario está en casa.**
B: **Ah, sí. Está enfermo.**

A: Mario is at home.
B: Pardon?
A: I'm saying that Mario is at home.
B: Oh, yes. He's ill.

Exercise 8

Match the word in the left column with its opposite on the right.

1	**cerca**	(a) **subir**
2	**acá**	(b) **barato**
3	**caro**	(c) **rápido**
4	**lento**	(d) **lejos**
5	**bajar**	(e) **allá**

Reading ▣

México

México es el país más poblado de habla castellana. Su población llega a más de 80 millones. Su capital, la ciudad de México, tiene casi 20 millones de habitantes. Otras dos ciudades importantes son Guadalajara y Monterrey.

México es el principal productor de plata del mundo. Es también un importante exportador de petróleo. Entre los productos agrícolas que ofrecen beneficios para el país están el algodón, la caña de azúcar, el café, el cacao y el garbanzo. El turismo es también una importante fuente de divisas.

poblado	populated	**algodón**	cotton
de habla	Spanish-	**cacao**	cacao
castellana	speaking	**garbanzo**	chickpea
plata	silver	**fuente de divisas**	source of foreign exchange

Exercise 9

Based on the paragraph above, say if the following statements are **verdadero** (true) or **falso** (false).

1 **México es el país con más población de habla castellana.**
2 **Monterrey no es una ciudad de México.**
3 **México no exporta petróleo.**
4 **El comercio de algodón y caña de azúcar ofrece beneficios al país.**
5 **El turismo no aporta beneficios económicos.**

6 De compras

Shopping

By the end of this chapter you should be able to:

- Make comparisons using adjectives
- Express possibility or impossibility
- Express likes and dislikes
- Use radical changing verbs

Comprando regalos

Martha works in a gift shop. A customer wants to buy a present and is comparing two ornaments

CLIENTE:	¿Cuánto cuesta ese adorno?
MARTHA:	Doscientos cuarenta el grande y ciento noventa el más pequeño.
CLIENTE:	¿Puedo ver el grande un momento?
MARTHA:	Por supuesto. Puede ver los dos.
CLIENTE:	Los dos son lindos, pero prefiero el grande. ¿Acepta tarjetas de crédito?
MARTHA:	Sí, aceptamos todas las principales tarjetas de crédito.

CUSTOMER:	*How much is that ornament?*
MARTHA:	*Two hundred and forty for the big one and one hundred and ninety for the smaller one.*
CUSTOMER:	*Can I have a look at the big one for a moment?*
MARTHA:	*Of course. You can have a look at both of them.*
CUSTOMER:	*Both are pretty, but I prefer the big one. Do you take credit cards?*
MARTHA:	*Yes, we accept all major credit cards.*

Language points

El grande/el chico

The big one/the small one

To avoid the repetition of a noun or noun phrase it is possible to use only the article + the adjective. In these cases in English you would use the adjective + 'one', as in 'the small one'.

¿Le gusta el plato grande o el chico?	Do you like the big plate or the small one?
A: **Tengo una camiseta roja y una azul.**	A: I have a red T shirt and a blue one.
B: **La roja, por favor.**	B: The red one, please.
¿Qué modelo busca, el liviano o el pesado?	Which model are you looking for, the light one or the heavy one?

Lindo

The word **lindo/linda** is very much used in Latin American Spanish to mean 'pretty, nice, beautiful'. In Peninsular Spanish **bonito/bonita** is preferred.

Tu hija es muy linda.	Your daughter is very pretty.
¡Qué linda casa!	What a beautiful house!

Radical changing verbs

These are verbs in Spanish which undergo a change of the stem vowel (i.e. the vowel in the part of the verb that remains the same when it is conjugated) when you conjugate them. In these verbs the vowel -**e**- in the stem becomes -**ie**-, and the vowel -**o**- becomes -**ue**-. The exception is the first person plural.

-e- → -ie-

preferir (to prefer)

prefiero	**preferimos**
prefieres	**prefieren**
prefiere	**prefieren**

pensar (to think)

pienso	**pensamos**
piensas	**piensan**
piensa	**piensan**

-o- → -ue-

dormir (to sleep)

duermo	**dormimos**
duermes	**duermen**
duerme	**duermen**

volver (to return)

vuelvo	**volvemos**
vuelves	**vuelven**
vuelve	**vuelven**

Some other common radical changing verbs are:

With vowel change **-e- → -ie-**

cerrar (to close)

cierro	**cerramos**
cierras	**cierran**
cierra	**cierran**

perder (to lose)

pierdo	**perdemos**
pierdes	**pierden**
pierde	**pierden**

pedir (to ask for)

pido	**pedimos**
pides	**piden**
pide	**piden**

empezar (to begin)

empiezo	empezamos
empiezas	empiezan
empieza	empiezan

With vowel change -o- → -ue-

morir (to die)

muero	morimos
mueres	mueren
muere	mueren

encontrar (to find)

encuentro	encontramos
encuentras	encuentran
encuentra	encuentran

recordar (to remember)

recuerdo	recordamos
recuerdas	recuerdan
recuerda	recuerdan

soñar (con) (to dream (of))

sueño	soñamos
sueñas	sueñan
sueña	sueñan

Exercise 1

Rewrite the following phrases using the correct form of the verb in brackets.

1 **¿A qué hora (empezar) la reunión?**
2 **Yo (recordar) la visita a Costa Rica.**
3 **Nosotros siempre (cerrar) a las 7.30.**
4 **Muchas personas (morir) de cáncer.**
5 **Enrique no (recordar) el problema.**

Language points

The comparatives

One way of comparing people or objects is by using **más** followed by the adjective, as in the examples:

más alto	taller, higher
más caro	more expensive
más grande	bigger, larger

Irregular comparatives

Some adjectives do not form their comparatives with **más**. They have a special form.

Adjective		*Comparative*	
bueno	good	**mejor**	better
malo	bad	**peor**	worse
mucho	a lot of	**más**	more
poco	little	**menos**	less

Más . . . que

When expressing comparison you usually use **más** + adjective + **que**:

Miami es más grande que Tampa.	Miami is bigger than Tampa.
En mi opinión el teatro es más interesante que el cine.	In my opinion, the theater is more interesting than the cinema.
El tabaco es más dañino que el café.	Tobacco is more harmful than coffee.

Exercise 2

Say if the following statements are true (**verdadero**) or false (**falso**):

1 **Londres es más grande que Nueva York.**

2 **Generalmente un televisor es más caro que un carro.**
3 **Una computadora es más inteligente que una persona.**
4 **Las 6 de la mañana es más tarde que las 10 de la mañana.**
5 **Un carro es más pequeño que un camión.**

Language point

The superlative

The superlative is formed by adding the definite article before the comparison:

El juguete más caro.	The most expensive toy.
El más flexible de todos los materiales.	The most flexible of all materials.
La película más interesante del festival.	The most interesting film of the festival.

If the adjective is in the plural, the superlative is formed with **los** or **las**:

Los juguetes más atractivos son japoneses.	The most attractive toys are Japanese.
Las bicicletas más caras están en esta sección.	The most expensive bicycles are in this section.

Exercise 3

Write an equivalent in Spanish for the following. See the glossary at the back of the book for the new words.

1 The most intelligent girl in the group.
2 It is the worst film in the festival.
3 The most functional models are here.
4 I would like the cheapest product.
5 It is the most difficult problem.

Language points

Poder

To ask if something is possible or permissible, the verb **poder** is used.

¿Puedo ver el grande?	Can I have a look at the big one?
¿Puedo usar esta computadora?	Can I use this computer?

The forms are as follows:

puedo	can I? *or* I can
puedes	can you? *or* you can (informal)
puede	can you? *or* you can (formal); can he/she? *or* he/she can
podemos	can we? *or* we can
pueden	can you? *or* you can (formal and informal)
pueden	can they? *or* they can

Notice that this is a radical changing verb.

¿Se puede? is used to ask if something can be done without referring to a particular subject in the sentence.

¿Se puede estacionar acá?	Can you park here?
¿Se puede fumar?	Is smoking allowed?

Exercise 4

Complete the following sentences with the correct form of **poder**.

1 (Yo) No _____ asistir a la clase mañana.
2 (Nosotros) ¿ _____ ayudar?
3 (Ella) ¿ _____ venir con nosotros?
4 Usted _____ hacerlo.
5 (Yo) No _____ empezar el trabajo hoy. No tengo los materiales.

Saber

To indicate ability, as in 'Can you play the piano?', the verb **saber** is used.

¿Sabes tocar el piano?	Can you play the piano?
¿Sabes nadar?	Can you swim?
¿Sabes manejar?	Can you drive?

The forms are as follows:

sé	**sabemos**
sabes	**saben**
sabe	**saben**

Language point

Ambos/los dos

Ambos and **los dos** are used with the meaning of 'both'. If you refer to a feminine pair, then **ambas** or **las dos** is used. **Los dos** and **las dos** are preferred in spoken language, **ambos** and **ambas**, in written language.

Los dos son lindos.	**Ambos son lindos.**
Las dos son chilenas.	**Ambas son chilenas.**
Las dos estudiantes tienen problemas.	**Ambas estudiantes tienen probemas.**

Both . . . and . . .

The structure 'both . . . and . . .' can be translated by **ambos/ambas . . . y . . .** or **los/las dos . . . y . . .**, but also by the structure **tanto . . . como . . .**. Again, **ambos . . . y . . .** is preferred in written language.

Ambos Julián y María aprobaron sus exámenes.
Los dos, Julián y María aprobaron sus exámenes.
Tanto Julián como María aprobaron sus exámenes.

Both Julián and María passed their examinations.

La nueva computadora 〔⚏〕

Lucrecia has just bought a new computer and is telling Alicia about it

LUCRECIA: Mira mi nueva computadora. Es más potente que la anterior. Ahora también tengo una impresora láser.

ALICIA: ¿Tienes pantalla en color o en blanco y negro?

LUCRECIA: Es de color. No se puede trabajar con gráficos en blanco y negro.

ALICIA: ¿Tienes agenda electrónica?

LUCRECIA: Sí. Presionas este botón y se pueden ver todas las citas de esta semana.
¿Te gusta mi escritorio?

ALICIA: Sí es muy funcional.

LUCRECIA: Ahora es más fácil que antes organizar mi trabajo.

LUCRECIA: *Look at my new computer. It's more powerful than the previous one. I also have a laser printer now.*

ALICIA: *Do you have a color or black and white monitor?*

LUCRECIA: *It's a color monitor. You can't work with graphics in black and white.*

ALICIA: *Does it have an electronic diary?*

LUCRECIA: *Yes. You press this button and you can see all the appointments for this week.*
Do you like my desk?

ALICIA: *Yes. It's very functional.*

LUCRECIA: *Now organizing my work is easier than before.*

Language point

Me gusta

In order to express likes and dislikes you can use **gustar** or **no gustar**. For example:

Me gusta la camisa azul.	I like the blue shirt.
Nos gusta caminar.	We like walking.
A Miguel no le gusta el café.	Miguel doesn't like coffee.

It is also possible to use them in questions:

¿Te gusta el hotel?	Do you like the hotel?
¿No le gusta el regalo a María?	Doesn't María like the present?

Here are all the forms:

me gusta	**nos gusta**
te gusta	**les gusta**
le gusta	**les gusta**

And here are more examples:

Nos gusta montar en bicicleta.	We like to ride a bicycle.
¿Te gusta el chocolate?	Do you like chocolate?
A Gloria le gusta la moda.	Gloria likes fashion.
A ustedes les gusta la clase?	Do you like the class?

Me gustan

If what is liked is plural, then the forms are as follows:

me gustan	**nos gustan**
te gustan	**les gustan**
le gustan	**les gustan**

Examples:

Me gustan los domingos.	I like Sundays.
A mis padres no les gustan las vacaciones en el extranjero.	My parents don't like holidays abroad.
¡Te gustan las frutillas!	You like strawberries!
Nos gustan los documentales.	We like documentaries.
No me gustan las comidas picantes.	I don't like spicy food.

Exercise 5

Complete the phrases stating whether you like or dislike the following:

1 _____ **los animales domésticos.**
2 _____ **las vacaciones en el extranjero.**
3 _____ **las ensaladas.**
4 _____ **visitar museos.**
5 _____ **escribir cartas.**
6 _____ **comprar regalos.**
7 _____ **levantarme temprano.**
8 _____ **comer chocolate.**
9 _____ **los niños.**
10 _____ **leer novelas.**

Exercise 6

The following are types of television programs. Which ones do you like? Which ones don't you like?

	ME GUSTAN	NO ME GUSTAN
Los noticieros		
Las películas del oeste		
Las telenovelas		
Los documentales		
Los dibujos animados		
Las entrevistas		
Los programas cómicos		
Los reportajes		
Los concursos		
Los programas musicales		
Otros		

noticieros	news	**entrevistas**	interviews
películas del oeste	westerns	**programas cómicos**	comedy programs
		reportajes	reports
telenovelas	soap operas	**concursos**	contests
documentales	documentaries	**programas musicales**	music programs
dibujos animados	cartoons		

Reading 📼

Read the information in the advertisement below and answer these questions:

How much discount are you given?
What kind of keyboard does the computer have?
Can you pay with a credit card?
Are these discontinued models?

PROMOCIÓN ESPECIAL
35% de descuento del precio de lista

CARACTERÍSTICAS

ÚLTIMA TECNOLOGÍA

Disco duro de 210 MB
(100 mil páginas de texto)

Memoria 4 MB

Sistema DOS

Teclado en castellano

Monitor alta resolución

Velocidad 66 MHz

100% compatible

Ranuras de expansión

Ratón incluido

Los precios se pueden pagar en
moneda nacional o en su
equivalente en dólares.

Precios válidos sólo en efectivo o con cheque.

---

precio de lista	list price	**ranuras de**	expansion slots
última tecnología	latest technology	**expansión**	
disco duro	hard disk	**ratón**	mouse
páginas	pages	**pagar**	to pay
teclado	keyboard	**en efectivo**	in cash
alta resolución	high resolution		

7 ¿Qué estás haciendo?

What are you doing?

By the end of this chapter you should be able to:

- Refer to actions in progress using the present continuous e.g. (I am working)
- Use possessive adjectives (my, your, etc.)
- Use demonstrative adjectives and pronouns (this, this one, etc.)
- Use exclamations with **que** + adjective/noun (e.g. **¡Qué bonito!**)

¡Qué lindas fotos! 📼

Ernesto is showing Maritza photographs of his birthday party

MARITZA: ¿Qué lindas fotos! ¿Qué estás haciendo en esa foto?
ERNESTO: Estoy celebrando mi cumpleaños.
MARITZA: ¿Y en esta foto?
ERNESTO: Julia y yo estamos bailando. Acá todos están brindando por mi cumpleaños.
MARITZA: Tú estás leyendo un discurso.
ERNESTO: Sí, algo chistoso.

MARITZA: *Nice photographs! What are you doing in that photograph?*
ERNESTO: *I'm celebrating my birthday.*
MARITZA: *And in this one?*
ERNESTO: *Julia and I are dancing. Here everybody is making a toast.*
MARITZA: *You're reading a speech.*
ERNESTO: *Yes, something funny.*

Language point

The present continuous tense

The present continuous tense is formed by using **estar** + the gerund form of the verb. The gerund ends in -**ando** or -**iendo** (-**ando** for -**ar** verbs; -**iendo** for -**er** and -**ir** verbs.) These forms correspond to the English ending '-ing', as in 'eating', 'running', etc.

estoy estudiando	I am studying
estás estudiando	you are studying (informal)
está estudiando	you are studying (formal); he/she is studying
estamos estudiando	we are studying
están estudiando	you are studying (formal and informal)
están estudiando	they are studying

The present continuous refers to an action which is in progress at the time of speaking.

Estoy estudiando para el examen de mañana.	I am studying for tomorrow's exam.
Estamos jugando a las cartas, ¿quieres jugar?	We are playing cards, do you want to play?

Reading 🔘

After reading the following extract from a TV report transcript, answer these questions:

Who is giving a speech?
What is the speaker trying to explain?
Are people interested in the message?

Rodolfo Arias is a current affairs reporter and is giving a live report by satellite on events in a neighboring country

LOCUTOR DE
 TELEVISIÓN: A continuación un informe de nuestro corresponsal en el extranjero.
RODOLFO: El presidente está hablando a la nación en estos momentos. Está dando un discurso de fin de año. La radio y la televisión están transmitiendo el mensaje.

El presidente está explicando los planes del gobierno para el próximo año. En estos momentos está tratando sobre el aumento de sueldos para los empleados públicos y privados. Sin duda, todo el país está escuchando.

a continuación	now follows	**está explicando**	is explaining
informe	report	**próximo**	next
corresponsal en el extranjero	foreign correspondent	**está tratando sobre**	is dealing with
la nación	the nation	**aumento de sueldos**	wage increase
dando un discurso	giving a speech	**sin duda**	no doubt
		todo el país	the whole country
de fin de año	end of the year	**está escuchando**	is listening

Exercise 1

Answer each question as in the example:

> **¿Qué está haciendo Silvia? (saltar)**
> **Está saltando.**

1 **¿Qué está haciendo Pepe? (estudiar)**
2 **¿Qué están haciendo Julia y Rosana? (escribir)**
3 **¿Qué estás haciendo? (trabajar en la oficina)**
4 **¿Qué están haciendo ustedes? (arreglar el jardín)**
5 **¿Qué están haciendo las chicas? (practicar el baile)**

saltar	to jump	**el jardín**	the garden
arreglar	to tidy up	**el baile**	the dance

Exercise 2

Read the following notice put up by the telephone company on the road. Answer these questions:

1 Is it an apology? If so, what is the expression used?
2 What is the reason for this apology?

> **Compañía de Teléfonos S.A.**
> **Disculpe la molestia.**
> **Estamos instalando nuevas líneas.**

| **disculpe la** | I/we apologize for | **instalar** | to instal |
| **molestia** | the inconvenience | **líneas** | lines |

Exercise 3

Give the equivalent in English for the following sentences:

1 **Estamos entrevistando para dos puestos de trabajo.**
2 **El grupo está incursionando en el mercado internacional.**
3 **La recuperación económica está empezando.**
4 **Estoy buscando una alternativa a este producto.**
5 **Genaro está trabajando en un nuevo proyecto.**

| **incursionar** | to make inroads | **puestos de trabajo** | jobs |
| **buscar** | to look for | | |

Language point

Possessive adjectives

Possessive adjectives appear in front of the noun they refer to and correspond to the English 'my', 'your', etc. They agree in number with the noun possessed. The possessive adjective for the first person plural ('our') also agrees in gender.

	Singular	Plural
my	**mi**	**mis**
your (informal)	**tu**	**tus**
your (formal)	**su**	**sus**
his/her/its	**su**	**sus**
our	**nuestro(/a)**	**nuestros(/as)**
your	**su**	**sus**
their	**su**	**sus**

Examples:

| **Mi casa está cerca.** | My house is near. |
| **Nuestra clase es a las nueve.** | Our lesson is at nine. |

Tus amigos están esperando.	Your friends are waiting.
¡Apúrate!	Hurry up!
Su opinión es muy importante.	Your opinion is very important.

Exercise 4

Rewrite the second sentence in each pair, adding at the beginning
the correct possessive adjective for the person mentioned or implied
in the first sentence.

Example:

Sandra tiene problemas.
Su madre está enferma.

1 **Marina y Lupe están adentro.**
   _____ **amigas también.**

2 **Felipe sabe manejar.**
   _____ **carro es nuevo.**

3 **El producto es bueno.**
   _____ **precio es competitivo.**

4 **Estoy contento.**
   _____ **padre ahora está bien.**

5 **Juan tiene una motocicleta.**
   _____ **hermano menor tiene una bicicleta.**

Language points

Demonstrative adjectives

The demonstrative adjectives 'this' and 'that' are translated by the
Spanish **este** and **ese** and other forms associated with them (see
below). They agree in number and gender with the noun they refer
to. **Aquel**, which also means 'that', is preferred to indicate something that is far away.

Singular		Plural	
masc.	*fem.*	*masc.*	*fem.*
este	esta	estos	estas
ese	esa	esos	esas
aquel	aquella	aquellos	aquellas

Examples:

Este periódico es el más popular.	This newspaper is the most popular one.
Esa camisa es cara.	That shirt is expensive.
Estos amigos viven en Guadalajara.	These friends live in Guadalajara.
Estas mesas son para el colegio.	These tables are for the school.
Esas chicas estudian medicina.	Those girls study medicine.
Aquel señor es el presidente del club.	That gentleman (over there) is the president of the club.
Aquellos animales son especies en peligro.	Those animals are endangered species.

Demonstrative pronouns

In spoken Spanish, demonstrative pronouns are identical in form to demonstrative adjectives. In writing, the difference is that the pronouns have an accent. 'This one' and 'that one' correspond to **éste** and **ése** and their associated forms. Again, **aquél** and related forms are used for something remote.

Singular		Plural	
masc.	*fem.*	*masc.*	*fem.*
éste	ésta	éstos	éstas
ése	ésa	ésos	ésas
aquél	aquélla	aquéllos	aquéllas

Examples:

No quiero este periódico, quiero aquél.	I don't want this newspaper, I want that one.
Quisiera comprar éstas.	I would like to buy these ones.
¿Cuánto cuestan éstos?	How much are these?

Ese video no me gusta. Prefiero éste.	I don't like that video. I prefer this one.

There are also the neuter pronouns **esto** and **eso** and **aquello**, as in ¿**Qué es esto?** 'What's this?', **Eso es todo** 'That's all'.

¡Qué!

The structure **qué** + adjective translates the English 'how + adjective'.

¡**Qué lindo!**	How lovely!
¡**Qué interesante!**	How interesting!
¡**Qué caro!**	How expensive!
¡**Qué tonta!**	How stupid!

The structure **qué** + noun corresponds to the English 'what (a) + noun'.

¡**Qué día!**	What a day!
¡**Qué tiempo!**	What weather!
¡**Qué película!**	What a film!
¡**Qué desastre!**	What a disaster!

Acá/aquí; allá/allí

The English 'here' is translated by **acá** or **aquí**; 'there' is translated by **ahí**, **allá** or **allí**. In Latin America, **acá** and **allá** are preferred. In Spain, **aquí** and **allí** are preferred. In both varieties of Spanish **ahí** is used regularly. **Acá/aquí** refers to a place near the speaker. **Ahí** refers to a place not far from the speaker, perhaps near the hearer. **Allá/allí** refers to a place far from the speaker.

Acá en la tienda tenemos una amplia variedad de productos.	Here in the shop we have a wide variety of products.
Allá en el norte se vive mejor.	People live better in the north.
Ahí está. Cerca de la puerta.	It's there. By the door.

Más fotos 📼

Ernesto and Maritza are looking at more photographs of his birthday party

ERNESTO: En esta foto estoy leyendo las tarjetas de saludos.
MARITZA: Mira, acá estás con un plato repleto.
ERNESTO: Y en ésta, Rosana está posando para el fotógrafo. Está mirando las flores.
MARITZA: Está muy bien.
ERNESTO: Sí, está bien.

ERNESTO: *In this photo I'm reading my cards.*
MARITZA: *Look, here you are with a huge serving on your plate.*
ERNESTO: *And in this one Rosana is posing for the photographer. She's looking at the flowers.*
MARITZA: *She looks great.*
ERNESTO: *Yes, she does.*

Language points

Leer → leyendo

When the verb has -**ee**- in the infinitive, there is a spelling change in the gerund ('-ing') form.

leer (to read)
Está leyendo en la biblioteca. He's reading in the library.

creer (to believe)
Creyendo que era fácil de hacer, empezó a pintar el retrato. Believing that it was easy to do, she started to paint the portrait.

Construir → construyendo

When the infinitive ends in -**uir**, there is also a spelling change.

construir (to build)
Están construyendo un colegio nuevo.   They are building a new school.

disminuir (to go down)
El nivel del agua está disminuyendo.   The water level is going down.

Exercise 5 🔘

Complete this dialogue, changing the verb in brackets to the continuous form.

Ana arrives home from work and finds her son in the kitchen.

ANA: ¿Qué estás (hacer)?
MARIO: Estoy (preparar) un informe.
ANA: Y Tomás, ¿qué está (hacer)?
MARIO: Está (escribir) una carta a una amiga.
ANA: ¿Dónde está?
MARIO: En su cuarto.

hacer	to do, to make
informe	report
carta	letter
cuarto	room, bedroom (note that other words used for bedroom are **pieza, alcoba, recámara, dormitorio**)

Exercise 6

Complete the following sentences with the correct form of **estar**.

1 **(Yo) _____ hablando por teléfono a Bogotá.**
2 **María _____ explicando el problema.**
3 **Dolores y Fernando _____ platicando.**
4 **El abuelo _____ tomando fotos a los niños.**
5 **Mi madre _____ exprimiendo las naranjas para el jugo.**

explicar	to explain	**exprimir**	to extract
platicar	to talk	**jugo**	juice
tomar fotos	to take photographs		

Exercise 7

Choose the correct answer from the words in brackets.

1 **(Maribel/Nosotros) está viendo televisión.**
2 **(Asunción y Genaro/Yo) están hablando por teléfono.**
3 **(Tú/Usted) está preparando el informe y (tú/usted) estás preparando los gráficos, ¿verdad?**
4 **(Maritza/Yo) estoy cantando en esta foto.**
5 **(La radio/Los periódicos) está transmitiendo el partido de fútbol.**

el informe	the report	**cantando**	singing
los gráficos	graphics	**transmitiendo**	broadcasting
¿verdad?	right?	**partido**	match

Language point

Conjunctions

The conjunctions **y** and **o** correspond to 'and' and 'or' in English and are used in a similar way.

When **y** precedes another word beginning with the sound **i**, it changes to **e**, as in **Felipe e Ignacio**.

When **o** precedes a word beginning with the sound **o**, it changes to **u**, as in **Aconsejar u orientar es difícil**. 'To advise or give guidance is difficult'.

Reading 🔊

While reading the passage below, see if you can find answers to these questions:

What happens on the Day of the Dead according to popular belief?
What do children usually buy?

El Día de Muertos

El dos de noviembre en todo México se celebra el Día de Muertos, una de las fiestas más importantes del país. Se cree que los muertos vuelven a visitar a su familia y se les ofrece alimentos, frutas y flores. Además, se encienden velas y se quema incienso. Por todas partes hay calaveras de 'papier-maché' y los niños compran calaveras de dulce para comer.

muertos	the dead	**se encienden**	are lit
fiesta	festival	**velas**	candles
se cree	it is believed	**incienso**	incense
alimentos	food	**por todas partes**	everywhere
frutas	fruit	**calaveras**	skulls
flores	flowers	**dulce**	sweet

8 ¿Qué tengo que hacer?

What do I have to do?

By the end of this chapter you will be able to:

- Express necessity or obligation using **tener que** and **hay que**
- Talk about your routines at work and at home
- Describe a house
- Describe a room
- Use **con** + pronoun/**conmigo**, **contigo** (with me, with you, etc.)

Tengo que ir al banco ▣▣

Mark wants to change some traveler's checks

MARK: Tengo que cambiar cheques de viajero. Necesito más plata. Vamos a la casa de cambio.

CARMEN: No. El banco es mejor.

MARK: ¿Por qué?

CARMEN: El banco cobra menos comisión y paga más por dólar.

MARK: Entonces, vamos al banco.

CARMEN: Tenemos que ir rápido. El banco cierra a las tres. ¡Apúrate! Quedan diez minutos.

MARK: *I have to change some traveler's checks. I need some more money. Let's go to the Bureau de Change.*

CARMEN: *The bank would be better.*

MARK: *Why?*

CARMEN: *The bank charges less commission and pays more per dollar.*

MARK: *Then let's go to the bank.*

CARMEN: *We have to rush. The bank closes at three. Hurry up!*
We've got ten minutes.

Language point

Tener que

To explain that something has to be done the expression **tener que** is used. This is the equivalent of the English 'to have to'. Here are all the forms:

tengo que	I have to
tienes que	you have to (informal)
tiene que	you have to (formal); he/she has to
tenemos que	we have to
tienen que	you have to (formal and informal)
tienen que	they have to

The expression **tener que** is always followed by a verb in the infinitive.

Tengo que cambiar cheques de viaje.	I have to change traveler's checks.
Tenemos que terminar pronto.	We have to finish soon.

Exercise 1

Which of these things do you do at work and at home? Use the expression **tener que** to say what you have to do both at home and at work. Then write the phrases down in your notebook.

Example:

En el trabajo tengo que presentar informes.

En el trabajo (At work)

1 **abrir la correspondencia**
2 **enviar faxes**
3 **escribir cartas**

4 **supervisar la producción**
5 **trabajar hasta tarde**
6 **presentar informes**
7 **llamar por teléfono**
8 **tratar con el público**
9 **utilizar la computadora**

En casa (At home)

1 **preparar la comida**
2 **limpiar**
3 **pasar la aspiradora**
4 **planchar**
5 **ayudar a los niños con sus tareas**
6 **contestar el teléfono**
7 **atender el jardín**
8 **hacer reparaciones**

enviar	to send	**ayudar**	to help
hasta tarde	until late	**tareas**	homework
pasar la aspiradora	to vacuum	**atender**	to attend to
planchar	to iron	**hacer reparaciones**	to do repairs

Now practise the same sentences again, adding some expressions of frequency.

generalmente	generally
normalmente	normally
a veces	sometimes
siempre	always
nunca	never

Examples:

En casa, generalmente tengo que contestar el teléfono.
En el trabajo siempre escribo cartas.

Reading

A professor of Economics is talking about the problems of the nation

'En mi opinión, el gobierno tiene que rebajar las tasas de interés, el sector privado tiene que invertir más, los sindicatos tienen que moderar sus expectativas, y todos tenemos que trabajar juntos para estimular la economía del país.'

gobierno	government	**sindicatos**	trade unions
rebajar	to reduce	**moderar**	to tone down,
tasas de interés	interest rates		to moderate
sector privado	private sector	**expectativas**	expectations
invertir	to invest	**juntos**	together

Exercise 2

People from various sources mentioned in the speech above have commented on the contents of it. Are they in favor (**en favor**) or against (**en contra**) what was said in the speech?

1 **Vocero del gobierno: '. . . las tasas de interés están bien . . .'**
2 **Sociedad de Empresarios: 'Tenemos que invertir más capital . . .'**
3 **Líder sindical: 'Tenemos que luchar por un salario justo.'**

vocero	spokesperson	**luchar**	to fight
sociedad de	industrialists'	**salario**	salary
empresarios	confederation	**justo**	fair, just
líder sindical	union leader		

Exercise 3

Mr Miller has a few things to do during his one-day business visit to a Latin American client. In what order does he have to do things, do you think? Write it down in your notebook. The following expressions may help you to link your sentences:

primero	first
después	afterwards
luego	next, then
entonces	then
más tarde	later
por último	lastly

Example:

Primero, tiene que preparar el informe.

tiene que visitar la fábrica
tiene que discutir precios
tiene que ver muestras
tiene que probar el producto
tiene que estudiar el contrato

la fábrica	the factory	**probar**	to try, to test
discutir	to discuss	**muestras**	samples
precios	prices		

Tareas de la casa 🔲

While reading the dialogue below, see if you can find answers to this question:

Does Sra Huertas do housework or does she do a paid job from home?

Sra Huertas explains some of the things she has to do at home

ENTREVISTADOR: ¿Qué tareas domésticas tiene que hacer en la casa Sra Huertas?

SRA HUERTAS: Tengo que lavar la ropa, tengo que lavar los platos, tengo que limpiar la casa, tengo que preparar el desayuno, tengo que llevar a los niños al colegio . . .

INTERVIEWER: *What sort of housework do you have to do, Mrs Huertas?*

MRS HUERTAS: *I have to do the washing, I have to do the washing up, I have to clean the house, I have to prepare breakfast, I have to take the children to school . . .*

Language point

Personal a

After certain verbs, such as **conocer** (to know), **llevar** (to carry), **acompañar** (to accompany), **ver** (to see), **visitar** (to visit), it is necessary to use the 'personal' **a** when the direct object (i.e. the person, animal or thing directly affected by the verb) that follows is a person or the name of a person. You do not need the 'personal' **a** if the direct object is not a person.

Me gusta visitar a mi tía.	I like to visit my aunt.
Me gusta visitar Chile.	I like to visit Chile.
Llevo a los niños al colegio.	I take the children to school.
Llevo muchas cosas al colegio.	I take many things to school.

Exercise 4

Study the following examples:

Tengo que llevar mi carro al trabajo.	I have to take my car to work.
Tenemos que llevar a Julia al centro.	We have to take Julia to town.

Now make similar sentences including other things or people you have to take somewhere, e.g. **al colegio** (to school), **al trabajo** (to work), **al parque** (to the park), etc., either regularly or occasionally.

Language point

Hay que

Another way of expressing that something needs to be done is by using **hay que** followed by the infinitive.

| Hay que parar la guerra. | The war must be stopped. |
| Hay que comprar por docenas. | You have to buy by the dozen. |

In this case the expression is more impersonal than **tener que** since you do not refer to any person in particular. The emphasis is on the need to perform the action.

Exercise 5

Match the possible solutions to the problems in the following troubleshooting chart for a television set.

PROBLEMA	SOLUCIÓN POSIBLE
1 **Imagen imperfecta.**	(a) **Hay que regular el contraste.**
2 **Buen sonido, pero la pantalla no está iluminada.**	(b) **Hay que ajustar la antena.**
3 **Imagen lluviosa y ruido.**	(c) **Hay que chequear la conexión de la antena.**
4 **Aparecen líneas horizontales.**	(d) **Hay que regular el brillo.**

imagen	TV picture	**lluviosa (imagen)**	snowy (TV picture) (literally, 'rainy')
ajustar	adjust		
sonido	sound	**regular**	adjust
pantalla	screen	**ruido**	noise
antena	aerial	**líneas**	lines
		brillo	brightness

Exercise 6

Here are the names of well-known daily newspapers from Latin America. Use the map below to match each paper with the country where it is published.

1	**Excelsior**	(a)	Venezuela
2	**El Mercurio**	(b)	Argentina
3	**La Nación**	(c)	Colombia
4	**El Comercio**	(d)	Chile
5	**El Espectador**	(e)	México
6	**ABC**	(f)	Paraguay
7	**El Universal**	(g)	Perú

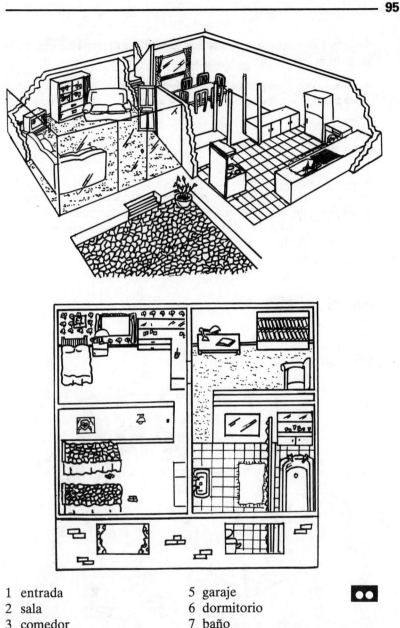

1 entrada
2 sala
3 comedor
4 cocina

5 garaje
6 dormitorio
7 baño

Al entrar a la casa, en la planta baja a la izquierda está la sala. A la derecha está el patio. Más adentro, a la izquierda está el comedor y a la derecha está la cocina. En la planta alta hay dos dormitorios y un baño. También hay un estudio.

Note: in Latin America **entrar a** is usually the preferred form, while in Spain **entrar en** predominates.

al entrar	as you go in	**planta alta**	upstairs
planta baja	downstairs	**más adentro**	further inside

Exercise 7

Based on the description above, now try to describe your own house. You can start by saying: **Vivo en una casa** 'I live in a house' or **Vivo en un departamento** 'I live in a flat/apartment' and then describe the layout, i.e. **Al entrar a la casa/al departamento . . .** 'As you go into the house/flat . . .'.

Reading 📼

Mi cuarto

Mi cuarto es chico, pero cómodo. A la izquierda está mi cama. Al lado de la cama está el ropero. A la derecha está mi estéreo. También a la derecha hay estantes para libros. En los estantes tengo mi cámara fotográfica y fotos. Cerca de la puerta están mis zapatos y zapatillas. La ventana es grande y da al jardín.

chico	small	**estantes**	shelves
cómodo	comfortable	**ventana**	window
cama	bed		

Note: Spanish speakers in Latin America prefer the word **chico/chica** to mean 'small'. In Spain **pequeño/pequeña** is preferred.

Now try to describe in Spanish your own room and some of the things there are in it:

    ¿Cómo es tu cuarto?   What's your room like?
    ¿Qué tienes en tu cuarto?   What do you have in your room?

Hablando por teléfono ▄▄

Ana María and Adela are talking on the phone

ANA MARÍA: ¿Adela? ¿qué estás haciendo?
ADELA: Estoy escuchando mis 'compact discs'. ¿Quieres escuchar música conmigo?
ANA MARÍA: Bueno.
ADELA: Ven a mi casa, entonces.
ANA MARÍA: Sí, voy ahorita.

ANA MARÍA: *Adela? What are you doing?*
ADELA: *I am listening to my compact discs. Shall we listen to music together?*
ANA MARÍA: *Alright.*
ADELA: *Come round, then.*
ANA MARÍA: *Yes, I'll come round straight away.*

Language points

Ahorita

This word is used to indicate that something will be done straight away, without delay. In Spain the equivalent expression is **enseguida**.

Conmigo/contigo

The special forms **conmigo** and **contigo** are used for 'with me' and 'with you'. For other persons **con** + pronoun is used.

conmigo	with me
contigo	with you (singular)
con él	with him
con ella	with her
con nosotros	with us
con ustedes	with you (plural)
con ellos	with them
con ellas	with them (if all are female)

Examples:

Ven conmigo.	Come with me.
¿Quieres ir a comer con ellos?	Do you want to go out for a meal with them?

Note: if you want to refer to a mixed group of people, the masculine plural form is used.

Exercise 8

Give the Spanish equivalent for the following phrases.

1 I want to go with you.
2 Sra Rosas lives in a small house with them (two daughters).
3 Come with me.
4 They want a meeting with you.
5 He always arrives with them (all male).

Reading 🔘

Here is a message from a charity collecting donations for Christmas. While reading the text, see if you can find answers to these questions:

What are they collecting for?
How can you make a donation?

CONTAMOS CONTIGO

Esta Navidad con la ayuda de todos vamos a lograr sonrisas. Como siempre, esperamos contar contigo. Toda ayuda será bienvenida: ropa, medicinas, juguetes. Llama al teléfono 49 – 4949 de 8 de la mañana a 6 de la tarde para ofrecer tu donativo.

Navidad	Christmas	**contar**	to count on
vamos a lograr	we are going to get	**bienvenida**	welcome
sonrisa	smile	**juguetes**	toys
como siempre	as always	**ofrecer**	offer
esperamos	we hope	**donativo**	donation

9 He perdido . . .

I have lost . . .

By the end of this chapter you will be able to:

- Refer to recent events using the present perfect tense (e.g. I have finished, we have eaten, etc.)
- Use the present perfect continuous tense (e.g. I have been working)
- Give a basic physical description of objects and materials
- Use **por** and **para**

He perdido mi pasaporte

JAIME:	¿Qué pasa?
CATHERINE:	He perdido mi pasaporte.
JAIME:	¿Dónde? ¿Cómo?
CATHERINE:	No sé. No estoy segura. Quizás en el mercado.
JAIME:	Hay que ir a la comisaría y luego al consulado.
CATHERINE:	Sí. Necesito uno nuevo.

JAIME:	*What's the matter?*
CATHERINE:	*I've lost my passport.*
JAIME:	*Where? How?*
CATHERINE:	*I don't know. I'm not sure. Perhaps in the market.*
JAIME:	*We must go to the police station and then to the consulate.*
CATHERINE:	*Yes. I need a new one.*

Language points

¿Qué pasa?

This question is used to find out what the matter is with somebody. It is similar to 'What's happening?/What's the matter?'

The present perfect tense

The present perfect tense is formed by the auxiliary verb **haber** and the past participle of the main verb of the sentence.

Example:

He perdido mi maletín.   I have lost my briefcase.

The forms of **haber** are:

he	I have
has	you have (informal)
ha	you have (formal); he/she has
hemos	we have
han	you have (plural)
han	they have

Note: when the meaning of 'to have' is 'to possess', then you must use **tener** and not **haber**, i.e. **tengo** (I have), **tienes** (you have), etc., as in

Tengo un modem en mi   I have a modem in my computer.
computadora.

You form the past participle of a verb by replacing the infinitive ending -**ar** by the ending -**ado**, and the endings -**er** and -**ir** by -**ido**.

trabajar	**trabajado**
comer	**comido**
vivir	**vivido**

The most common irregular past participles are:

abrir (to open)	**abierto**
decir (to say)	**dicho**
escribir (to write)	**escrito**

hacer (to do, to make)	**hecho**
morir (to die)	**muerto**
poner (to put)	**puesto**
romper (to break)	**roto**
ver (to see)	**visto**
volver (to return)	**vuelto**

The present perfect is used to indicate that an event has happened in a period of time in the past but which includes the present or whose effects still bear on the present.

He perdido mi pasaporte.	I have lost my passport.
Hemos terminado.	We have finished.
¿No ha llegado?	Hasn't he/she arrived?

The present perfect continuous

This tense is used to indicate that an action has been in progress over a period of time and continues to be in progress at the time of speaking. It is formed by using **haber** plus the past participle plus the gerund (e.g. **escribiendo** 'writing', **viajando** 'traveling').

Examples:

Hemos estado trabajando todo el día en este asunto.	We have been working on this matter all day.
¿Has estado estudiando todo el tiempo?	Have you been studying all the time?

Desde

The word **desde** is the equivalent of 'since'.

He estado trabajando desde las siete y media.	I have been working since half past seven.
Hemos estado preparando el congreso desde enero.	We have been preparing the conference since January.

The following structure in Spanish:

desde + hace + period of time

is similar to the English structure 'for' + period of time.

Examples:

Trabajo acá desde hace dos años.	I have been working here for two years.
¿Desde hace cuánto tiempo que estás en Santiago?	How long have you been in Santiago?
Estudio en la universidad desde hace dos meses.	I have been studying at the university for two months.

Exercise 1

Translate the following into Spanish:

1 I have finished my work.
2 I have been writing this letter for two hours.
3 Elena and I have written a letter to the newspaper.
4 Roger has been in Cali for a week.
5 Carlos Fuentes has published a new book.
6 You have lived in Paraguay for a long time.
7 The bank has opened a new branch.
8 We haven't seen Lorena since this morning.
9 They have arrived.
10 Haven't you finished?

Exercise 2

Here are two things you may have done today. Continue the list with other things you have completed during the day – on your own or with somebody else.

He escrito una carta.
Mi madre y yo hemos preparado el desayuno.

En la comisaría

While reading the dialogue below, see if you can find answers to these questions:

Why is Mark at the police station?
Would you carry the same things in your briefcase if you visited a Latin American country?

Mark has lost his briefcase and is reporting the loss at a police station

POLICÍA: Buenas tardes.
MARK: He perdido mi maletín con documentos personales.
POLICÍA: Su nombre, por favor.
MARK: Mark Williams.
POLICÍA: ¿Qué hay en su maletín?
MARK: Un momento, por favor. He escrito una lista. Acá está: mi pasaporte, boleto de avión, cheques de viajero, una guía de Latinoamérica, una lista de hoteles y una agenda.
POLICÍA: Voy a apuntar los detalles.
MARK: Quisiera una copia del informe policial. Es para el seguro.
POLICÍA: Sí, por supuesto.

POLICEMAN: *Good afternoon.*
MARK: *I've lost my briefcase with all my documents in it.*
POLICEMAN: *Your name, please.*
MARK: *Mark Williams.*
POLICEMAN: *What is in the briefcase?*
MARK: *Just a moment, please. I've made a list. Here it is. My passport, flight ticket, traveler's checks, a guide to Latin America, a list of hotels and a diary.*
POLICEMAN: *I'll write down the details.*
MARK: *I would like a copy of the police report. It's for the insurance.*
POLICEMAN: *Yes, of course.*

Language point

Por/para

Por usually indicates the source of the action ('because of, by, through'). **Para** usually expresses destination or purpose ('to, in order to'). These two prepositions can often be confusing to English speakers because both may also translate the English preposition 'for'.

Fue elegida por su experiencia.	She was elected for her experience.
Contestar por fax.	Answer by fax.
Por María aceptó la invitación.	Because of María he accepted the invitation.
Este regalo es para ti.	This present is for you.
¿Qué estás haciendo? Estoy mirando por la ventana.	What are you doing? I'm looking through the window.
Empuje la palanca para abrir la puerta.	Push the lever to open the door.
¿Para qué quieres esto? Para arreglarlo.	What do you want this for? To fix it.

Por is also used in the following idiomatic expressions:

por ahora	for the time being
por el momento	for the moment
por otra parte	on the other hand
por si acaso	just in case
por ejemplo	for example
por fin	at last

Exercise 3

Complete these sentences choosing **por** or **para**.

1 **Este libro es _____ Susana.**
2 **¿_____ qué no has terminado tu comida?**
3 **Estoy preparando la agenda _____ la reunión.**
4 **¿Vas _____ la tienda?** (on your way to)
5 **Hay que salir _____ esta puerta.**

Exercise 4

These are features you might find in a Latin American publication. Write down those which also belong to the journal/magazine that you usually read. Are there any others you can name?

- **Edición actualizada**
- **450 páginas**
- **53 cuadros estadísticos**
- **90 gráficos**

- **Glosario técnico**
- **Terminología en castellano, francés e inglés**
- **Mapas y fotos**
- **Temas: sociedad, nutrición, pobreza, mujer, sector informal, pequeña y mediana empresa.**

actualizada	up to date	**nutrición**	nutrition
cuadro		**pobreza**	poverty
estadístico	chart	**sector informal**	the 'informal'
gráfico	graphics		sector (of the
temas	topics, themes,		economy)
	subjects	**empresa**	firm, company
sociedad	society		

Reading

While reading the passage below, see if you can find answers to these questions:

Why are there so many street vendors in Latin America?
How do they announce the goods they sell?

Vendedores ambulantes

Los vendedores ambulantes, hombres, mujeres y niños, llenan las calles de las principales ciudades latinoamericanas. Ofrecen todo tipo de productos, alimentos, artículos de tocador importados, verduras, bebidas gaseosas, etc. El desempleo y la pobreza obligan a muchos a trabajar horas y horas voceando sus productos. Son parte del sector informal de la economía.

vendedores	street sellers	**verduras**	vegetables
ambulantes		**bebidas gaseosas**	soft drinks
llenan	fill	**voceando**	shouting
artículos de		**desempleo**	unemployment
tocador	toiletries	**pobreza**	poverty

Are there any street sellers in your city/town/village? What do they sell? Can you think of the names of some of their products in Spanish?

¿Por qué estás triste? 📼

Mark has not yet recovered his briefcase

DELIA: ¿Por qué estás triste?
MARK: Porque he perdido mi maletín con mi agenda.
DELIA: ¿Cuándo?
MARK: El otro día. He ido a la comisaría, pero no han encontrado el maletín.
DELIA: ¿Por qué no te compras otra agenda?
MARK: Ya tengo una nueva. Pero he perdido nombres y direcciones con contactos importantes.

DELIA: *Why are you sad?*
MARK: *Because I've lost my briefcase with my diary in it.*
DELIA: *When?*
MARK: *The other day. I've been to the police station, but they haven't found the briefcase.*
DELIA: *Why don't you buy another diary?*
MARK: *I've got a new one. But I've lost the names and addresses of important contacts.*

Language point

¿Por qué?/porque

¿Por qué?, the equivalent of 'why?', is written as two words.
Porqué, the equivalent of 'because', is one word.

¿Por qué no ha venido Sofía?	Why hasn't Sofía come?
Porque está enferma.	Because she is ill.

Exercise 5

Below is a list of possible presents. Which one would you choose for . . .

un enamorado/una enamorada	a boyfriend/girlfriend
tu niño o niña	your child
tu abuela	your grandmother
un amigo	a friend
tu oficina	your office
¿y para ti?	and for you?

Juegos de construcción
en plástico sólido
transparente y cálido.

Carpeta para guardar
facturas o apuntes.
Hecha de plástico.
Muy útil.

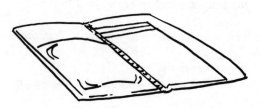

Silla plegable. El asiento es de lona y cuero. Para
conciertos al aire libre. Es cómoda.

Sortija de plata. Elegante.

Llavero de oro. Atractivo.

Caja fuerte de acero. Con sistema
electrónico. Muy segura.

Poleras/Polos de algodón.
De moda.

Abrigos de lana.
Gruesos.

Algunos otros materiales:

madera	wood
metal	metal
cartón	cardboard
fibra de vidrio	glass fiber
vidrio	glass
plástico	plastic
tela	fabric

Reading 📼

While reading the passage below, see if you can find answers to these questions:

When did Europeans arrive in Latin America?
What does Latin America buy from industrialized countries?
Does your own country produce or import one or more of these products?

Latinoamérica exporta

Desde la llegada de los europeos en el siglo XVI, América Latina ha exportado materias primas y ha importado productos manufacturados de los países industrializados. Algunas de las principales materias primas que exporta Latinoamérica son petróleo, café, azúcar de caña, algodón y cobre.

desde la llegada	since the arrival	**petróleo**	oil
siglo	century	**café**	coffee
materias primas	raw materials	**azúcar de caña**	cane sugar
países	countries	**algodón**	cotton
algunas	some	**cobre**	copper

10 ¿Qué vamos a hacer hoy?

What are we going to do today?

> **By the end of this chapter you should be able to:**
>
> - Explain what you intend to do using **ir a**
> - Order a meal and/or a drink
> - Use subject relative clauses (e.g. the music that I like)
> - Use expressions of agreement (e.g. according to)

En Lima

While reading the dialogue below, see if you can find answers to these questions:

What are the tourists going to visit?
Are they going to do anything in the afternoon?

A group of tourists are visiting Lima. The travel agent is talking to them about their itinerary for the day

TURISTA: ¿Qué vamos a hacer hoy?

GUÍA: Primero, vamos a visitar el Museo Arqueológico. Aparte de la exposición van a ver un video de diez minutos y luego vamos a almorzar en un restaurante criollo. En la tarde vamos a recorrer las iglesias antiguas de la capital y a comprar recuerdos. El guía va a explicar . . .

TOURIST: *What are we going to do today?*

GUIDE: *First, we are going to visit the Archaeological Museum. Apart from the exhibition, you are going to watch a ten-minute video and then we are going to have lunch in a typical restaurant. In the afternoon we are going to go round the old churches in the capital and we are going to buy souvenirs. The guide is going to explain . . .*

Language point

ir a *+ infinitive*

One way of expressing the future is by using the present tense of the verb **ir** (to go) followed by **a** plus the infinitive expressing the intended action. This is similar to the English structure 'to be going to + infinitive'

Vamos a visitar el museo.   We are going to visit the museum.
Elena va a viajar a México.   Elena is going to travel to Mexico.

Here are all the forms of the verb **ir + a**:

voy a	I am going to
vas a	you are going to (informal)
va a	you are going to (formal); he/she/it is going to
vamos a	we are going to
van a	you are going to
van a	they are going to

Exercise 1

This is what a tourist intends to do one day while visiting Lima:

1 **Voy a visitar el Museo de la Inquisición.**
2 **Voy a pasear por el malecón.**
3 **Voy a nadar en el mar.**
4 **Voy a mirar tiendas.**
5 **Voy a tomar helados.**
6 **Voy a cambiar plata.**

And this is what a local person has to say about each activity. Can you match the comment with the corresponding sentence above?

(a) **En el mercado paralelo pagan más.**
(b) **Es muy romántico.**
(c) **Está cerca de la catedral.**
(d) **El de frutilla es muy rico.**
(e) **Yo prefiero la piscina.**
(f) **Hay un centro comercial muy cerca.**

pasear	to walk about,	**tomar helados**	to have ice cream
	to go for a stroll	**mercado paralelo**	free rate
malecón	promenade		currency market
nadar	to swim	**frutilla**	strawberry
mar	sea	**piscina**	swimming pool
mirar tiendas	window shopping	**cambiar plata**	change money

Exercise 2 🔳

¿Qué vas a hacer?

This is a list of possible activities for the week ahead. Look at the example and practise similar questions and answers for each day. Use **y también** 'and also' to link both sentences.

Example:

¿Qué vas a hacer el lunes?
El lunes voy a telefonear a casa y también voy a preparar la reunión.

LUNES	telefonear a casa
	preparar la reunión
MARTES	asistir a la reunión
	comer en un restaurante céntrico
MIÉRCOLES	estudiar el reglamento
	escribir cartas
JUEVES	probar el equipo nuevo
	entrevistar a posible jefe de ventas
VIERNES	recoger la nueva impresora láser
	comprar 'compact discs'
SÁBADO	descansar
DOMINGO	descansar

asistir	to attend	**jefe de ventas**	head of sales
reglamento	regulations	**recoger**	to pick up
equipo	equipment	**impresora**	printer
entrevistar	to interview	**descansar**	to rest

Some more useful connectors:

en primer lugar	first, in the first place
luego	then
más adelante	later
finalmente	finally, lastly

Exercise 3

Say what you are going to do at the weekend. Use events from the list below. Here is an example:

A: **¿Adónde vas a ir el viernes?**
B: **Voy a ir a la Exposición de Juguetes.**
A: **¿Dónde es?**
B: **En el Museo Antropológico.**
A: **¿A qué hora?**
B: **A las cinco de la tarde.**

Guía de Fin de Semana

VIERNES
P.M.
5.00   Exposición. Ganadores del Concurso de Pintores Jóvenes. Auditorio Municipal.
5.00   Exposición. Juguetes de otra época. Museo Antropológico. Sala Especial 1.
8.00   El grupo Arena interpreta los temas de su nuevo compact. Restaurante Bartolo. Playa Las Piedritas.
9.00   La cantante Tania ofrece una noche de rock en el teatro La Primavera. Cerca de la Catedral.

SÁBADO
P.M.
4.00   Exposición fotográfica. 'Paisajes y personas'. En blanco y negro y en color. Entrada gratis. Instituto de Cultura.
7.00   Ballet Nacional. Danzas folklóricas y modernas. Palacio de la Música.
8.00   Teatro Marsano. Obra cómica. 'Las Brujas'. Décima semana en cartelera.
9.30   Bar El Auténtico. Jazz hasta las 2 de la madrugada.

DOMINGO
A.M.

9.00	Competencia automovilística. En la Vía Expresa.
10.00	Exposición de monedas antiguas. Banco Central.
2.00	Final del Campeonato de Vóley. Estadio Nacional.

fin de semana	weekend	**entrada**	admission, ticket
ganadores	winners	**obra cómica**	comedy
concurso	competition	**en cartelera**	on at the theater or
juguetes	toys		cinema
otra época	bygone era	**madrugada**	early hours of the
sala	hall		morning
interpreta	sings	**monedas**	old coins
ofrece	gives	**antiguas**	
cantante	singer	**campeonato**	championship
paisajes	landscapes	**estadio**	stadium

Exercise 4

RESTAURANTE 'TERRENAL'

Dirección:	Lisina 844
Teléfono:	343–9983
Tarjetas:	Visa y Diners
Horario:	Lunes a Sábado a partir del mediodía
Reservas:	Recomendables
Nivel de Precios:	De $10 (menús especiales) a $25

tarjeta	card	**nivel de precios**	price range
horario	opening hours	**a partir de**	from, as from

Based on the information above, say which of the following statements are possible and which are not. Use the words **Sí es posible** 'It is possible' or **No es posible** 'It is not possible' for your answers.

1 **Voy a pagar con tarjeta Visa.**
2 **Vamos a almorzar el domingo.**
3 **Vamos a almorzar a las 11.30 de la mañana.**
4 **Voy a pedir el menú más barato de diez pesos.**
5 **Vas a reservar una mesa por teléfono.**

Language point

The relative pronoun que

Que is the relative pronoun normally used to link two phrases in one sentence. In English it can be 'that', 'which' or 'who':

Los jóvenes *que* prefieren un Young people *who* prefer a quiet
ambiente tranquilo. atmosphere.
El restaurante *que* está en la The restaurant *which* is on the
esquina. corner.
El plato *que* me gusta. The dish *that* I like.

En el restaurante

After reading the dialogue below and looking at the menu, answer the following questions:

Do the customers both choose the same?
What would you choose?

A couple are choosing something to eat from the menu below at a restaurant in Buenos Aires

CLIENTE: (*To the waiter*) ¿Qué es lenguado? ¿Carne? ¿Pescado? ¿Verdura?
MOZO: Es pescado. Es muy agradable.
CLIENTE: Para mí un lomo. Para mi esposo, lenguado con jenjibre.
MOZO: ¿Para beber?
CLIENTE: Vino blanco, por favor.

CUSTOMER: *What is 'lenguado'? Meat? Fish? Vegetable?*
WAITER: *It's fish. It's very nice.*
CUSTOMER: *A steak for me. For my husband, sole with ginger.*
WAITER: *Something to drink?*
CUSTOMER: *White wine, please.*

```
★ MENU TRADICIONAL ★
          10 pesos

Ensaladas    A escoger del bar de las ensaladas
(Salads)     (To choose from the salad bar)

Broqueta de pollo          (Chicken brochettes)
Broqueta de carne          (Meat brochette)
Panqueques de espinaca     (Spinach pancakes)
Milanesas                  (escalope)

Ensalada de fruta con helado (Fruit salad and ice cream)

          ★ PLATOS ESPECIALES ★

Lomo con salsa de berenjenas
                          (Beefsteak in aubergine sauce)
Lenguado con jenjibre    (Sole with ginger)
'Hojas' de pollo con champiñones
                          (Chicken with mushrooms)
Parrillada               (Grilled meats)

              ★ POSTRES ★

Ensalada de frutas       (Fruit salad)
Torta de chocolate       (Chocolate cake)
```

Language point

Para mí

To indicate for whom something is intended, such as a meal at a restaurant or a drink at a bar, the usual expression is **para** followed by the object of the order. Here are all the forms:

para mí	for me
para ti	for you (informal)
para usted	for you (formal)
para él	for him
para ella	for her

para nosotros	for us
para ustedes	for you (formal and informal)
para ellos	for them (all masculine or mixed group)
para ellas	for them (all feminine)

Examples:

| **La chica es para Mariana.** | The small one is for Mariana. |
| **Estos regalos son para ustedes.** | These presents are for you. |

Reading

In each issue a weekly magazine recommends some restaurants following the International Classification System, giving points for cooking, service, decoration, etc. Read this week's results and then answer the questions in Exercise 5:

CLASIFICACIÓN

0–10 puntos	Malo/Regular
11–15 puntos	Promedio
16–20 puntos	Bueno
21–25 puntos	Muy bueno
26–30 puntos	Excelente

Según el sistema de clasificación internacional, se otorgan puntos por cada aspecto del restaurante: cocina, servicio, decorado, etc.

Esta semana recomendamos

24 puntos   *El Jardín*, Calle Ugarteche 315. Reservas al 802–1555. Cocina argentina moderna y de rápida preparación 'fast-food'. Broquetas de langostinos y champiñones. Todos los días desde las 12 del mediodía hasta las 4 de la madrugada. De \$10 a \$30 por persona.

18 puntos   *The Grill*, Calle Reconquista 1875. Reservas al 312–2477. Cocina inglesa y porteña. Lunes a viernes mediodía y noche. \$20 a \$40 por persona.

17 puntos	*Marítimo*, Costanera Norte. Reservas al 788–0409. Pescados y mariscos. Broqueta de pez espada con tagliatelle. Todos los días al mediodía y por la noche. $30 a $40 por persona.
14 puntos	*Sabor*, Pelliza 319. Reservas al 726–5341. Cocina europea. Martes a domingo por la noche. $30 a $50 por persona.

Exercise 5

Decide if the following statements are true (**verdadero**) or false (**falso**).

1 **El Jardín está en la calle Ugarteche.**
2 **El Jardín abre sólo por las tardes.**
3 **El Grill es un restaurante promedio.**
4 **El Marítimo se especializa en pescados.**
5 **El Sabor es un restaurante malo.**

Language point

Según

This word means 'according to', as in **Según el gobierno, la inflación está bajo control.** 'According to the government, inflation is under control.'

Other expressions with similar meaning are:

de acuerdo con
conforme a
de conformidad con

Conforme a and **de conformidad con** are used in a more formal or legal context.

De acuerdo con las normas.	According to the rules.
De conformidad con la ley actual.	According to current legislation.

Reading

While reading the advertisement below, see if you can find answers to these questions:

Is the advertisement offering travel abroad?
What does the Gran Hotel offer, and what is required from you?

★ **EL GRAN HOTEL** ★
PRESENTA

NOCHE CUBANA
NOCHE BRASILEÑA
NOCHE PERUANA
NOCHE PARAGUAYA
NOCHE MEJICANA

Cada fin de semana viaje
con su imaginación a otros países.

Nosotros ofrecemos el ambiente,
la música, el baile, la comida
adecuada.

Usted aporta su grata presencia.

---

viaje	travel	**comida**	food
imaginación	imagination	**aporta**	contribute
ambiente	atmosphere	**grata**	pleasant
baile	dance	**presencia**	presence

Reading

While reading the list of food and drinks from a health food shop, see if you can find answers to these questions:

Can you ask them to deliver or do you have to collect?
How many dishes a day are recommended?

tarta de verduras	vegetable pie	**bizcochuelo de**	carrot cake
tarta dulce	low-fat sweet pie	**zanahoria**	
dietética		**pan de salvado**	bran bread
bocaditos	'healthy' snacks	**pan de queso**	cheese bread
dietéticos		**elaboramos**	we make
empanadas	low-fat pasties	**bajar de peso**	to loose weight
dietéticas		**mantener el peso**	to maintain a
jugos y licuados	isotonic drinks		certain weight
energéticos		**deseado**	that you want
budín dietético	low-fat bread	**reparto a**	home delivery
	pudding	**domicilio**	

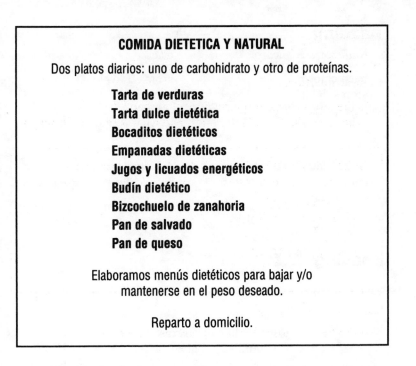

COMIDA DIETETICA Y NATURAL

Dos platos diarios: uno de carbohidrato y otro de proteínas.

Tarta de verduras
Tarta dulce dietética
Bocaditos dietéticos
Empanadas dietéticas
Jugos y licuados energéticos
Budín dietético
Bizcochuelo de zanahoria
Pan de salvado
Pan de queso

Elaboramos menús dietéticos para bajar y/o
mantenerse en el peso deseado.

Reparto a domicilio.

Note: health food shops usually announce their products as
dietéticos .

Exercise 6

Match the food/drink on the left with the country on the right where
it is a typical dish/drink. The glossary at the back of the book might
help.

1	**chipa**	(a)	Perú
2	**guacamole**	(b)	Colombia
3	**carapulcra**	(c)	Paraguay
4	**tinto**	(d)	México
5	**mate**	(e)	Argentina

Exercise 7

You have just ordered sole as the main course. Which of these two
wines goes well with it?

VINOS

Naturaleza Blanca	*Clásico*
buen color	aroma tradicional
aroma débil	neutro
algo dulce	frutal
ligero	cuerpo medio
agradable	
Buena combinación con jamón, melón o con frutas en general.	Adecuado para acompañar a mariscos o pescados asados.

Reading 📼

While reading the passage below, see if you can find answers to these questions:

What's the atmosphere like in this restaurant?
What are the restaurant's special attractions?

El restaurante 'La Plata'

El restaurante 'La Plata' está situado en la zona del sur de la Plaza de Mayo en Buenos Aires, donde hay un ambiente romántico y melancólico. Los restaurantes tienen un aire de antiguos, aunque muchos son edificios nuevos. La zona es concurrida por adultos y también por jóvenes que prefieren un ambiente tranquilo. Esta parte de Buenos Aires es diferente del norte o del oeste. El restaurante 'La Plata' está en un inmenso local decorado con pinturas modernas. Se utiliza un proyector de video láser para mostrar video clips sobre una amplia pared.

está situado	is located	**concurrido**	well attended,
zona	area		busy (of a place
ambiente	atmosphere		but not a person)
tiene un aire de	has an air of	**jóvenes**	young people
antiguo	old	**tranquilo**	quiet
edificio	building	**norte**	north

sur	south	**pinturas**	paintings
este	east	**se utiliza**	it is used
oeste	west	**mostrar**	to show
inmenso local	huge premises	**amplia pared**	large wall

11 Se dice que . . .

It is said that . . .

By the end of this chapter you should be able to:

- Make impersonal statements using **se**
- Understand basic travel and leisure information
- Use some expressions of comparison with **tan . . . como** (as . . . as)
- Make comparisons using **más de** (more than) and **menos de** (less than) followed by numbers or quantities

Turismo en Mar Del Plata 🔘

While reading the dialogue below, see if you can find answers to these questions:

Is tourism on the increase?
What has been done to attract more tourists?

The mayor of Mar del Plata is being interviewed about tourism in his town

ENTREVISTADOR: Este año el turismo muestra un incremento del 30 por ciento. ¿Cómo se logró esto?

ALCALDE: Se trabaja para el crecimiento. Anualmente se destina 25 por ciento de los recursos a obras públicas. Se ha reducido el personal (en 35 por ciento). Se mejora continuamente la limpieza de plazas, paseos y calles. Hay que atraer al turista.

ENTREVISTADOR: ¿Qué otros planes hay?

ALCALDE: Se van a construir atracciones deportivas y culturales. El turismo está relacionado con el deporte y la cultura.

INTERVIEWER: *This year tourism has shown an increase of 30 per cent. How was this achieved?*
MAYOR: *We are working for growth. We allocate 25 per cent of resources to public works annually. Staff have been reduced by 35 per cent. Cleanliness is improved continuously in squares, promenades and streets. We have to attract tourists.*
INTERVIEWER: *What other plans are there?*
MAYOR: *Sport and cultural venues will be built. Tourism is linked to sport and culture.*

Language point

Impersonal se

Se with a third person verb usually has an impersonal meaning. In English, the usual equivalent is a sentence in the passive voice. (See also Chapter 19.)

Examples:

Se dice que tiene cáncer.	It is said that he/she has cancer.
Se iniciará en 1999.	It will be started in 1999.
Se van a construir veinte casas.	Twenty houses are going to be built.
Se ha aumentado el precio.	The price has been increased.
Se habla español.	Spanish spoken.
El grupo musical 'Los Gitanos' se presenta en distintos estadios en las próximas semanas.	The band 'Los Gitanos' will perform in various stadia in the next few weeks.
Las canciones de Daniela se inspiran en su trabajo de maestra.	Daniela's songs are inspired by her work as a teacher.
Con una computadora:	With a computer,
se puede procesar textos	you can do word processing
se puede hacer una base de datos	you can create a database

| **se puede emplear una hoja de cálculo** | you can use a spreadsheet |
| **se puede hacer gráficos** | you can create graphics |

Exercise 1

Give the equivalent in Spanish using the impersonal **se**.

1 It opens early.
2 Cars are made here.
3 Computers repaired.
4 A report is prepared daily.
5 It is said that he is very ill.

Exercise 2

Read the following information about holidays and then complete the chart given below.

CHARTERS EXCLUSIVOS – CONFIRMACIÓN INMEDIATA - SALIDAS VIERNES

De lujo

Hotel Amsterdam

7 noches en Hotel de Primera Categoría con desayuno, piscina. Precio incluye pasaje aéreo y asistencia médica durante la estadía.

$495

****

Especial

Hotel Central

5 noches, con desayuno. Incluye pasaje aéreo. Entrada al casino. Asistencia médica durante la estadía.

$435

****

Alojamiento independiente

7 noches en apartamentos de dos ambientes con kitchenette. Auto compacto con kilometraje ilimitado. El precio incluye el pasaje aéreo y la asistencia médica durante toda la estadía.

$680

(Precio por persona. Base cuádruple.)

Based on the information about holidays above, complete the following:

Hotel	Nº de noches	desayuno	piscina	pasaje incluido	asistencia médica incluida
Amsterdam					
Central					
Apartamento					

Reading

Read the following information about a weekly publication called *Pasatiempo*, devoted to outdoor activities, then answer the following questions:

What are the main features of the magazine?
What are the activities covered?
Which of the activities mentioned do you like?

Pasatiempo

Una publicación semanal completa y actualizada para planificar su fin de semana.

Información indispensable:

lugares   hojas de ruta
paseos   tarifas

atracciones	medios de transporte
campings	itinerarios
hoteles	pronóstico del tiempo

La revista para los que gustan del descanso. Para disfrutar del tiempo libre en contacto con la naturaleza y el aire puro.

Actividades que incluimos:

turismo	montañismo
salidas cortas	fauna
campamentismo	bicicleta de montaña
pesca	todo terreno
buceo	aventuras

Exercise 3

Match each present to the most suitable recipient:

1 **billetera para hombre**
2 **cartera en negro y marrón**
3 **garrafa de vidrio para vino**
4 **reloj despertador**
5 **mochila colegial**
6 **malla entera de baño**
7 **lapicero**
8 **adorno de porcelana**

(a) **esposo**
(b) **esposa**
(c) **enamorado**
(d) **enamorada**
(e) **una joven de 15 años**
(f) **una abuela**
(g) **tu mejor amigo**

billetera	wallet	**malla entera de baño**	one-piece swimsuit
cartera	purse	**lapicero**	ball-point pen
garrafa	carafe	**adorno**	ornament
reloj	watch/clock	**esposo**	husband
despertador	alarm clock	**esposa**	wife
mochila	rucksack	**enamorado**	boyfriend
colegial	school (adjective)		

enamorada	girlfriend	**abuela**	grandmother
una joven	a young lady	**mejor amigo**	best friend

Suggest other suitable presents for the people mentioned above.

Una bici 🔊

While reading the dialogue below, see if you can find answers to these questions:

When does the child want the bike?
Why is it a good time to buy one now?

HIJO: Papi, quiero una bici. Una bicicleta de montaña.
PADRE: Tienes que esperar hasta la Navidad. Además las bicicletas de montaña son más caras que las bicicletas tradicionales.
HIJO: Pero ahora están de oferta hasta el sábado.
PADRE: Montar en bicicleta puede ser peligroso.
HIJO: Sí, pero voy a usar un casco protector. He visto uno amarillo que me gusta. No es tan grande como un casco para ir en moto.

SON: *Dad, I want a bike. A mountain bike.*
FATHER: *You'll have to wait until Christmas. Besides, mountain bikes are more expensive than ordinary bicycles.*
SON: *But they are on special offer until Saturday.*
FATHER: *Riding a bike can be dangerous.*
SON: *Yes, but I'm going to wear a helmet. I've seen a yellow one I like. It's not as big as the one you need to go on a motorbike.*

Language point

Tan . . . como

When you compare in terms of equality you use the expression **tan . . . como**. It translates as 'as . . . as', often with an adjective in the middle. The adjective describes the nature of the equality. Here are some examples:

La bicicleta es tan necesaria como el aire puro.	A bicycle is as necessary as fresh air.
Yo tengo 49 años. Tú tienes 20. Yo no soy tan joven como tú.	I am 49 years old. You are 20. I am not as young as you are.
El otro libro no es tan interesante como éste.	The other book is not as interesting as this one.

Exercise 4

Express the following comparisons as in the example, using the clue in brackets.

Example:

El mapa cuesta 20 pesos. El libro cuesta 250 pesos. (caro)
El mapa no es tan caro como el libro.

1 **Carlos vive a dos horas de aquí. Graciela vive a cinco horas de aquí. (cerca)**
2 **Carolina mide 1.78m y su hermano José también mide 1.78m (alto/a)**
3 **La rosa es una flor muy linda. El clavel también es una flor muy linda. (linda/o)**
4 **Mi televisor es de 14". El televisor de mi novia es de 17". (grande)**
5 **Esta impresora produce 4 páginas por minuto. La otra impresora produce 8 páginas por minuto. (rápida)**

Exercise 5

Read the following advertisement offering prizes, then match the prizes 1 to 5 with their use (a) to (e).

(a) para escuchar música en diversas formas
(b) para ver programas
(c) para pasear
(d) para preparar la comida
(e) para grabar música

BICI REINA

Con la compra de una Bici Reina recibes un termo de regalo.
En el termo hay un cupón para un sorteo de grandes premios.

PREMIOS PARA LOS COMPRADORES:

1 Un ciclomotor 50 cc.
2 Un televisor a color de 14".
3 Un equipo de sonido.
4 Una cocina de 4 hornallas.
5 Una radiograbadora stereo.

Fecha del sorteo: 22 de diciembre

Reading

While reading the advertisement below, see if you can find answers to these questions:

Can you win a prize if you buy this product?
How do you enter the draw?

ADELGAZAR CON 'GELA SLIM'

Más sabor y más color

Gela Slim es un 'postre' que adelgaza. Es una gelatina deliciosa con todo su color y sabor.

Sólo 1.8 calorías en cada porción de 100 gramos.
Consumir media hora antes de las comidas.

Gela Slim absorbe grasas y azúcares.

Menos de 2 calorías. Más de 10 sabores para escoger.

Es posible ganar un automóvil 0 km.

En cada envase de Gela Slim hay un formulario. Rellenar los espacios con sus datos y a participar en el sorteo.

(Concurso sin obligación de compra.)

adelgazar	to slim	**formulario**	form
sabor	flavor, taste	**rellenar**	to fill in
todo	all	**datos**	information, data
porción	portion, serving	**sorteo**	draw, raffle
antes de	before	**concurso**	contest,
comidas	meals		competition
grasas	fats	**sin**	without
azúcares	sugars	**obligación**	obligation
ganar	to win	**compra**	purchase
envase	packet, container		

Note: the phrase **Concurso sin obligación de compra** is the equivalent of the English 'No purchase necessary'.

Language point

Más de/menos de

The expressions **más de** and **menos de** ('more than' and 'less than') are used to establish comparison before numbers or quantities.

Hay más de 10 sabores.	There are more than 10 flavors.
Tiene menos de 2 calorías.	It has less than 2 calories.
Hay más de 100 personas.	There are more than 100 people.
Hay menos de 50 dólares en la cuenta.	There is less than 50 dollars in the account.

Exercise 6

Complete with **más de** or **menos de**:

1 **Tienen 23 empleados. Tienen _____ de veinte empleados.**
2 **Hay 1,050 asistentes. Hay _____ mil asistentes.**
3 **Cuesta $64.99 por semana. Cuesta _____ sesenta y cinco dolares.**
4 **Ha viajado 32,045 km. en ese carro. Ha viajado _____ treinta y cinco mil km.**
5 **Normalmente asisten 107 diputados. Normalmente asisten _____ de cien diputados.**

Exercise 7

Read the following advertisements:

INSTITUTO INTERNACIONAL
Turno diurno y nocturno
Inglés
Procesamiento de textos
Computación
Mecánica de automóviles
Jr Córdoba 911

FUNDACIÓN LEXIS
Cursos por correspondencia
Manualidades en 10 lecciones
Pintura sobre madera en 12 lecciones
Contabilidad básica en 15 lecciones
Precio de cada lección $20
Pagar al cartero
Solicite información al 825 3257

INSTITUTO DE DEPORTES
Natatorio climatizado
Clases individuales y grupales de natación
Bebés – Niños – Adultos
Jr Zepita 765

Say if the following statements are **verdadero** (true) or **falso** (false) based on the three advertisements above.

1 **Para estudiar inglés se puede ir al Instituto de Deportes.**
2 **Es posible estudiar inglés por correspondencia en la Fundación Lexis.**
3 **Manualidades por correspondencia se estudia en diez lecciones.**
4 **El curso de contabilidad básica cuesta $300.**
5 **Cuando se estudia por correspondencia en Fundación Lexis se paga directamente en la oficina principal.**
6 **Procesamiento de textos es un curso que ofrece el Instituto Internacional.**
7 **Sólo se puede estudiar de día en el Instituto Internacional.**
8 **Pintura sobre madera lleva más tiempo que manualidades.**
9 **Un niño de seis meses puede empezar a nadar en el Instituto de Deportes.**
10 **Se puede aprender mecánica de automóviles por correspondencia.**

Exercise 8

Read the following invitation:

CLUB DE TENIS

Se invita a los socios a una reunión el miércoles 3 de diciembre a partir de las 19.30 horas, a fin de conformar la subcomisión de tenis del club.

Based on the information above, say if the following statements are **verdadero** (true) or **falso** (false).

1 Members and non-members are invited.
2 The meeting is on a Friday.
3 The meeting starts at 7.30 p.m.
4 The purpose of the meeting is to form a subcommittee.
5 The meeeting is at the beginning of the year.

a partir de	as from, beginning from	**reunión**	meeting
a fin de	in order to	**subcomisión**	sub-committee

12 ¿Qué hiciste?

What did you do?

By the end of this chapter you should be able to:

- Use the past tense with regular verbs
- Use the past tense with irregular verbs
- Use a range of expressions for past time reference

Reading

Below are some news headlines from a newspaper.

LOS TITULARES

- Ayer llegó a Lima el nuevo embajador de la República de Chile.
- El dólar subió diez céntimos en el mercado de cambios.
- Empatamos en fútbol, ganamos en vóley.
- Anoche terminó la Primera Jornada de Educadores Latino-americanos.
- Volvió la cantante Tania Libertad.

THE HEADLINES

- The new ambassador from Chile arrived in Lima yesterday.
- The dollar rose ten cents in the currency market.
- We drew in football and won in volleyball.
- The first conference of Latin American teachers came to an end last night.
- The singer Tania Libertad is back.

Note: it is not unusual to find headlines written in the past tense in Latin American newspapers.

Language points

The past tense or preterite

The past tense, or preterite, is used to express an action in the past already complete at the time of speaking.

Ayer comimos en un restaurante.	Yesterday we went to a restaurant for a meal.
Al fin terminamos el proyecto.	At last we finished the project.
Vivimos en Quito durante dos años.	We lived in Quito for two years.

Regular verbs

The past tense of regular verbs, i.e. those which follow a certain pattern or rule, is formed using endings which vary according to the person.

-ar verbs: **terminar** (to finish)

terminé	I finished
termin*aste*	you finished (informal)
termin*ó*	you finished (formal); he/she/it finished
termin*amos*	we finished
termin*aron*	you finished
termin*aron*	they finished

Note that the form for the first person plural is the same as the present tense. The context of the sentence, or the addition of a reference to the time when the action took place, usually avoids any confusion.

-er verbs: **comer**

com*í*	com*imos*
com*iste*	com*ieron*
com*ió*	com*ieron*

-ir verbs: **vivir**

viv*í*	viv*imos*
viv*iste*	viv*ieron*
viv*ió*	viv*ieron*

El fin de semana 🔲

Carola tells Elsa about her weekend in Lima

CAROLA: Hola, cuéntame de tu fin de semana.
ELSA: El viernes por la noche comimos en un restaurante típico. Bailamos 'landó' y luego regresamos al departamento. El sábado por la mañana compramos varias cosas en el centro, luego compramos comida para llevar y almorzamos en el departamento. Por la tarde vimos una película en un cine de estreno y luego vimos la obra *No me toquen ese vals* en un teatrito de la Avenida Brasil. Muy linda la obra.
CAROLA: ¿Y el domingo?
ELSA: El domingo, descansamos.

CAROLA: *Hello! Tell me about your weekend.*
ELSA: *On Friday evening we had a meal in a typical restaurant. We danced 'landó' and then we went back to the apartment. On Saturday morning we went to town and bought a few things. Later we bought some take-away food and had lunch in the apartment. In the afternoon we saw a film at the cinema and then we saw the play* Don't Play That Waltz *in a little theater on Avenida Brasil. A beautiful play.*
CAROLA: *And on Sunday?*
ELSA: *On Sunday, we had a rest.*

Note: **landó** is a type of Afro-Peruvian music.

Exercise 1

Give an account in Spanish of your (or somebody else's) weekend in Lima, based on the information below. Say the sentences in the preterite, and in the order that you find most suitable. Omit some and/or add others if you wish.

Useful connectors:

después	afterwards
luego	then
más tarde	later

Comprar la revista *Quehacer.*
Ver una obra de teatro en Barranco.
Visitar una exposición de pintura en la galería Forum.
Asistir a la clase de quena.
Llamar por teléfono a un amigo/una amiga.
Bailar en la discoteca.
Practicar aeróbicos en el gimnasio.
Comer un cebiche.
Preparar unos cocteles.

Quehacer	current affairs publication in Perú
Barranco	district of Lima where many cultural events take place and where many restaurants which offer live shows are located
pintura	painting
Forum	well-known art gallery in Lima
asistir	to attend (a lesson, a meeting, etc.)
quena	traditional Andean musical instrument
llamar	to call
cebiche	popular dish made with raw fish marinated in lemon
coctel	cocktail

Language points

Expressions of time in the past ▫▫

Here are some useful expressions for specific reference to time in the past.

ayer	yesterday
anteayer	the day before yesterday
anoche	last night
la semana pasada	last week
el lunes pasado	last Monday
el viernes pasado	last Friday
el mes pasado	last month

As you can see, **pasado/a** can be used to form a number of expressions in the past. It is not the literal translation of 'last' (**último**). **Último** is used to indicate that something or somebody is the last of

a series; that there are no more, as in: **Esta es la última función.**
'This is the last show'.

Hace

Hace is used to indicate how long ago something happened.

Examples:

¿Cuándo llegó? Hace dos días.	When did she arrive? Two days ago.
Terminó la universidad hace un año.	He finished college a year ago.

Exercise 2

Match the phrases 1 to 5 with the phrases (a) to (e).

1 **Leí un cuento . . .**
2 **Vimos una linda pintura modernista . . .**
3 **Visitamos tres iglesias . . .**
4 **Anoche . . .**
5 **Rellenamos el formulario . . .**

(a) **. . . en la galería Forum.**
(b) **. . . para renovar el pasaporte.**
(c) **. . . en el centro de la capital.**
(d) **. . . soñé contigo.**
(e) **. . . en la biblioteca.**

cuento	short story	**soñar**	to dream (of)
renovar	to renew		

¿Dónde nació? 🔲

Here is an interview with a young painter from Paraguay

PERIODISTA: ¿Dónde nació?
COLLAR: Nací en Itauguá Guazú en 1964.
PERIODISTA: ¿Dónde pasó sus primeros años?

COLLAR:	Pasé mis primeros años con mi abuela materna. Aprendí guaraní como primera lengua. Luego me adapté al castellano.
PERIODISTA:	¿Tuvo una infancia feliz?
COLLAR:	Desde los diez años tuve que trabajar. Primero en una farmacia y luego como ayudante de imprenta. Luego tuve mi propia oficina de diseño gráfico.
PERIODISTA:	¿Cómo nace su trabajo de pintor?
COLLAR:	Estudié en la Escuela de Bellas Artes. Poco a poco participé en muestras individuales y colectivas.
PERIODISTA:	¿Qué premio importante ha obtenido?
COLLAR:	Recientemente gané el Premio Martel de Artes Plásticas.

JOURNALIST:	*Where were you born?*
COLLAR:	*I was born in Itauguá Guazú in 1964.*
JOURNALIST:	*Where did you spend the first years of your life?*
COLLAR:	*I was with my maternal grandmother. I learnt Guarani as my first language. Later I got used to speaking Spanish.*
JOURNALIST:	*Did you have a happy childhood?*
COLLAR:	*I had to work from the age of ten. First in a chemist's and then as an apprentice in a printing workshop. After that I had my own graphic design studio.*
JOURNALIST:	*How did your work as a painter start?*
COLLAR:	*I studied in the School of Fine Arts. Gradually I took part in individual and group exhibitions.*
JOURNALIST:	*Have you won any awards?*
COLLAR:	*I recently won the Martel Prize for the Arts.*

Reading 📼

De visita en ciudad de México

Ayer empezamos nuestra visita de la ciudad de México. Primero partimos del Zócalo y fuimos al Palacio de Bellas Artes que está construido de mármol. Luego estuvimos en el Museo Antropológico y más tarde en el Museo de Arte Moderno. De ahí, fuimos al Bosque de Chapultepec, que está muy cerca del Museo de

Arte Moderno. Yo compré artesanía de Oaxaca en un mercado local. Los tapetes son lindos. La señora Chávez va muy seguido a ese mercado. Dice que allí venden más barato.

empezamos	we started	**tapetes**	tapestries
partimos	we set off	**lindos**	pretty
mármol	marble	**muy seguido**	very often
artesanía	handicraft	**barato**	cheap

Language points

Irregular verbs in the past

Irregular verbs do not follow the rules which apply to the majority of verbs. Their stems or their endings differ from those of regular verbs.

Compare these verbs in the past:

escribir (regular)   **ir** (irregular)

escribí	**escribimos**	**fui**	**fuimos**
escribiste	**escribieron**	**fuiste**	**fueron**
escribió	**escribieron**	**fue**	**fueron**

As you see, the stem in the past forms of **ir** has changed.

comer (regular)   **hacer** (irregular)

comí	**comimos**	**hice**	**hicimos**
comiste	**comieron**	**hiciste**	**hicieron**
comió	**comieron**	**hizo**	**hicieron**

Other frequently used irregular verbs in the past are:

ser   **venir**

fui	**fuimos**	**vine**	**vinimos**
fuiste	**fuisteis**	**viniste**	**vinisteis**
fue	**fueron**	**vino**	**vinieron**

tener   **estar**

tuve	**tuvimos**	**estuve**	**estuvimos**
tuviste	**tuvieron**	**estuviste**	**estuvieron**
tuvo	**tuvieron**	**estuvo**	**estuvieron**

saber		dar	
supe	supimos	di	dimos
supiste	supieron	diste	dieron
supo	supieron	dio	dieron

Exercise 3

Replace the infinitives with the correct past form.

1 **La semana pasada (ir)(yo) al Museo de Arte Moderno.**
2 **(Nosotros)(ver) obras de Frida Kahlo.**
3 **Ayer Julián y Carmela (visitar) Guadalajara por primera vez.**
4 **(Yo)(comprar) dos libros en la librería del Sótano.**
5 **¿(Tú)(visitar) el Salón de la Informática en el Hotel María Isabel – Sheraton?**
6 **¿Cuándo (Ud.)(llegar) a Ciudad de México?**
7 **(Yo)(aprender) el castellano en la escuela secundaria.**
8 **Anoche (nosotros)(estar) en el restaurante Santa Anita.**
9 **(Nosotros)(ver) mariachis y otros conjuntos musicales.**
10 **María (escribir) dos cartas muy largas a sus hermanos.**

Exercise 4

Somebody attended a short training course for two weeks. Say in Spanish what this person did during that time based on the information below. Consult the glossary at the end of the book if necessary.

You can start your sentences like this:

En la primera semana . . .	The first week . . .
En la segunda semana . . .	The second week . . .

Semana 1
Estudiar el sistema operativo.
Escribir texto y fórmulas.
Imprimir la hoja de trabajo.
Diseñar pantallas.
Alimentar datos.

Semana 2
Analizar economía empresarial.

Preparar estrategias financieras.
Aplicar estadísticas y probabilidades.
Desarrollar métodos de valuación de proyectos.

Exercise 5

Change these sentences to the preterite using the information in brackets.

Example:

> **Compro una revista de deportes. (ayer)**
> **Ayer compré una revista de deportes.**

1 **Escucho un programa de radio. (anoche)**
2 **Marcelo y Estela diseñan ropa para una firma extranjera. (el año pasado)**
3 **Carlos imita a Elvis Presley en la tele. (el sábado pasado)**
4 **La revista *Decoración* sale los viernes. (ayer)**
5 **El servicio médico es criticado siempre. (ayer)**
6 **Siempre gana las carreras. (el sábado pasado)**
7 **Pochita entrena todos los domingos. (ayer y anteayer)**
8 **Leonardo come en casa. (anoche)**
9 **El jefe organiza una reunión de ejecutivos cada semana. (el viernes pasado)**
10 **Steven vuelve los lunes. (hace dos horas)**

Reading 🔲

While reading the passage below, see if you can find answers to these questions:

> Are working hours in Uruguay the same as in your own country?
> Do banks open on Saturdays in Uruguay?

Horarios de trabajo

Los horarios promedio para la actividad comercial son de 9.00 de la mañana a 7.00 de la noche, de lunes a viernes y de 8.30 de la mañana a 12.30 de la tarde los sábados. Los servicios esenciales públicos y privados se mantienen sin interrupción todo el día. Las oficinas públicas, los bancos e industrias no trabajan sábado ni domingo. La mayor parte abre de 12.00 a 5.00 de la tarde y algunos sólo cierran a las siete de la noche. Las oficinas privadas y la industria abren desde las 9.00 de la mañana hasta las 5.00 de la tarde.

horarios	opening hours	**la mayor parte**	most
promedio	average	**algunos**	some

13 Irán al mercado

They will go to the market

By the end of this chapter you should be able to:

- Express ideas using the future tense (I will)
- Use specific time reference in the future
- Use irregular verbs in the future tense

Reading 🔘🔘

While reading the following newspaper article, see if you can find answers to these questions:

Have the price increases taken effect already?
What is the highest increase expected in domestic bills?

Tarifas de electricidad aumentarán entre el 5% y 10%

El incremento se efectivizará en julio. La próxima semana se publicarán las tarifas que cobrarán a los usuarios.

Las tarifas eléctricas se incrementarán entre 5% y 10% a partir del primero de julio. Así lo manifestó el Presidente de la Comisión de Tarifas Eléctricas.

Las tarifas de los consumos industriales y comerciales experimentarán un incremento promedio de 10%. El incremento máximo de las tarifas de consumo doméstico será de 5%. Con estos aumentos las tarifas comerciales e industriales estarán muy cerca de las tarifas objetivo.

Electricity prices to go up between 5% and 10%

The increase will be implemented in July. The new prices to be charged to the users will be published next week.

Electricity prices will be increased between 5% and 10% from 1 July, said the Chairman of the Electricity Price Regulation Committee.

Prices for industrial and commercial consumption will go up by an average of 10%. The maximum increase in domestic electricity prices will be 5%. After this adjustment, prices for commercial and industrial consumption will be very near the target price.

Language points

The future tense

To form the future of regular verbs you add the same endings to the infinitive of all -**ar**, -**er** or -**ir** verbs.

trabajar	**comer**	**vivir**
trabajaré	**comeré**	**viviré**
trabajarás	**comerás**	**vivirás**
trabajará	**comerá**	**vivirá**
trabajaremos	**comeremos**	**viviremos**
trabajarán	**comerán**	**vivirán**
trabajarán	**comerán**	**vivirán**

Examples:

La empresa ampliará sus actividades.	The firm will expand its activities.
El gobierno aplicará las medidas necesarias.	The government will take the necessary action.

The future tense is used mainly in written language. In conversation the future tense is less common than its equivalent in English. Spanish speakers tend to prefer the '**ir + a** + verb' structure (see Chapter 10) to express ideas in the future.

El Presidente viajará a Europa.	The President will travel to Europe.
El nuevo entrenador del equipo llegará esta noche.	The new team manager will arrive tonight.
Mañana vamos a ir a la playa.	We are going to go to the beach tomorrow.

Voy a empezar un curso de castellano.	I am going to start a Spanish course.

Exercise 1

Change these sentences to the future tense.

Example:

   Voy a ir al centro en la mañana.
   Iré al centro en la mañana.

 1 **Vamos a comer juntos.**
 2 **Marcelo va a preparar la comida mañana.**
 3 **Esteban y yo vamos a escribir el informe.**
 4 **Vamos a esperar hasta que llegue la nueva computadora.**
 5 **Van a abrir a las 9.30, en vez de las 10.00.**
 6 **Tú vas a venir mañana temprano, ¿no?**
 7 **Se van a llevar todo.**
 8 **Elena va a empezar a trabajar el lunes.**
 9 **La reunión va a ser en mi despacho.**
10 **Voy a dejar a mi hija en la escuela.**

El próximo/la próxima

When expressing ideas in the future, such phrases as **la próxima semana**, **el próximo domingo**, etc., may be useful. Generally speaking, **próximo/próxima** means 'next', as in 'next week'.

   el próximo lunes
   la próxima semana
   el próximo mes
   el próximo verano
   las próximas vacaciones
   el próximo año

El lunes que viene

Another way to express a specific moment in the future is by using the phrase **que viene** (literally 'the one which is coming').

el lunes que viene
la semana que viene
el mes que viene
el verano que viene
las vacaciones que vienen
el año que viene

Expressions with **que viene** have the same meaning as and are interchangeable with those using **el próximo/la próxima**, especially in spoken Spanish.

There is a tendency in Spanish to prefer expressions of time at the beginning of a sentence rather than at the end, although both are correct.

Example:

Mañana iremos al centro.   We will go to town tomorrow.

Exercise 2

Translate these sentences into Spanish:

1 Ann and I will go to the travel agent's next Tuesday.
2 I will travel to Guatemala and Nicaragua next year.
3 We will discuss prices at our next meeting.
4 The company will grow in the next few years.
5 New prices for gas will be announced next week.

Exercise 3

Rewrite these sentences using the alternative way of expressing time.

Example:

El próximo año visitaremos Cuba.
El año que viene visitaremos Cuba.

1 **La próxima semana saldremos de paseo al campo.**
2 **El próximo lunes firmaremos el contrato.**
3 **El próximo semestre será decisivo para la empresa.**
4 **El próximo mes terminamos el proyecto.**
5 **La próxima entrevista será con el Director.**

Language point

Dentro de

To explain when something will be completed, Spanish uses the expression **dentro de** followed by the period of time.

Dentro de dos días se clausurará la Feria.	The Fair will close in two days' time.
El grupo rockero llegará dentro de tres semanas.	The rock band will arrive in three weeks' time.

Exercise 4

This is somebody's plan of activities for next week. Say what he or she will do each day and explain each action using the future tense. Then do it again using the '**ir + a** + verb' pattern. The glossary at the back of the book will help you with new vocabulary.

Example:

El lunes estará en una reunión de diez a once.

La próxima semana en el trabajo

LUNES	Estar en la reunión (10–11) Ir a la feria de informática Comprar nuevo equipo
MARTES	Visitar la tienda de repuestos
MIÉRCOLES	Enviar fax a las sucursales Informar sobre cambios en el horario
JUEVES	Terminar el informe anual
VIERNES	Empezar las negociaciones con nuevo socio

Say what your main activities at work or at home will be next week. Again, use the future tense. Write them down in your notebook. You might start like this:

El lunes iré a la oficina a las ocho.

Exercise 5

Read the following paragraph and then answer the questions below.

Al mercado

Ana y María irán al mercado a las ocho de la mañana el sábado. Comprarán frutas y verduras. A eso de las nueve, se reunirán con Javier en la cafetería El Sol para tomar un refresco o un café. Luego a las diez y media estarán en casa de Cecilia, una amiga de los tres. Los cuatro amigos saldrán para el centro de la ciudad a las doce. Almorzarán en un restaurante céntrico y luego asistirán a una exposición de pintura en un parque situado en el Norte de la ciudad. Quizás comprarán uno o dos cuadros y más tarde tomarán helados con un grupo de tres amigos de la universidad.

Are the following **verdadero** (true) or **falso** (false)?

1 **Ana y María irán al mercado el sábado a las ocho.**
2 **Más tarde tomarán un café o refresco.**
3 **No irán al centro de la ciudad.**
4 **A sus amigos no les gustan los helados.**
5 **Quizás comprarán cuadros en una exposición de pinturas.**

¿Qué harás?

Carmen and Santiago are making plans for the afternoon

CARMEN: ¿Qué vas a hacer esta tarde? ¿Irás al centro o vendrás a la universidad?

SANTIAGO: Iré a la universidad y pondremos el toque final al trabajo que estamos preparando. Los otros estudiantes de nuestro grupo querrán saber cómo va el proyecto. Tendremos una reunión a las siete en la cafetería. ¿Qué te parece?

CARMEN: Está bien. ¿Qué harás después de la reunión?

SANTIAGO: Raúl, Silvia y yo saldremos al cine. ¿Quieres ir también?

CARMEN: Sí, claro.

CARMEN: *What are you going to do this afternoon? Will you go to the town center or will you come to the university?*

SANTIAGO: *I'll go to the university and we'll put the finishing touches to the work we are preparing. The other students in our group will want to know how this project is coming on. We'll have a meeting at seven in the cafeteria. What do you think?*

CARMEN: *Fine. What are you going to do after the meeting?*

SANTIAGO: *Raúl, Silvia and I will go to the cinema. Do you want to go, too?*

CARMEN: *Yes, of course.*

Language point

Irregular verbs in the future

These are verbs which do not follow the standard rule or pattern of formation of verbs in the future.

vivir		**salir**	
viviré	**viviremos**	**saldré**	**saldremos**
vivirás	**vivirán**	**saldrás**	**saldrán**
vivirá	**vivirán**	**saldrá**	**saldrán**

Notice how the irregular verb **salir** undergoes changes in the stem as it is conjugated.

Here are the most common irregular verbs in the future:

decir		**hacer**	
diré	**diremos**	**haré**	**haremos**
dirás	**dirán**	**harás**	**harán**
dirá	**dirán**	**hará**	**harán**

poder		**poner**	
podré	**podremos**	**pondré**	**pondremos**
podrás	**podrán**	**pondrás**	**pondrán**
podrá	**podrán**	**pondrá**	**pondrán**

querer		saber	
querré	querremos	sabré	sabremos
querrás	querrán	sabrás	sabrán
querrá	querrán	sabrá	sabrán

tener		venir	
tendré	tendremos	vendré	vendremos
tendrás	tendrán	vendrás	vendrán
tendrá	tendrán	vendrá	vendrán

Exercise 6

Complete the sentences with the future tense of the verb in brackets. Use the glossary at the back of the book to check the meaning of any new words.

1 Los visitantes (venir) a la reunión el próximo sábado.
2 La charla (empezar) a las diez de la mañana.
3 Nosotros (regresar) al local del sindicato a la una.
4 Leonor (poner) el anuncio en el periódico.
5 Ellos (establecer) nuevas normas de calidad para el producto.
6 El 23 de abril se (celebrar) el Día del Idioma.
7 Pronto (aparecer) un nuevo libro del mismo autor.
8 La Galería de Arte (presentar) una exposición de arte colonial.
9 Un especialista en el tema (hablar) a los asistentes.
10 Dentro de cinco minutos (ver) un video sobre el historial de la empresa.

Exercise 7

Match the phrases in 1 to 5 with (a) to (e).

1 Voy a llegar tarde a la reunión.
2 Estaremos en el centro mañana.
3 Ayer compramos un nuevo juego de muebles.
4 Se ha dislocado el brazo.
5 Hace frío.

(a) Hay que llevarla al hospital.
(b) Ponte una chaqueta.
(c) No hay problema. Se ha postergado para mañana.
(d) ¿Es de roble o caoba?
(e) Yo también. Tengo que hacer compras.

Reading 📼

El Día de la Tierra

El 22 de abril se celebrará el Día de la Tierra. La municipalidad entregará distinciones a los pioneros de la conservación local. El acto tendrá lugar el viernes 22 a las 8.00 de la noche en el auditorio municipal. El sábado 23 habrá un gran concierto en el auditorio del Parque Central en el cual tomarán parte varios grupos musicales que interpretarán temas ecologistas. El concierto se llevará a cabo a partir de las 6.00 de la tarde. Este evento durará aproximadamente tres horas.

entregar	to give, to deliver	**tomar parte**	to take part
pioneros	pioneers	**llevar a cabo**	to take place,
conservación	conservation		to carry out
el acto	the event	**temas**	themes
tener lugar	to take place	**durar**	to last

Exercise 8

Answer the following questions stating whether each statement is **verdadero** (true) or **falso** (false) based on the reading passage above.

1 **El Día de la Tierra no se celebra.**
2 **Los pioneros de la conservación recibirán distinciones.**
3 **Habrá un concierto en el Parque Central.**
4 **El concierto terminará a las seis de la tarde.**
5 **El concierto incluye temas ecologistas.**

14 Yo estudiaba . . .

I used to study . . .

By the end of this chapter you should be able to:

- Use the imperfect tense (e.g. I used to study)
- Use the imperfect continuous tense (e.g. I was studying)
- Use negative words

Yo estudiaba por la noche 📼

Ramón is telling Julia about his time at college

RAMÓN: En esa época, yo estudiaba en la universidad. Era una casona antigua donde había patios y balcones. Las clases se daban desde las cuatro de la tarde hasta las diez de la noche. Muchos de los estudiantes trabajaban y por eso el horario era conveniente.

JULIA: ¿Era difícil estudiar y trabajar?

RAMÓN: Sí. Llegábamos a clases medio dormidos. Estábamos cansados por el trabajo durante el día. A veces perdíamos la primera hora de clase y sólo asistíamos a partir de la segunda hora.

JULIA: ¿Cómo hacían para estar al día?

RAMÓN: Los fines de semana nos reuníamos en grupos y tratábamos de ponernos al día en todos los cursos.

RAMÓN: *At that time, I was studying at the university. It was an old mansion with courtyards and balconies. The lessons were from four in the afternoon until ten at night. Many of the students worked, so the evening lessons were convenient.*

JULIA: *Was it difficult to study and work?*

RAMÓN: *Yes. We used to arrive at the university half asleep. We*

*were tired due to our work during the day. Sometimes we
would miss the first hour and would only start to attend
from the second lesson.*

JULIA: *How did you manage to keep up to date?*

RAMÓN: *We used to gather in groups at weekends and try to catch
up with work on our course.*

Language points

The imperfect indicative tense

The imperfect tense is used to indicate a habitual or repeated action
in the past. It is the equivalent of verbs with 'used to' or 'was' in
English.

Los fines de semana nos reuníamos en grupos.	We used to gather in groups at the weekends.
Íbamos a la playa todos los domingos durante el verano.	We used to go to the beach every Sunday during the summer.

It is also used to describe characteristics in the past when such
characteristics continued to exist for a period of time. In the
preterite actions are finite.

La gata se llamaba Magdalena. (imperfect)	The cat used to be called/was called Magdalena.
Tomás llamó a su gata. (preterite)	Tomás called for his cat.

More examples with the imperfect:

La casa estaba muy cerca del centro.	The house was very near the center of town.
Todo costaba menos en aquellos días.	Everything cost less in those days.

Regular verbs have their forms in the imperfect indicative as
follows:

comprar	vender	vivir
compraba	vendía	vivía
comprabas	vendías	vivías
compraba	vendía	vivía

comprábamos	vendíamos	vivíamos
compraban	vendían	vivían
compraban	vendían	vivían

There are only three verbs which are irregular in the imperfect indicative:

ir	ser	ver
iba	era	veía
ibas	eras	veías
iba	era	veía
íbamos	éramos	veíamos
iban	eran	veían
iban	eran	veían

Examples:

Entonces iba al colegio a pie.	Then I used to go to school on foot.
Eramos veintitres en la clase.	We used to be twenty-three in our class.
Antes veía mucha televisión.	She used to watch television a lot.

The imperfect continuous tense

Example:

Estaba estudiando.	I was studying.

This tense in Spanish is very similar in use to its English equivalent. In Latin America it is very common. In Spain however, there is a tendency to use the imperfect indicative instead (**estudiaba**).

The imperfect continuous is used to refer to an action already in progress in the past when something else happened, interrupting the first action.

Estaba escuchando música cuando sonó el timbre.	I was listening to music when the bell rang.
El cartero llegó cuando estaba tomando desayuno.	The postman arrived when I was having breakfast.
Estábamos preparando el almuerzo cuando se apagó la luz.	We were making lunch when there was a power cut.

In the imperfect continuous you use the verb **estar** in the imperfect indicative together with the continuous form of the main verb.

estaba trabajando	**estábamos trabajando**
estabas trabajando	**estaban trabajando**
estaba trabajando	**estaban trabajando**

Exercise 1

Complete the sentences with either the preterite or the imperfect of the verb in brackets.

1 **Antes (trabajar) los sábados. Ahora ya no.**
2 **Cuando era niña (ir) al cine con su mamá.**
3 **Ayer (llegar) el nuevo director de la empresa.**
4 **Este periódico (costar) un dólar hasta el año pasado.**
5 **El sábado pasado (llamar) a mi hermana que vive en Panamá.**
6 **Ana y Julio (ir) al mercado a comprar y (volver) hace una hora.**
7 **Fue a la tienda y (comprar) frutas exóticas.**
8 **Antes no (tener) aire acondicionado. Ahora lo han instalado.**
9 **La casa (tener) cuatro habitaciones. Luego la ampliaron.**
10 **Anoche (volver) Estela.**

Exercise 2

Give the English equivalent for these sentences.

1 **Iris trabajaba en una agencia de viajes.**
2 **Nosotros estudiábamos por la noche.**
3 **Estábamos mirando la televisión cuando llegó Rosana.**
4 **Todos los domingos venía a visitar a sus abuelos.**
5 **Las computadoras estaban a disposición de los estudiantes.**

Exercise 3

Give the Spanish equivalent for these sentences.

1 What were you doing when the telephone rang?
2 The airplane was landing when we heard the explosion.
3 He used to travel a lot.
4 Food was cheap in those days.
5 The office used to be on the second floor.

Exercise 4

Below is information from an old leaflet used to promote a private school ten years ago. Read it and then answer the questions that follow.

Colegio San Antonio
Avenida de la Montaña 2759
Tel. 782–9981

Primaria
Secundaria
Bachillerato Internacional
Laboratorio de Idiomas
Educación personalizada
Estudio dirigido
Orientación personal
Olimpiadas estudiantiles
Viajes estudiantiles a Brasil, EE. UU, Canadá, Inglaterra y
España y Japón.

Campo de deportes propio	**Gimnasio cubierto**
(50 hectáreas)	**4 canchas de tenis**
Estadio	**2 piletas de natación**
Pista de Atletismo	

idiomas	languages	**campo de deportes**	sports field
dirigido	planned, directed		
orientación	guidance, counselling	**estadio**	stadium
		pista	track
olimpiadas estudiantiles	school sports festival including many or all of the games which are part of the Olympics	**atletismo**	athletics
		gimnasio cubierto	indoor gymnasium
		cancha	court
		pileta	swimming pool
		natación	swimming
viajes estudiantiles	school trips		

1 **¿Cómo se llamaba el Colegio?**
2 **¿Dónde estaba el Colegio?**
3 **¿Qué facilidades tenía para aprender idiomas?**
4 **¿Qué viajes hacían?**
5 **¿Aconsejaban a los alumnos?**
6 **¿Qué deportes practicaban?**

7 ¿El campo de deportes era grande?
8 ¿Ofrecía sólo primaria y secundaria?
9 ¿Cuántas canchas de tenis había?
10 ¿Había pista de atletismo?

Language point

Había

The imperfect of **hay** (there is/there are) is **había** and only the singular form exists.

Había dos canchas de tenis.	There were two tennis courts.
Había una pista de atletismo.	There was an athletics track.

Nadie tenía carro

Ramón continues to talk about his university days

JULIA: ¿Cómo iban a la universidad?
RAMÓN: Era difícil llegar al campus. En mi grupo nadie tenía carro. Ninguno de nosotros tenía suficiente dinero para comprar ni siquiera un auto chico usado. Todos teníamos que ir en omnibús que se demoraba casi una hora para recorrer diez kilómetros. Nada me molestaba más que viajar parado una hora. Aunque tenía veinte años, ya tenía artritis reumatoide.

JULIA: *How did you travel to the university?*
RAMÓN: *It was difficult to reach the campus. In my group nobody had a car. None of us had enough money to afford even a small used car. We all had to go by bus, which used to take one hour to cover ten kilometers. Nothing was more irritating for me than having to travel standing for one hour. Although I was 20, I already had rheumatoid arthritis.*

Language points

Negative words

As in English, negative words, e.g. **nada** (nothing), **nadie** (nobody), **ni** (nor), may precede a verb.

Nadie tenía dinero.	Nobody had money.
Ninguno quería viajar en omnibús.	No one wanted to travel by bus.
Nada parecía apropiado.	Nothing seemed suitable.

When the negative word appears after the verb, there must be another negative word before the verb.

Nunca venía nadie a la tienda.	Nobody would ever come to the shop.
No habla ni inglés ni francés.	She speaks neither English nor French.

The most frequently used negative words are:

nada	nothing
nadie	nobody
ninguno/ninguna	no one
ni	nor
nunca	never

No más

In Latin American Spanish this expression is more frequently used than in Spain, with the meaning of 'just', 'only' or 'no more'. In Spain **nada más** is preferred.

Cincuenta gramos no más. (Latin America)	Just fifty grams.
Cincuenta gramos nada más. (Spain)	

Una no más. (Latin America)	Only one.
Una nada más. (Spain)	

The expression **no más** also has other meanings peculiar to Latin American Spanish:

to encourage others to do something

Sírvete no más.	Do help yourself.
Escríbeme no más. Yo te contesto enseguida.	Do write to me. I'll answer straight away.

to convey the idea of 'very recently' or 'very near'

Llegó ayer no más.	He only arrived yesterday.
Aquí no más voy.	I am not going very far.
Voy a la tienda no más.	I'm just going to the shop.

Exercise 5

Give the English equivalent for the following:

1 **Nadie tiene nada.**
2 **Nunca compra ningún regalo.**
3 **Estela no come ni carne ni huevos.**
4 **Nadie aprende un idioma en un día.**
5 **Aquí no más está el museo.**

Reading 🔲

While reading the following passage, see if you can find answers to these questions:

In which present day countries did the Maya civilization flourish?
What were their main interests?

Los Mayas

Los antiguos Mayas ocupaban la península de Yucatán al sur de México y la mayor parte de lo que hoy es Guatemala. Los Mayas empezaron a construir su civilización en el siglo V antes de Cristo. Los mayas se dedicaban a la arquitectura, escultura, pintura, escritura jeroglífica, matemáticas y astronomía.

antiguos	old
se dedicaban a	were devoted to
escritura jeroglífica	hieroglyphic writing
astronomía	astronomy

15 Espero que puedas

I hope you can

By the end of this chapter you should be able to:

- Use the present subjunctive with regular verbs
- Use the present subjunctive with irregular verbs
- Use expressions related to health (e.g. I've got a headache)

Estoy buscando a alguien que me oriente

Tania hopes to find somebody to help her with her project

TANIA: Estoy buscando a alguien que me oriente sobre el proyecto de consultoría.

LAURA: No creo que tengas que buscar más. Yo conozco a una persona con mucha experiencia en el asunto. Es Iris Vidal, Directora de una firma de Consultoría y Asesoramiento de Empresas.

TANIA: ¿Me puedes dar su número de teléfono?

LAURA: Claro. Acá lo tengo en mi agenda.

TANIA: *I'm looking for somebody who can give me some guidance regarding the consultancy project.*

LAURA: *I don't think you need to look any further. I know a person with a lot of experience in this matter. It's Iris Vidal, head of a Business Consultancy and Advice Bureau.*

TANIA: *Could you give me her telephone number?*

LAURA: *Sure. I have it here in my diary.*

Language points

The present subjunctive

The subjunctive is a mood which denotes attitude and is mainly used in sentences expressing wish, hope or doubt. It is used to indicate actions which are only hypothetical or a possibility in the future, at the moment of speaking.

Espero que puedas venir a la fiesta.	I hope you can make it to the party.
Quisiera que ayudes a Isabel.	I would like you to help Isabel.
Rosa me ha pedido que vaya a la oficina.	Rose has asked me to go to the office.
Su papá lo ha convencido para que vaya a Quito.	His dad has persuaded him to go to Quito.

The present subjunctive of regular verbs is formed as follows:

trabajar	**comer**	**vivir**
trabaje	**coma**	**viva**
trabajes	**comas**	**vivas**
trabaje	**coma**	**viva**
trabajemos	**comamos**	**vivamos**
trabajen	**coman**	**vivan**
trabajen	**coman**	**vivan**

Examples:

No quiero que trabaje.	I don't want her to work.
Quizás trabajemos el sábado.	We may go to work on Saturday.
Es importante que comamos frutas y verduras.	It is important for us to eat fruit and vegetables.
No creo que coman en casa esta noche.	I don't think they will eat at home tonight.
Le han recomendado que viva en el campo.	They have recommended that he should live in the countryside.
No creo que tengan una casa tan grande.	I don't believe that they own such a big house.

The most commonly used irregular verbs in the present subjunctive are:

dar	dé, des, dé, demos, den, den
decir	diga, digas, diga, digamos, digan, digan
estar	esté, estés, esté, estemos, estén, estén
haber	haya, hayas, haya, hayamos, hayan, hayan
hacer	haga, hagas, haga, hagamos, hagan, hagan
ir	vaya, vayas, vaya, vayamos, vayan, vayan
oir	oiga, oigas, oiga, oigamos, oigan, oigan
poder	pueda, puedas, pueda, podamos, puedan, puedan
poner	ponga, pongas, ponga, pongamos, pongan, pongan
querer	quiera, quieras, quiera, querramos, quieran, quieran
saber	sepa, sepas, sepa, sepamos, sepan, sepan
salir	salga, salgas, salga, salgamos, salgan, salgan
ser	sea, seas, sea, seamos, sean, sean
tener	tenga, tengas, tenga, tengamos, tengan, tengan
traer	traiga, traigas, traiga, traigamos, traigan, traigan
valer	valga, valgas, valga, valgamos, valgan, valgan

Use of the subjunctive

A first use of the subjunctive is after verbs indicating the exercise of some kind of influence (persuasion, recommendation, etc.). Commonly used verbs in this context are **querer** (to want) **aconsejar** (to advise), **recomendar** (to recommend), **sugerir** (to suggest).

Quiero que termines pronto.	I want you to finish soon.
Recomiendo que salgan por la puerta lateral.	I recommend that you leave through the side door.
La señora dice que vuelva mañana.	The lady says that you should come back tomorrow.
Sugerimos que viajen durante la noche.	We suggest that you travel overnight.

Quizá tenga el número

Lola and Mirtha are talking about a mutual friend

LOLA: Es una pena que José no esté en su casa.
MIRTHA: Sí. Yo creo que es necesario que le llamemos.
LOLA: Quizá tenga el número en mi cartera. A ver . . . Sí acá

está. No creo que se sorprenda cuando escuche mi voz.
Pero nunca se sabe.

MIRTHA: ¿Cuándo hablaste con él por última vez?

LOLA: Hace tres o cuatro días. Sara y yo estábamos en el centro y él se acercó.

MIRTHA: ¿Cuándo volverá por acá?

LOLA: No creo que sea esta semana.

LOLA: *It's a shame that José is not at home.*

MIRTHA: *Yes. I think we need to give him a ring.*

LOLA: *Perhaps I have his number in my handbag. Let's see . . . Yes. Here it is. I don't think he will be surprised to hear my voice. But you never know.*

MIRTHA: *When did you talk to him last?*

LOLA: *Three or four days ago. Sara and I were in the town centre and he came up to us.*

MIRTHA: *When will he be back?*

LOLA: *I don't think it will be this week.*

Language point

More uses of the subjunctive

After expressions which indicate judgement or emotion:

Es necesario que vengas a la oficina.	It is necessary that you come to the office.
¡Qué pena que Carlos no esté!	What a shame Carlos is not in!
¿No te fastidia que te hable de ese modo?	Are you not bothered that he talks to you like that?
Es mejor que no salgas. Está lloviendo mucho.	It's better if you don't go out. It's raining heavily.

After expressions which indicate probability, possibility or doubt:

Es posible que traiga la maqueta esta noche.	It is possible that he will bring the scale model tonight.
Dudo que compre más de una docena.	I doubt whether she will buy more than a dozen.
No creemos que salga bien.	We don't think it will work out well.

When the person or object is not specified, and you use words like **alguien** (somebody), **algo** (something), etc.

Estoy buscando a alguien que me oriente en este asunto.	I am looking for somebody to give me some guidance in this matter.
Quiero algo que me alivie el dolor.	I want something to relieve the pain.

After **¡qué!** or **¡ojalá!** (expressions of hope or wish):

¡Qué te vaya bien!	Have a good time!
¡Qué te diviertas!	Enjoy it!
¡Ojalá no necesite una operación!	Let's hope he doesn't need an operation.
¡Ojalá esté en casa!	Let's hope she is at home.

Exercise 1

Give English equivalents for these sentences.

1 **No creo que termine todo.**
2 **Qué interesante que incluya esto en su libro.**
3 **Es probable que salga esta noche.**
4 **Quiero que vayas al médico.**
5 **Te pido que continúes en tu puesto.**
6 **No les parece que ofrezca posibilidades.**
7 **Nos molesta que no llegue temprano.**
8 **Es importante que comamos verduras y frutas.**
9 **Dudamos que escriba desde Ecuador.**
10 **Lamento que usted no pueda venir a la reunión.**

Exercise 2

Give Spanish equivalents for these sentences. Use the subjunctive in your answers.

1 It is necessary that you eat less.
2 It's interesting that she answers in Spanish.
3 I am looking for something that will help everybody.
4 We advise you to do it.
5 They ask you to answer promptly.

Language point

Another use of the subjunctive

The subjunctive is always used after these expressions:

antes que	before
para que	in order that
con tal que	provided that
a menos que	unless

Examples:

Terminaremos antes que venga tu amiga.	We will finish before your friend arrives.
Aquí está el dinero para que compres los regalos.	Here is the money so that you buy the presents.
Puedes llevarte el libro, con tal que lo devuelvas mañana.	You can take the book, provided you return it tomorrow.
A menos que diga dónde está, no lo encontraremos.	Unless she says where it is, we will not find it.

Exercise 3

Complete the sentences with the correct form, choosing from the ones given in brackets.

1 **Carlos (vendrá/venga) el viernes a la casa.**
2 **Espero que Linda (vendrá/venga) mañana.**
3 **Quiero que (prepare/prepara) este informe para el lunes.**
4 **Esteban (trajo/traiga) la nueva computadora ayer.**
5 **Le recomiendo que no (comprará/compre) el tamaño grande.**
6 **¡Qué pena que Marcelo (estuvo/esté) ocupado mañana!**
7 **Dudamos que (encontrará/encuentre) al encargado.**
8 **Puedes comer dulces con tal de que no (es/sea) en exceso.**
9 **Creo que me (escuchará/escuche) cuando (habla/hable) con él.**
10 **El próximo domingo (empezarán/empiecen) las clases.**

Exercise 4

Explain that you would like to see the following features in your new car. Make use of the subjunctive in your sentences.

Example:

Tener levantacristales eléctricos.
Quiero que tenga levantacristales eléctricos.

1 **Tener capacidad para cinco pasajeros.**
2 **Ser económico con el combustible.**
3 **Ser de tamaño mediano.**
4 **Incluir cierre electrónico de puertas.**
5 **Contar con motor de 1,300 o 1,400 centímetros cúbicos.**
6 **Venir con caja de cambios de cinco velocidades.**
7 **Ser de un precio razonable.**
8 **Funcionar con gasolina sin plomo.**
9 **Ofrecer fiabilidad.**
10 **Estar entre los líderes del mercado.**

Exercise 5

Match each of the expressions 1 to 10 with one of the responses (a) to (j).

1 **Tiene hambre la niña.**
2 **No arranca el coche.**
3 **Necesitamos una secretaria más para mañana.**
4 **Casi se ha terminado el dinero en efectivo.**
5 **Tenemos que pagar la cuenta del teléfono.**
6 **No saben adónde ir a comer.**
7 **¿Vendrá Carlos hoy?**
8 **Le duele la muela.**
9 **¿Qué dice del informe?**
10 **¿Puede llevarse la guía telefónica?**

(a) **No creo que venga.**
(b) **Que coma algo en el comedor.**
(c) **Dile al encargado que saque dinero de la cuenta corriente.**
(d) **Siempre que la devuelva pronto.**
(e) **Que llamen al mecánico.**
(f) **Dile que haga una cita con el dentista.**
(g) **Recomiéndales el restaurante típico de la esquina.**

(h) **Espera que no tengas que volver a escribirlo.**
(i) **Pide a la secretaria que pague mañana.**
(j) **Es posible que contraten a otra esta tarde.**

Exercise 6

Choose the correct alternative for each sentence.

1 **Espero que (tienes/tengas) plata. Yo no tengo.**
2 **No creo que (sea/es) auténtico.**
3 **Este carro (tiene/tenga) cuatro puertas.**
4 **Milagros (dice/diga) que quiere hablar contigo.**
5 **Dudo que (preparará/prepare) un informe.**
6 **Puedes llevarte el libro con tal que lo (devolverás/devuelvas).**
7 **Juan Carlos (llegue/llegará) mañana.**
8 **¡Ojalá (traen/traigan) una muestra!**
9 **No esperamos que nos (ayudan/ayuden).**
10 **Mañana (sea/será) la reunión.**

¡Qué te diviertas!

While reading the dialogue below, see if you can find the answer to this question:

Has Genaro actually forgotten something?

Genaro is about to leave for the airport. Luisa is seeing him off, trying to make sure he hasn't forgotten anything.

GENARO: Bueno. Me voy. Tengo que llegar al aeropuerto en veinte minutos.
LUISA: Sí apúrate. No te olvides de nada.
GENARO: Todo está en la maleta.
LUISA: ¡Qué te vaya bien! ¡Qué te diviertas!
GENARO: Gracias. Vuelvo el domingo.

GENARO: *Well. I'm off. I have to be at the airport in twenty minutes.*
LUISA: *Yes, hurry up. Don't forget anything.*
GENARO: *Everything is in the suitcase.*
LUISA: *I hope everything goes well! Have a good time!*
GENARO: *Thanks. I'll be back on Sunday.*

Language point

Apurarse

This verb in Latin America has the meaning of 'to hurry up', while in Spain it is mainly used to mean 'to worry'.

¡Apúrate! ¡Van a cerrar la tienda!	Hurry up! The shop is going to close!
No te apures. Hay tiempo.	Don't rush. There's time.

Me duele la cabeza 🔘

While reading the dialogue below, see if you can find the answer to this question:

What will Olga do if she can't get rid of her headache?

Elisa realizes that Olga is not feeling well

ELISA: ¿Qué te pasa?
OLGA: No me siento bien. Me duele mucho la cabeza.
ELISA: Toma una pastilla para calmar el dolor.
OLGA: Ya tomé una y no me pasa. Creo que voy a acostarme.
ELISA: Sí. Te hará bien.
OLGA: Si no me pasa, consultaré al médico mañana.
ELISA: Avísame, y te acompaño.
OLGA: Gracias. Te llamaré mañana a las diez.
ELISA: Chau.
OLGA: Chau.

ELISA: *What's the matter?*
OLGA: *I don't feel well. I've got a bad headache.*
ELISA: *Take a tablet to relieve the pain.*
OLGA: *I've already taken one and the pain is still there. I think I'll go to bed.*
ELISA: *Yes. It'll do you good.*
OLGA: *It the pain doesn't go, I'll go to the doctor tomorrow.*
ELISA: *Let me know and I'll go with you.*
OLGA: *Thanks. I'll give you a ring tomorrow at ten.*

ELISA: *Bye.*
OLGA: *Bye.*

Language point

Me duele

To explain that you have some kind of pain you use the expression
Me duele followed by the part of the body that hurts.

> **Me duele la cabeza**
> **la muela**
> **el oído**
> **la pierna**
> **el brazo**
> **el pie**
> **la mano**
> **la espalda**
> **el estómago**
> **la garganta**

It is possible to use **Tengo dolor de** instead of **Me duele**. In this case
you do not use the article **el** or **la**.

> **Tengo dolor de cabeza.**
> **Tengo dolor de muela.**

Reading

While reading the passage below, see if you can find answers to
these questions:

Is the airport near the center of town?
What are the main destinations of the national airline?

El transporte aéreo en Uruguay

El aeropuerto internacional de Carrasco se encuentra ubicado a 17 km de Montevideo. En este aeropuerto operan las líneas aéreas internacionales y hay un servicio diario de puente aéreo con Argentina. Un taxi del aeropuerto al centro de Montevideo cuesta aproximadamente veinte dólares. La línea aérea nacional controlada por el estado se llama PLUNA. Vuela a Europa y a países cercanos al Uruguay, especialmente a Argentina, Brasil, Chile y Paraguay.

ubicado	located
puente aéreo	shuttle service
cercano	nearby

16 Me gustaría . . .

I would like . . .

By the end of this chapter you should be able to:

- Use the conditional tense (e.g. I would go, etc.)
- Use ordinal numbers (first, second, etc.)
- Use the imperative (i.e. the command form)

¿Qué le gustaría?

While reading the dialogue below, see if you can find answers to these questions:

Do all the people interviewed agree?
Are there any advantages in having a tram service?

Some people are being asked about their views on a local issue

ENTREVISTADOR: ¿Le gustaría tener un servicio de tranvías por aquí?

TRANSEÚNTE 1: No. Sería una pérdida de dinero público y destruiría el ambiente de la calle principal que data de tiempos coloniales.

ENTREVISTADOR: ¿Estaría de acuerdo con un servicio de tranvías por aquí?

TRANSEÚNTE 2: Sí. Primero, porque sería más rápido que los omnibús y segundo porque es más limpio. Menos contaminante. Pero supongo que costaría más, ¿no?

ENTREVISTADOR: ¿Le parecería bien tener un servicio de tranvías por aquí, por la calle principal?

TRANSEÚNTE 3: Sí, claro. Necesitamos transporte rápido. Hace años había tranvías. Eran una gran cosa.

Interviewer:	*Would you like a tram service around here?*
Passer-by 1:	*No. It would be a waste of public money and it would destroy the atmosphere of the main street which goes back to the colonial days.*
Interviewer:	*Would you support a tram service around here?*
Passer-by 2:	*Yes. First, because it would be faster than buses and second, because it would be cleaner. Less pollution. Mind you, I guess it would be dearer.*
Interviewer:	*Would you say that it is a good idea to have a tram service running here, along the main street?*
Passer-by 3:	*Yes, of course. We need fast transport. Years ago we used to have trams. It was great.*

Language points

The conditional tense

The conditional tense (in English 'I would go', etc.) is formed by adding the following endings to the infinitive: **-ía, -ías, -ía, -íamos, -ían**. The same endings are used with the three conjugations.

trabajar	**comer**	**vivir**
trabajaría	**comería**	**viviría**
trabajarías	**comerías**	**vivirías**
trabajaría	**comería**	**viviría**
trabajaríamos	**comeríamos**	**viviríamos**
trabajarían	**comerían**	**vivirían**
trabajarían	**comerían**	**vivirían**

Examples:

Caroline dijo que estaría en su casa.	Caroline said that she would be at home.
¿Dónde te gustaría vivir?	Where would you like to live?
¿Irías al cine con Julián?	Would you go to the cinema with Julián?

Irregular verbs in the conditional tense

Some verbs are irregular. Although the endings present no irregularities in the conditional, the stem of the verb shows variations. Here are the main irregular verbs:

decir	haber	hacer
diría	habría	haría
dirías	habrías	harías
diría	habría	haría
diríamos	habríamos	haríamos
dirían	habrían	harían
dirían	habrían	harían

poder	poner	querer
podría	pondría	querría
podrías	pondrías	querrías
podría	pondría	querría
podríamos	pondríamos	querríamos
podrían	pondrían	querrían
podrían	pondrían	querrían

salir	tener	venir
saldría	tendría	vendría
saldrías	tendrías	vendrías
saldría	tendría	vendría
saldríamos	tendríamos	vendríamos
saldrían	tendrían	vendrían
saldrían	tendrían	vendrían

Ordinal Numbers

primero	first	**sexto**	sixth
segundo	second	**séptimo**	seventh
tercero	third	**octavo**	eighth
cuarto	fourth	**noveno**	ninth
quinto	fifth	**décimo**	tenth

Primero to **décimo** are used in everyday speech. When preceding nouns there must be agreement in gender and number. After **décimo**, there is a tendency to use the cardinal numbers (**once** 'eleven', **doce** 'twelve', etc.)

Es la primera vez que lo hace.	It is the first time she has done that.
El cuarto concursante de hoy.	The fourth contestant today.
Los europeos llegaron en el siglo XVI (dieciseis).	The Europeans arrived in the sixteenth century.

Note that **primero** and **tercero** become **primer** and **tercer** when they precede a noun.

Vive en un departamento   del primer piso.

She lives in an apartment on the first floor.

Gané el tercer premio.   I won the third prize.

Exercise 1

¿Qué programas te gustaría ver?

Say what kind of programs you might like to watch on TV. Use the expression **Me gustaría ver . . . .** Choose from the list below. Write the sentences down in your notebook.

Programas de televisión

informativos	cómicos
noticiarios	infantiles
culturales	musicales
telenovelas	femeninos
películas	deportivos
concursos	reportajes
policiales	ninguno
documentales	No veo televisión

Exercise 2

Match the situations in the column on the left with the possible course of action you would take from the list on the right.

1	**Un incendio**	(a) **Llamaría a un médico**
2	**El teléfono no funciona**	(b) **Encendería la calefacción**
3	**No comprendo una palabra**	(c) **Cambiaría la cinta**
4	**El carro no arranca**	(d) **Tomaría una bebida refrescante**
5	**Tienes hambre**	(e) **La limpiaría**
6	**Tienes sed**	(f) **Llamaría a los bomberos**
7	**Alguien está enfermo**	(g) **Me comunicaría con la compañía telefónica**
8	**La impresora matricial no imprime bien**	(h) **Comprobaría la batería**
9	**La mesa está sucia**	(i) **La buscaría en el diccionario**
10	**Hace frío en la casa**	(j) **Comería algo**

Ponga la cebolla a macerar 🔲

Adela is explaining how to prepare a typical dish

ADELA: Exprima los 4 limones y ponga la cebolla a macerar en este jugo luego de picarla. Sancoche y luego pele las papas.

MARIANA: ¿Se forma una masa?

ADELA: Sí. Machuque las papas y forme una masa con la papa machucada, la cebolla y el jugo de limón. Añada aceite si es necesario. Coloque la masa en un molde y decore con mitades de huevo duro, aceitunas y queso.

ADELA: *Squeeze the four lemons and after chopping the onions marinate them in this juice. Boil the potatoes and then peel them.*

MARIANA: *Do you mash them?*

ADELA: *Yes, mash the potatoes, onions and lemon juice. Add oil if necessary. Put the mixture in a mould and garnish with boiled eggs, olives and cheese.*

Language point

The imperative

The imperative form is used to give commands, orders or instructions.

Prepare un informe para mañana. (usted)	Prepare a report for tomorrow.
Toma estas pastillas. (tú)	Take these tablets.

The imperative for the second person singular informal (**tú**) is the same as the form for the third person singular in the present indicative, in the case of regular verbs.

preparar	**prepar***a*
comer	**com***e*
subir	**sub***e*

Examples:

Prepara la camioneta. Vamos a salir.	Have the van ready. We are going out.

Come toda tu comida.	Eat your meal up.
Sube al carro.	Get in the car.

There are some irregular verbs. The most frequently used irregular verbs in the imperative for the second person informal (**tú**) are:

decir	**di**	**salir**	**sal**
estar	**está**	**ser**	**sé**
hacer	**haz**	**tener**	**ten**
ir	**ve**	**venir**	**ven**
oír	**oye**		

The imperative for the second person singular formal (**usted**) is the same as the present subjunctive for **usted**, **él** or **ella**.

preparar	**prepare**
comer	**coma**
subir	**suba**

Examples:

Prepare el informe para mañana.	Have the report ready for tomorrow.
Coma antes de ir al examen médico.	Eat before going to the medical examination.
Suba al cuarto piso.	Go up to the fourth floor.

The imperative for the second person plural (**ustedes**) is the same as the present subjunctive for **ustedes**, **ellos** or **ellas**.

preparar	**preparen**
comer	**coman**
subir	**suban**

Examples:

Preparen todo enseguida.	Have everything ready straight away.
Coman despacio.	Eat slowly.
Suban por la escalera, no por el ascensor.	Go up the stairs, not the lift.

Negative commands

These are formed using the negative particle **no** before the imperative. The negative imperative in the informal singular uses the present subjunctive.

Affirmative	*Negative*
prepara	*no* **prepar***es*
come	*no* **com***as*
sube	*no* **sub***as*

Examples:

No prepares nada.	Don't prepare anything.
No comas antes de acostarte.	Don't eat before going to bed.
No subas al despacho hasta las diez.	Don't go to the office until ten.

The negative imperative in the formal singular also uses the subjunctive.

Affirmative	*Negative*
prepare	**no prepare**
coma	**no coma**
suba	**no suba**

Examples:

No prepare una presentación larga.	Don't prepare a long presentation.
No coma dulces.	Don't eat sweet things.
No suba por el ascensor.	Don't go up in the elevator.

The negative imperative in the plural is the same as the affirmative, but preceded by **no**.

no **preparen**
no **coman**
no **suban**

Examples:

No preparen las cuentas hasta mañana.	Do not prepare the accounts until tomorrow.
No coman muy tarde.	Do not eat too late.
No suban al tren cuando esté en movimiento.	Do not board the train while it is moving.

Exercise 3

Change these commands to the negative.

Example:

> **Compren revistas.**
> **No compren revistas.**

1 **Vengan a la fiesta.**
2 **Llama a tu novia.**
3 **Compra cigarrillos.**
4 **Abra la ventana.**
5 **Copien el documento en diskette.**
6 **Pide diez cuadernos.**
7 **Ven con tu novio.**
8 **Tome fotos.**
9 **Prepare el plato que le recomendé.**
10 **Instala la antena.**

Exercise 4

Change the following sentences to the imperative form.

Examples:

> **Ustedes deben venir mañana.**
> **Vengan mañana.**
>
> **Tienes que decir cuál es el problema.**
> **Di cuál es el problema.**

1 **Tienes que bajar al primer piso.**
2 **Usted debe ser más eficiente.**
3 **Tienes que tomar esto.**
4 **Ustedes deben revisar este contrato.**
5 **Debes regresar pronto.**
6 **Tienes que comer más proteinas.**
7 **Usted debe enviar el paquete por vía aérea.**
8 **Tiene que ir el próximo domingo.**
9 **Tienes que hacer lo que dice esta señorita.**
10 **Ustedes deben vender la máquina.**

Reading

While reading the passage below, see if you can find answers to these questions:

Does Colombia have a strategic location?
Which racial group is in the majority in Colombia?

Colombia

Colombia tiene costas en el Océano Pacífico y en el Océano Atlántico. Su situación geográfica es muy estratégica. Además está cerca del Canal de Panamá. Como el resto de América Latina, su población crece aceleradamente. La mitad de la población es mestiza, alrededor del 20 ciento es blanca, otro 20 por ciento está formado por mulatos y zambos y el resto por gente de raza negra e india.

estratégica	strategic
como el resto	like the rest, like the others
crece	grows
aceleradamente	fast
mitad	half
mestiza	Spanish and indigenous mixed-blood race
mulatos	people who have one white and one black parent
zambos	people who have one black and one Indian parent

17 Si yo tuviera . . .

If I had . . .

By the end of this chapter you should be able to:

- Use the imperfect subjunctive
- Use open conditional sentences (e.g. If I arrive early)
- Use remote/hypothetical conditional sentences (e.g. If I had a car)

Si yo tuviera un ingreso extra ▣

After reading the dialogue below, see if you can find answers to these questions:

Would both people do the same things with the extra money?
What would you do?

Two people are talking about hypothetical plans

GENARO: Si tuviera un ingreso extra, compraría algo para la casa.
ALAN: ¿Qué comprarías?
GENARO: Compraría una nueva aspiradora, porque la que tenemos ya es muy antigua, y también un escritorio para los chicos.
ALAN: ¿Pagarías a crédito?
GENARO: Sí. Hay buenas ofertas para pagar en 24 meses sin intereses.

GENARO: *If I had some extra income, I would buy something for the house.*
ALAN: *What would you buy?*
GENARO: *I would buy a new vacuum cleaner, because the one we have is very old, and also a writing desk for the kids.*

ALAN: *Would you buy on credit?*
GENARO: *Yes. There are good offers on 24-month interest-free credit.*

Language point

The imperfect subjunctive

Similar to the present subjunctive, the imperfect subjunctive indicates actions which are hypothetical, but also remote possibilities at the time of speaking. Compared to the present subjunctive, the action is less likely to take place. The imperfect subjunctive is used for sentences expressing hopes or wishes which are unlikely to happen. (Another use, in hypothetical conditional sentences, is explained later in this chapter.)

Ojalá llame.	I hope he rings. (And he probably will.)
Ojalá llamase.	I wish he would ring. (But he probably won't.)

The imperfect subjunctive has two alternative conjugations, which are interchangeable.

Examples of regular verbs:

trabajar

trabajara	**trabajase**
trabajaras	**trabajases**
trabajara	**trabajase**
trabajáramos	**trabajásemos**
trabajaran	**trabajasen**
trabajaran	**trabajasen**

comer

comiera	**comiese**
comieras	**comieses**
comiera	**comiese**
comiéramos	**comiésemos**
comieran	**comiesen**
comieran	**comiesen**

vivir

viviera	**viviese**
vivieras	**vivieses**
viviera	**viviese**
viviéramos	**viviésemos**
vivieran	**viviesen**
vivieran	**viviesen**

The most common irregular verbs used in the imperfect subjunctive are:

dar	diera, dieras, diera, diéramos, dieran, dieran
decir	dijera, dijeras, dijera, dijéramos, dijeran, dijeran
estar	estuviera, estuvieras, estuviera, estuviéramos, estuvieran, estuvieran
haber	hubiera, hubieras, hubiera, hubiéramos, hubieran, hubieran
hacer	hiciera, hicieras, hiciera, hiciéramos, hicieran, hicieran
ir	fuera, fueras, fuera, fuéramos, fueran, fueran
oir	oyera, oyeras, oyera, oyéramos, oyeran, oyeran
poder	pudiera, pudieras, pudiera, pudiéramos, pudieran, pudieran
poner	pusiera, pusieras, pusiera, pusiéramos, pusieran, pusieran
querer	quisiera, quisieras, quisiera, quisiéramos, quisieran, quisieran
saber	supiera, supieras, supiera, supiéramos, supieran, supieran
salir	saliera, salieras, saliera, saliéramos, salieran, salieran
ser	fuera, fueras, fuera, fuéramos, fueran, fueran
tener	tuviera, tuvieras, tuviera, tuviéramos, tuvieran, tuvieran
traer	trajera, trajeras, trajera, trajéramos, trajeran, trajeran
valer	valiera, valieras, valiera, valiéramos, valieran, valieran
venir	viniera, vinieras, viniera, viniéramos, vinieran, vinieran
ver	viera, vieras, viera, viéramos, vieran, vieran

Note: **yo/usted/él/ella** share the same verb form, e.g. **viera**, and **ustedes/ellos/ellas** share the same verb form, e.g. **vieran**.

Si quieres . . . 🔲🔲

Two friends are making arrangements to meet

ALBERTO: Si vienes esta tarde, salimos al cine juntos.
EMILIA: Bueno, ya que insistes.
ALBERTO: ¿A qué hora vienes?
EMILIA: No sé. Depende. Quizás vaya en el auto o quizás vaya a pie. Como vives tan cerca.
ALBERTO: Si vienes en el auto llegas rápido y podemos ir a la primera función. Si quieres, luego podemos ir a tomar algo.
EMILIA: Me parece bien. Voy en el auto.

ALBERTO: *If you come this afternoon, we can go to the cinema.*
EMILIA: *All right. Since you insist.*
ALBERTO: *What time are you coming?*
EMILIA: *I don't know. It depends. Perhaps I'll come by car or perhaps I'll walk. Since you live so close.*
ALBERTO: *If you come by car you'll be here soon and we can go to the first show. If you want, we can go and have a drink afterwards.*
EMILIA: *That's fine. I'll come by car.*

Language points

Open conditional sentences

In an open conditional sentence (e.g. If I go . . .) you use the present indicative.

Condition	*Conclusion*
si + present indicative	present indicative

Examples:

| **Si vienes temprano, vamos al cine.** | If you come early, we can go to the cinema. |
| **Si mandas el formulario, recibes un cupón a vuelta de correo.** | If you send the form, you get a voucher by return of post. |

Como

In the appropriate context the word **como** means 'since'/'because', as in these examples:

Como vives cerca, voy a pie. Since you live nearby I'll walk.
Como no tienes los boletos, Since you don't have the tickets,
no podemos entrar. we can't go in.
Como pasaste los exámenes, Since you passed your exams,
te compramos una bici. we'll buy you a bike.

Si tuviera la plata 📼

JOSÉ LUIS: Si tuviera la plata, compraría la computadora que queremos.
MARCELO: No importa. Mi papá dijo que es posible que la compremos a plazos.
JOSÉ LUIS: Pero mi mamá dudaba que mi papá pudiera pagar las cuotas mensuales ya que está pagando también el carro.
MARCELO: Si tuvieramos la oportunidad de trabajar este verano durante las vacaciones, podríamos ayudar a pagar cada mes.
JOSÉ LUIS: Vamos a hablar con Antonio.
MARCELO: Sí, vamos.

JOSÉ LUIS: *If I had the money, I would buy the computer we want.*
MARCELO: *Never mind. Dad says that perhaps we might pay for it in instalments.*
JOSÉ LUIS: *But mum didn't think my dad could afford the monthly payments since he also has to pay for the car.*
MARCELO: *If we had the chance to work this summer during the holidays, we could help with the monthly payments.*
JOSÉ LUIS: *Let's have a word with Antonio.*
MARCELO: *Yes, let's.*

Language point

Remote/Hypothetical conditional sentences

In a remote/hypothetical conditional sentence (e.g. If I had the money I would buy it.) you use the imperfect subjunctive for the condition and a conditional tense in the conclusion. When you use this type of conditional sentence the conclusion is hypothetical, since the condition expressed by the imperfect subjunctive is contrary to fact or unlikely to be fulfilled. (The imperfect subjunctive is discussed earlier in this chapter and the conditional tense appears in Chapter 16.)

Condition	*Conclusion*
si + imperfect subjunctive	conditional tense

Examples:

Si tuviera un diccionario, buscaría la palabra.	If I had a dictionary, I would look the word up.
Si fueran puntuales, no causarían problemas.	If they turned up on time, they would not cause problems.
Si la tienda estuviera en el centro, iría ahorita.	If the shop was in the town center, I would go right now.
Si vendiésemos más, podríamos ampliar la gama.	If we sold more, we could extend the range.

Compare the following examples of two types of conditional sentences:

Si tengo tiempo, te escribo.	If I have time, I'll write to you. (I think it is likely that I will have the time.)
Si tuviera tiempo, te escribiría.	If I had time, I would write to you. (But I don't have the time.)
Si eres socio te dejan entrar.	If you are a member, they let you in. (There is a possibility that you will become one.)
Si fueras socio, te dejarían entrar.	If you were a member, they would let you in. (But you are not and probably will never become one.)

Exercise 1

Si usted tuviera un ingreso extra a partir de este mes, ¿a qué lo destinaría?
If you had extra income as from this month, what would you use it for?

Answer the survey question above, putting yourself in the position of (a), (b) and (c) below:

(a) If you were unemployed.
(b) If you and your partner had a secure job.
(c) If you were leaving secondary school.

Start your answers using:

Si tuviera un ingreso extra lo destinaría a . . .
If I had extra income I would use it for . . .

ahorros	savings
alimentación	food
artículos para el hogar	household goods
vestido/calzado	clothes/footwear
inversión	investment
estudios	studies
diversión	entertainment
otra	other
no precisa/no responde	don't know

Exercise 2

Write an English equivalent for the following sentences.

1 **Si pudiera, viajaría más.**
2 **Si Marcelo fuese mejor organizado, tendría óptimos resultados.**
3 **Como vienes en auto llegarás antes que Alberto.**
4 **Si escribes un cheque deletrea bien el nombre.**
5 **Si me dieran la oportunidad, trabajaría en Uruguay.**
6 **Visitaría la capital si tuviera más tiempo, pero sólo estaré dos días por aquí.**
7 **Lo traería en diskette, si fuera compatible.**
8 **Si las cifras indicasen lo contrario, tendríamos que hacer una investigación.**
9 **Si la novela fuera más corta, tendría más éxito.**
10 **Si sabes la respuesta, ¿por qué no la dices?**

Exercise 3

Write a Spanish equivalent for the following sentences:

1 If there is a problem, I will send you a fax.
2 I do not think Helen will go to work tomorrow.
3 Would you go back if you had the chance to do so?
4 Since you only have one, take these other two.
5 If he rings, we will give him the details.

Exercise 4

Match the phrases in the first group (1 to 5) with those in the second group ((a) to (e)).

1 **¿Quisieras ir al teatro mañana?**
2 **¿Irías a la inauguración de la nueva tienda?**
3 **¿Volverías a este lugar?**
4 **En ese caso, Estela repetiría el mismo error.**
5 **Norma esperaría hasta que lleguen los pedidos.**

(a) **Sólo de vacaciones.**
(b) **Si me invitan, si iría.**
(c) **No puedo, voy a ir a hacer unas compras urgentes.**
(d) **Sí, para ver los detalles de la factura.**
(e) **Sí. Es difícil corregirla.**

Si pudiera

Enrique wishes he could buy something

ENRIQUE: Si pudiera, yo lo comprara inmediatamente.
ROSARIO: Sería una decisión apresurada.
ENRIQUE: Si fueras tú, posiblemente hicieras lo mismo.
ROSARIO: Tienes razón.

ENRIQUE: *If I could I would buy it immediately.*
ROSARIO: *It would be a rushed decision.*
ENRIQUE: *If it was you, you would possibly do the same.*
ROSARIO: *You're right.*

Language points

The subjunctive used instead of the conditional

Frequently in spoken Spanish the **-ra** form of the subjunctive is used instead of the conditional. This makes the sentence sound more informal and therefore is used by native speakers in colloquial, familiar language. While the following example is not grammatically correct, this type of language is often heard in everyday usage.

Si pudiera, lo comprara inmediatamente.	If I could, I would buy it immediately.

Tener razón

This expression is used to indicate that somebody is right or to accept somebody's argument.

tengo razón	**tenemos razón**
tienes razón	**tienen razón**
tiene razón	**tienen razón**

Examples:

Creo que son nueve, no diez como dices tú. Sí, tienes razón.	I think there are nine, not ten as you said. Yes, you're right.
Miguel, tú siempre tienes razón.	Miguel, you're always right.

Si tuviera más tiempo ▣▣

Elena and Jorge are discussing business plans

ELENA: Si yo tuviera más tiempo prepararía la base de datos que necesitamos. Creo que tendremos que pedir ayuda a alguna firma de consultoría.

JORGE: Estoy de acuerdo. No podemos seguir adelante sin tener toda nuestra información bien organizada antes de discutir nuestros planes de expansión.

ELENA: El año pasado cuando tuvimos problemas de producción vinieron dos consultores de una firma internacional a o rientarnos y lo hicieron muy bien. Creo que podríamos ponernos en contacto con ellos nuevamente.

JORGE: Sí. Tenían un enfoque muy profesional y abordaron el problema con gran eficiencia. Vamos a ponernos en contacto con ellos otra vez.

ELENA: Aquí tengo el teléfono. Voy a llamarlos.

ELENA: *If I had more time, I would prepare the database we need. I think we will have to ask for help from a consultancy.*

JORGE: *I agree. We cannot carry on without having all our information properly organized before discussing our expansion plans.*

ELENA: *Last year when we had production problems two consultants from an international firm came to give us guidance and they did it very well. I think we could contact them again.*

JORGE: *Yes, they had a very professional approach and dealt with the problem very efficiently. Let's contact them again.*

ELENA: *I've got their telephone number here. I'll give them a ring.*

Exercise 5

Translate the following sentences into Spanish:

1 If we had more personnel we could achieve better results.
2 We need to ask a consultancy for help.
3 Our company would expand into foreign markets if we had a better export policy.
4 Their approach is not very professional.
5 I think it is not a very good idea.

Exercise 6

Read the following advertisements:

TODATALLA

Importador directo de Europa
Sacones
Pantalones
Vestidos
Ropa de cuero

Tarjetas
Planes hasta 6 pagos

Sábados abierto hasta las 19 horas

Av. Córdoba 321

UNIVERSO

**Módulos multifunción para estantería.
En roble y nogal. En blanco y negro.**

**Lunes a sábados: 9 a 17 horas
Domingos: 15 a 19.30 horas**

**Venta directa de fábrica.
Av. Mendoza 177**

ÓPTICA UNIVERSITARIA

Lentes de Contacto
Descartables 12 pares
Importados USA $140
Blandos color importados $150

Entrega inmediata

Calle San Marcelo 3522
Tel 931 3992

Based on the information above, indicate if the following statements are **verdadero** (true) or **falso** (false)

1 Si quisiera comprar lentes de contacto los encontraría en Óptica Universitaria.

2 En la tienda Universo se podrían comprar muebles de caoba.

3 Si comprara los lentes de contacto descartables, éstos serían europeos.

4 Los domingos a las seis de la tarde sería posible comprar módulos para estantería en la tienda universo.

5 La tienda Todatalla no vende ropa de cuero.

6 Si quisiera pagar con tarjeta de crédito, la aceptarían en la tienda Todatalla.

7 La tienda Universo es un distribuidor.

8 Solamente se puede pagar al contado en Todatalla.

9 Si quisiera visitar la Óptica Universitaria y la tienda Universo iría a la misma calle.

10 Los módulos de Universo son en blanco y negro.

Reading 📼

Read the following passage and answer these questions:

Where is Honduras?
Are there four well defined seasons during the year?

Honduras

Honduras está situada en América Central. Tiene 112,000 kilómetros cuadrados y limita con tres países: Guatemala, Nicaragua y El Salvador. Prácticamente sólo hay dos estaciones durante el año: la época de lluvias y la estación seca. La época de lluvias es de junio a octubre. Durante esta época del año las temperaturas van de 15°C en las zonas altas a 30°C en las zonas bajas. Las temperaturas son más altas en la época seca, que va de noviembre a mayo.

cuadrados	square	época del año	time of the year
limita con	has borders with	época de lluvias	rainy season
estaciones	seasons		

18 Si hubieras enviado . . .

If you had sent . . .

By the end of this chapter you should be able to:

- Use the pluperfect subjunctive. (e.g. If I had known)
- Use the conditional perfect (e.g. I would have come)
- Use expressions of concession (although, despite, etc.)
- Use **demasiado** + noun (e.g too many problems)
- Use **demasiado** + adjective (e.g. too long, too expensive)

Si hubieras enviado la carta 📼

Juan and Mariela talk about things that should have been done

JUAN: Si hubieras enviado la carta, habrías obtenido la información necesaria. Así no habrías tenido que volver otra vez esta mañana con todos los documentos.

MARIELA: Lo que pasó fue que no tenía la dirección exacta. Si tú me hubieras dado los datos completos, entonces habría podido enviar la carta. ¡Pero faltaba el nombre de la calle! En fin, ya no importa.

JUAN: Discúlpame. Si hubiera notado que faltaba algo, te habría enviado un fax o te habría llamado por teléfono.

MARIELA: Está bien. Todo está resuelto ahora.

JUAN: *If you had sent the letter, you would have had the necessary information. Then you wouldn't have had to come back this morning with all the documents.*

MARIELA: *What happened was that I did not have the full address. If you had given me all the information, then I would have been able to send the letter. But the name of the*

> *street was missing! Anyway, it doesn't matter now.*

JUAN: *I'm sorry. If I had noticed that something was missing, I would have sent you a fax or would have given you a ring.*

MARIELA: *It's all right. It's all sorted out now.*

Language points

The conditional perfect tense

The verb haber in the conditional tense (habría, habrías, etc.) together with the past participle of the main verb are used to form the conditional perfect tense which is mainly used together with the pluperfect subjunctive in conditional sentences of the third type. Here are the forms of trabajar in the conditional perfect.

habría trabajado	I would have worked
habrías trabajado	you would have worked (informal)
habría trabajado	you would have worked (formal); he/she would have worked
habríamos trabajado	we would have worked
habría trabajado	you would have worked
habrían trabajado	they would have worked

The pluperfect subjunctive

To form the pluperfect subjunctive, you use the imperfect subjunctive of **haber** together with the past participle of the main verb. Here are the forms of **comprar** in the pluperfect subjunctive:

hubiera comprado	I would have bought
hubieras comprado	you would have bought (informal)
hubiera comprado	you would have bought (formal); he/she would have bought
hubiéramos comprado	we would have bought
hubieran comprado	you would have bought
hubieran comprado	they would have bought

As in the case of the imperfect subjunctive, it is possible to use the alternative form -**se**. They are interchangeable.

hubiese comprado	**hubiésemos comprado**
hubieses comprado	**hubiesen comprado**
hubiese comprado	**hubiesen comprado**

Conditional sentences of the third type

The pluperfect subjunctive is used together with the conditional perfect tense to form conditional sentences which refer to conditions that cannot be fulfilled at the time of speaking or conditions which are contrary to fact.

Condition	*Conclusion*
si + pluperfect subjunctive	conditional perfect

Examples:

Si hubiera traído el mapa, habríamos encontrado la ruta.	If I had brought the map, we would have found the route.
Muchas personas habrían muerto en la explosión si no hubiese ocurrido un domingo.	Many people would have died in the explosion if it had not happened on a Sunday.
Si hubiéramos tenido una cámara de video, habríamos grabado durante la fiesta.	If we had had a video camera, we would have recorded the party.

Exercise 1

Change the sentences below as in the example.

Example:

> **No visité Colombia. (tiempo)**
> **Si hubiera tenido tiempo habría visitado Colombia.**

1 **No terminé la pintura. (tiempo)**
2 **No fuimos al teatro. (entradas)**
3 **No compraste el regalo. (suficiente dinero)**
4 **Ustedes no vinieron a la fiesta. (invitación)**
5 **No preparé el informe. (datos necesarios)**

Yo que tú

SIMÓN: Yo que tú no aceptaría esas condiciones.
TERESA: No tengo alternativa. Necesito el préstamo. Si yo fuera
         una persona con un trabajo estable, entonces podría ir al
         banco a solicitar un préstamo.
SIMÓN: Tienes razón. Cuando consigas un trabajo a tiempo com-
         pleto tendrás mayor seguridad económica.
TERESA: Ojalá que sea pronto.

SIMÓN: *If I were you I would not accept those conditions.*
TERESA: *I have no choice. I need the loan. If I was somebody with
         a steady job I would be able to go to the bank to ask
         for a loan.*
SIMÓN: *You're right. When you get a full-time job you will have
         more financial security.*
TERESA: *I do hope it is soon.*

Language point

Yo que tú/usted

Although 'If I were you' can be translated as **Si yo fuera tú/usted**, a
more colloquial form is preferred in everyday speech, **Yo que
tú/usted**. The same applies to a third person, e.g. **Yo que Esteban** 'If
I was Esteban'.

Yo que usted no vendría más a este lugar.	If I were you I would not come back to this place.
Yo que tú lo mandaría por vía aérea.	If I were you I would send it by air mail.

Exercise 2

Match each statement in the group 1 to 10 with a suitable one from
the group (a) to (j).

1 **Me duele el estómago.**
2 **No funciona la linterna.**
3 **He traído un libro para leer durante el viaje.**
4 **La chaqueta le queda chica.**

5 **El modelo es anticuado.**
6 **No había nada de comer.**
7 **¡Cuánta gente!**
8 **Ojalá estuviera Rosana con nosotros.**
9 **Este periódico no tiene mucha información.**
10 **No encuentro la dirección de mi tía María.**

(a) **Deberíamos haber comido en casa.**
(b) **No deberías haber comido tanto.**
(c) **Deberías haber comprado uno más moderno.**
(d) **Una talla más grande habría sido mejor.**
(e) **Ojalá tuviéramos más sillas.**
(f) **Ojalá hubiera traído mi agenda. Por lo menos te podría haber dado su teléfono.**
(g) **Debería haber comprado una revista especializada.**
(h) **Sí. Nos habría ayudado mucho.**
(i) **Deberíamos haber traído más pilas.**
(j) **Si hubieras traído dos me podrías prestar uno.**

Aunque los gráficos son buenos . . . 🔊

Sr Sosa and Sr Méndez are discussing the graphics to appear in an advertisement

SR MÉNDEZ: ¿Qué le parece la publicidad que se ha preparado para el producto?

SR SOSA: Aunque los gráficos en el anuncio publicitario son muy buenos, creo que el texto es demasiado largo. Hay que recortarlo.

SR MÉNDEZ: Quizá es largo, pero así recortáramos el texto, habría que incluir suficiente información sobre las especificaciones técnicas del producto. Es un punto muy importante para atraer a los posibles compradores. Es ahí donde tenemos ventajas sobre nuestros competidores.

SR SOSA: Pienso que es cuestión de opinión. Para mí, la imagen dice más que las palabras. Quisiera que estudiases la posibilidad de recortar el texto, digamos en un quince a veinte por ciento.

SR MÉNDEZ: Bueno, a pesar de que ya pasó el plazo para entregar el texto al Departamento de Publicidad de la revista, voy a averiguar si podemos hacer algunos cambios.

MR MÉNDEZ: *What do you think about the publicity for the product?*

MR SOSA: *Although the graphics are very good, I think the text is too long. It has to be shortened.*

MR MÉNDEZ: *It may be long, but even if we shorten the text, we would have to include enough information on the technical specifications of the product. It is a very important point to attract potential customers. It is here that we have an edge over our competitors.*

MR SOSA: *I believe it is a matter of opinion. For me, the picture is worth more than the words. I would like you to consider the possibility of shortening the text, let's say by 15 to 20 per cent.*

MR MÉNDEZ: *All right, despite the fact that the deadline for submission of material to the advertising department of the magazine has passed, I'll find out if we can make some changes.*

Language points

Aunque

This expression of concession is used in a similar way to its English equivalent 'although'. In Spanish it can be followed by a verb in the indicative or in the subjunctive. Generally speaking they are interchangeable.

Aunque los gráficos son buenos, hay demasiado texto.
Although the graphics are good, there is too much text.

Aunque los gráficos sean buenos, hay demasiado texto.

Aunque el producto es bueno, su presentación es deficiente.
Although the product is good, its presentation is poor.

Aunque el producto sea bueno, su presentación es deficiente.

A pesar de que

This is another expression of concession which is also similar in use to its English equivalent 'despite the fact that'.

A pesar de que no hay subsidios o incentivos del estado, se ha logrado superar la falta de inversión en el sector de la construcción.	In spite of the fact that there aren't state subsidies or incentives, it has been possible to overcome the lack of investment in the construction sector.
A pesar de que no puede utilizar su brazo derecho, logró rescatar a la niña.	In spite of the fact that she can't use her right arm, she managed to rescue the girl.

Demasiado

When **demasiado** is used as an adjective, meaning 'too much/many', it agrees in number and gender.

Hay demasiadas fallas en esta máquina.	There are too many faults in this machine.
Tenemos demasiados problemas que resolver.	We have too many problems to solve.

When **demasiado** is used as an adverb meaning 'too/too much', it remains the same in all cases.

El texto es demasiado largo.	The text is too long.
Los vehículos todo-terreno son demasiado caros.	All-terrain vehicles are too expensive.
La cotización del dólar es demasiado baja.	The dollar exchange is too low.
Las excavaciones son demasiado profundas.	The excavations are too deep.

Exercise 3

Join the two phrases using **aunque** as in the example.

Example:

> **Iremos esta tarde. El museo está lejos.**
> **Aunque el museo está lejos, iremos esta tarde.**

or

> **Aunque el museo esté lejos, iremos esta tarde.**

No compramos las camisas. Estaban rebajadas.
Aunque estaban rebajadas, no compramos las camisas.

or

Aunque estuvieran rebajadas, no compramos las camisas.

1 Manejó el auto. No tenía licencia de conducir.
2 Pagó al contado. Tenía tarjetas de crédito.
3 Compro en una tiendecita. El supermercado está cerca.
4 Le regaló una loción para después de afeitarse. No se afeita.
5 No contestó. Recibió su carta.
6 Organizó una reunión para la mañana siguiente. Llegaba de madrugada.
7 No es compatible con las demás de la oficina. La computadora es nueva.
8 No le gusta la comida picante. Es latinoamericano.
9 No tiene sistema computarizado. Es el archivo más grande del país.
10 No bajó de peso. Estuvo a dieta todo el año pasado.

Exercise 4

Give Spanish equivalents for the following:

1 There are too many students in this room.
2 Everything is too hot.
3 The temperature is too cold for this time of year.
4 It is too high. She cannot reach.
5 I put too many coins in the machine. It doesn't work.

Exercise 5

Give English equivalents for the following:

1 A pesar de que no tenía dinero, pidió comida cara.
2 Terminamos a pesar de que las condiciones eran negativas.
3 A pesar de sus quejas no recibe ayuda.
4 Visita a sus nietos muy seguido a pesar de tener muchos años.
5 A pesar de las oportunidades que tuvo, nunca triunfó.
6 A pesar de tener un gran reparto, la película no es buena.
7 A pesar de sus problemas de salud, sigue jugando fútbol.
8 No sale a pesar de que el médico se lo aconsejó.
9 A pesar de la lluvia, caminaron toda la tarde.
10 A pesar de tener un sueldo muy alto, siempre pide préstamos.

Suponiendo que . . . 🔳

JUAN: Suponiendo que no lleguen, ¿qué hacemos?
MARÍA: Nada. Hay que esperar y luego ya veremos.
JUAN: Yo creía que tú querías resolver las cosas rápido. Me parecía que no ibas a esperar.
MARÍA: Cambié de opinión.
JUAN: Así lleguen tarde, sería mejor a que no lleguen.

JUAN: *Supposing they don't arrive, what shall we do?*
MARÍA: *Nothing. We have to wait and then we will see.*
JUAN: *I thought you wanted to solve things quickly. I thought you were not going to wait.*
MARÍA: *I changed my mind.*
JUAN: *Even if they arrive late, it would be better than not arriving at all.*

Language points

Suponiendo que . . .

Supposing . . .

This expression of concession is always followed by the subjunctive.

Suponiendo que esté armado, ¿qué medidas tomará la policía?	Supposing he is armed, what action will the police take?
Eso es suponiendo que pudiera asistir a la reunión.	That is supposing he was able to attend the meeting.

Así

Even if

Apart from its usual use (the equivalent of 'so', 'thus' in English), in Latin American Spanish **así** can be used as an alternative to **aunque**.

Así lo castiguen, seguirá creyendo en sus ideales.	Even if he is punished, he will continue to believe in his ideals.

No irá, así lo amenacen.	He will not go, even if he is threatened.

Exercise 6

Give the English equivalent for these phrases.

1 **No responderá a las preguntas, así lo torturen.**
2 **Esperará a su hijo, así llegue muy tarde.**
3 **Iremos, así llueva toda la noche.**
4 **Te avisaríamos, así fuera muy tarde.**
5 **En mi caso te habría telefoneado, así hubiera sido domingo.**

Reading

While reading the passage below, see if you can find answers to these questions:

Is the lack of water going to affect Latin America in the same way as the industrialized countries?
Which sector of the economy is going to suffer most?

Falta de agua

En un futuro cercano será mayor la falta de agua en Latinoamérica. Aunque en Europa y en el resto de los países industrializados el agua disponible por habitante se reducirá en los próximos años, en Latinoamérica esta reducción será más pronunciada. Las sociedades actuales deben detener el derroche existente y la mala utilización de este elemento vital, de lo contrario habrá repercusiones para los distintos sectores económicos, especialmente para la agricultura.

la falta	lack	**sociedades**	societies
disponible	available	**derroche**	waste
se reducirá	will be reduced	**de lo contrario**	otherwise
pronunciada	marked		

19 Ha sido . . .

It has been . . .

By the end of this chapter you should be able to:

- Use the passive voice (e.g. It has been returned)
- Use the impersonal **se** in place of the passive voice
- Distinguish between **pero** and **sino**

Han sido entrevistados

While reading the dialogue below, see if you can find the answer to this question:

Do Laura and Eduardo know exactly what happened?

Laura and Eduardo are in their office talking about something in the news

LAURA: ¿Qué sabes del asunto?

EDUARDO: Sólo lo que dice el periódico. Escucha. Han sido entregados dos de los tres expedientes que se perdieron de la oficina. Los directores han sido entrevistados por la policía. Los documentos han sido devueltos esta mañana. No se sabe quién los devolvió.

LAURA: Es un misterio. Vamos a preguntar a tu hermano. Quizás él tenga más noticias.

EDUARDO: Sí, vamos.

LAURA: *What do you know about this matter?*

EDUARDO: *Only what is in the newspaper. Listen. Two of the three dossiers which went missing have been returned. The directors have been interviewed by the police. The documents have been returned this morning. It is not known who handed them back.*

LAURA: *It's a mystery. Let's go and ask your brother. He may have more news.*

EDUARDO: *Yes, let's go.*

Language point

The passive voice

The verb **ser** is used with the past participle to form the passive voice. There is agreement in number and gender with the subject of the verb **ser**. The passive voice is used to put the emphasis on the action taking place rather than on the subject performing the action (as in the active voice).

Los expedientes han sido devueltos.	The dossiers have been returned.
Los trabajadores son llevados en vehículos de la empresa.	The workers are transported in company vehicles.

The following are examples of the passive voice in various tenses.

Present	*Imperfect*
soy llevado	**era llevado**
eres llevado	**eras llevado**
es llevado	**era llevado**
somos llevados	**éramos llevados**
son llevados	**eran llevados**
son llevados	**eran llevados**

El dinero es llevado al banco en cantidades pequeñas.	The money is taken to the bank in small amounts.
Ese día los tres eran llevados a la comisaría.	That day the three of them were being taken to the police station.

Preterite	*Future*
fui llevado	**seré llevado**
fuiste llevado	**serás llevado**
fue llevado	**será llevado**
fuimos llevados	**seremos llevados**

fueron llevados   serán llevados
fueron llevados   serán llevados

El ataúd fue llevado por sus   The coffin was carried by his
   amigos más íntimos.   closest friends.
Todos seremos llevados a la   We will all be taken to room two.
   sala dos.

Conditional	*Present perfect*
sería llevado	he sido llevado
serías llevado	has sido llevado
sería llevado	ha sido llevado
seríamos llevados	hemos sido llevados
serían llevados	han sido llevados
serían llevados	han sido llevados

El cuadro sería llevado al   The painting would be taken to the
   museo si se garantizara la   museum if safe transport could be
   seguridad del transporte.   guaranteed.
Los acusados han sido   The accused have been taken to
   llevados al tribunal.   the court.

Pluperfect	*Future perfect*
había sido llevado	habré sido llevado
habías sido llevado	habrás sido llevado
había sido llevado	habrá sido llevado
habíamos sido llevados	habremos sido llevados
habían sido llevados	habrán sido llevados
habían sido llevados	habrán sido llevados

Para entonces los artículos   By then the stolen goods had
   robados ya habían sido   already been taken to another
   llevados a otro país.   country.
A principios del próximo   At the beginning of the next cen-
   siglo las muestras habrán   tury the samples will have been
   sido llevadas a otro planeta   taken to another planet in a
   en un laboratorio espacial.   space laboratory.

Conditional perfect
habría sido llevado
habrías sido llevado
habría sido llevado
habríamos sido llevados
habrían sido llevados
habrían sido llevados

Nosotros no habríamos sido llevados en ese helicóptero si las autoridades hubieran insistido en realizar más pruebas.	We wouldn't have been taken in that helicopter if the authorities had insisted on carrying out more tests.

The passive construction in continuous tenses, e.g. **estoy siendo llevado**, is not very common.

Exercise 1

Change the sentences to the passive voice.

Example:

El alcalde inauguró la feria.
La feria fue inaugurada por el alcalde.

Destruyeron la muñeca.
La muñeca fue destruida.

1 **Construyeron la nueva autopista.**
2 **La municipalidad aplicó la multa.**
3 **El gobierno aprobó el presupuesto.**
4 **La tienda rebajó los precios.**
5 **Terminaron la obra.**
6 **La casa editorial habría publicado la obra.**
7 **Los llevarían a todos a la comisaría.**
8 **El juez habrá interrogado a todos.**
9 **Nos han engañado.**
10 **Un gran número de personas leería el libro.**

Se sabe

Juan is explaining the virtues of a new material in the product he sells

JUAN: Se sabe que este material dura años sin perder color.
ALICIA: ¿Qué se tiene que hacer para mantenerlo limpio?
JUAN: Sólo se necesita pasar un trapo húmedo para limpiarlo y ya está.
ALICIA: ¿No se necesita también utilizar un limpiador abrasivo?
JUAN: No es necesario. Un trapo húmedo es suficiente.
ALICIA: Lo probaré.

JUAN: *It is known that this material lasts for years without fading.*
ALICIA: *What is needed to keep it clean?*
JUAN: *You only need to wipe it clean with a damp cloth and that's it.*
ALICIA: *Don't you also need to use an abrasive cleaner?*
JUAN: *It's not necessary. A damp cloth is enough.*
ALICIA: *I'll try it.*

Language point

The impersonal se

Se is used in spoken Spanish to replace the passive construction learned above, which is mainly used in written language.

Se sabe que no funciona.	It is known that it doesn't work.
Se espera que compren nuestros productos.	It is expected that they will buy our products.
Se decía que no tenía la información.	It was said that she did not have the information.
Finalmente se ha establecido por qué lo hicieron.	Finally it has been established why they did it.
Creo que se ha decidido que no asistirán al Congreso.	I think it has been decided that they will not attend the conference.

Exercise 2

Give a Spanish equivalent for the following sentences.

1 It has been decided that you will represent the company at the fair.
2 It is said that the competitors are demoralized.
3 It is explained in the leaflet.
4 It was accepted in the end.
5 It has been repeated for the third time.
6 It is known that this product affects the skin.
7 It is sent by post.
8 It is offered to members of the organization.
9 They are given in advance.
10 They will be returned the next day.

Exercise 3

Give an English equivalent for the following sentences.

1 **Se piensa que no habrá aumento de sueldos.**
2 **Se sabe que no llegarán hasta mañana.**
3 **Creo que ahora se entiende la idea.**
4 **Se ha terminado la sesión.**
5 **Primero, el producto se coloca en el interior de la máquina.**
6 **Se acordó durante la última reunión.**
7 **Se simplificarían trámites de exportadores para pagar impuestos.**
8 **El préstamo no se invertirá en obras públicas.**
9 **Se introducirá un nuevo sistema de clasificación.**
10 **La próxima semana se publicarán los nuevos precios del gas industrial.**

Language point

The passive with the subject performing the action

Although the passive construction and the impersonal **se** are inter-changeable in the cases introduced above, only the passive con-struction can be used when the subject who performs the action is mentioned.

La noticia fue revelada a la prensa por el presidente de la comisión.	The news was revealed to the press by the president of the committee.
La mayor inversión fue realizada por el sector de la construcción.	The biggest investment was made by the construction sector.

Exercise 4

Change the sentences from the active to the passive construction.

Examples:

El Rector clausuró el año académico.
El año académico fue clausurado por el Rector.

Los alumnos han organizado la reunión de mañana.
La reunión de mañana ha sido organizada por los alumnos.

1 **La Directora inauguró la exposición sobre comercio exterior.**
2 **Los comerciantes del centro publicarán una nueva revista.**
3 **El distribuidor reemplazará la máquina.**
4 **El Ministerio de Transportes reconstruirá más de cien kilómetros de la carretera al Norte.**
5 **La Compañía de Teléfonos introducirá una nueva gama de
productos.**
6 **El Ministerio del Interior ha distribuido la nueva tarjeta de
identificación.**
7 **La policía detuvo al delincuente.**
8 **Las empresas extranjeras entregaron el donativo.**
9 **El dueño de la tienda donó una computadora.**
10 **Los hinchas llevaron en hombros al entrenador.**

La puerta estaba abierta

CARLOS: Cuando llegué la puerta ya estaba abierta.
SANDRA: Yo llegué unos momentos antes cuando un empleado
estaba abriendo la puerta.
CARLOS: ¿Compraste algo?
SANDRA: Sí la ropa estaba bien rebajada. Compré una blusa para
mi hermana y dos para mí.
CARLOS: Estaba convencido de que encontraría algo para Celia,
pero al final no compré nada para ella.

CARLOS: *When I arrived the door was already open.*
SANDRA: *I arrived a few moments earlier when a shop assistant was
opening the door.*
CARLOS: *Did you buy anything?*
SANDRA: *Yes, clothes were reduced. I bought a blouse for my
sister and two for me.*
CARLOS: *I was sure I would find something for Celia, but in the end
I didn't buy anything for her.*

Language point

Estaba abierta

When you use the passive with **estar** you usually refer to a state which is the result of an action; the agent of the action (i.e the person who performs the action) is usually not included: e.g. **La puerta estaba abierta** 'The door was open'. When you use the passive with **ser**, you describe the action itself and you can add the agent: **La puerta fue abierta (por el vigilante)** 'The door was opened (by the guard)'.

Exercise 5

Give an English equivalent for the following phrases.

01 **El libro estaba destinado a ser un éxito.**
02 **El libro fue destinado al mercado exterior.**
03 **Julián estaba castigado por no terminar sus deberes.**
04 **Julián fue castigado por su madre.**
05 **Este material es procesado en una máquina muy moderna.**
06 **El alimento ya estaba procesado.**
07 **Los soldados eran instruidos cada mañana.**
08 **Las flores eran cortadas cuidadosamente por las mujeres que trabajaban allí.**
09 **Las flores estaban cortadas.**
10 **La capital fue atacada por tropas extranjeras.**

Es cara, pero es buena 🔲

Cecilia and Rosa are discussing the washing instructions on a label

CECILIA: Esta blusa es cara, pero el material es bueno.
ROSA: Es un material muy durable, pero también delicado. Cuando se ensucie no lo pongas en la lavadora sino lávalo a mano.
CECILIA: ¿Por qué?
ROSA: Acá dice en la etiqueta: 'Lavarse a mano'. Lo que pasa es que si no lo lavas a mano puede perder su forma o color en la lavadora.
CECILIA: Muy bien. Habrá que lavarlo a mano.

CECILIA: *This is an expensive blouse, but the material is good.*
ROSA: *It is a durable material, but it is a delicate fabric as well. When it gets dirty don't put it in the washing machine, but wash it by hand.*
CECILIA: *Why?*
ROSA: *It says here on the label, 'Hand Wash'. If you don't wash it by hand, what happens is that it may lose its shape or fade in the washing machine.*
CECILIA: *All right. It will have to be washed by hand.*

Language point

Pero/sino

The two words **pero** and **sino** mean 'but' in English. It is important to understand the difference in Spanish.

> **Sabe nadar, pero no va a la piscina muy seguido.** She can swim, but she doesn't go to the swimming pool very often.
> **No quiere nadar, sino bucear.** He doesn't want to swim, he wants to dive.

Pero is used to contrast the first statement but it does not contradict it. **Sino**, however, contradicts the first statement. Here are some more examples:

> **Quisiera ir a la fiesta, pero no puedo.** I would like to go to the party, but I can't.
> **No pedí vino tinto, sino blanco.** I did not order red wine, but white.

Exercise 6

Give a Spanish equivalent for the following phrases:

1 I do not want cheese, but ham.
2 She doesn't have a house now, but perhaps next year she will.
3 They do not have a cat, but a dog.
4 We do not want a single, but a return ticket.
5 He has gone to Mexico, but I do not know when he will be back.

Language point

Si no

This expression – written as two words – must not be confused with the one discussed above. In this case the meaning is 'if not', as in the following examples:

Debes pagar la cuenta de la luz, si no te la cortan.
You must pay the electricity bill, if not you will be cut off.

Tiene que cuidarse, si no se va a enfermar.
You have to look after yourself, if not you'll fall ill.

Reading 🔘

Argentina

Argentina cuenta con una población de más de 30 millones de habitantes. Es uno de los países con el más alto ingreso por habitante en Latinoamérica. El índice de alfabetismo (94%) es el más alto de América Latina. El país está situado en la zona templada, pero es posible hallar todo tipo de climas, desde el tropical en el norte, hasta el muy frío en las zonas altas andinas, en la Patagonia y en la Tierra del Fuego. La mayoría de la población argentina vive en las ciudades y casi la mitad del total de la población vive en la Provincia de Buenos Aires.

ingreso	income	**la mayoría**	most of, the majority
índice de alfabetismo	literacy rate		

Exercise 7

Based on the reading passage above, say if the following statements are **verdadero** (true) or **falso** (false).

1 **Argentina es uno de los países más pobres de América Latina.**
2 **Tiene el mayor número de alfabetos en América Latina.**
3 **Sólo hay clima templado en su territorio.**
4 **La mayoría de la población es rural.**
5 **Casi un cincuenta por ciento de la población vive en la Provincia de Buenos Aires.**

20 Repaso

Review

Fui al cine [cassette icon]

Sara and Pablo are talking about what they like to do

SARA: ¿Qué hiciste ayer?
PABLO: Fui al cine a ver una película francesa. Luego compré una revista para leer en el tren mientras volvía a casa.
SARA: ¿De qué se trata la revista?
PABLO: Trata de asuntos de actualidad.
SARA: ¿Es interesante?
PABLO: Sí. La compro todas las semanas. ¿Tú lees mientras viajas?
SARA: Sí, pero prefiero escuchar la radio.
PABLO: ¿Qué programas te gustan?
SARA: Me gusta un programa periodístico que se llama 'Primera Plana', otro que se llama 'Competencia' y es de deportes. También escucho el programa 'De noche' que es cultural, educativo y de servicio. El programa que más me gusta es 'Los 40 mejores'.
PABLO: ¿Qué tipo de programa es?
SARA: Es de música del momento.
PABLO: Sí, claro. Yo a veces lo escucho.

SARA: *What did you do yesterday?*
PABLO: *I went to the movies to see a French film. Then I bought a magazine to read on the train on the way home.*
SARA: *What kind of magazine is it?*
PABLO: *It deals with current affairs.*
SARA: *Is it interesting?*
PABLO: *Yes. I buy it every week. Do you read while you travel?*
SARA: *Yes. But I prefer to listen to the radio.*
PABLO: *What programs do you like?*
SARA: *I like a news program called 'Primera Plana', another called*

'Competencia' which is about sport. I also listen to the
program 'De noche'. It is cultural, educational and serves
the community. The program I like most is 'Los 40 mejores'.

PABLO: What kind of program is it?
SARA: It plays the latest music.
PABLO: That's right. I sometimes listen to it as well.

Exercise 1

Change these sentences to the preterite using the information in
brackets.

Example:

Compro una revista de deportes. (ayer)
Ayer compré una revista de deportes.

1 **Veo un programa de televisión. (anoche)**
2 **Marcelo y Estela diseñan interiores para una firma conocida. (el año pasado)**
3 **Cecilia imita a varios personajes en la tele. (el sábado pasado)**
4 **La telenovela 'Adoración' se transmite los viernes. (ayer)**
5 **El servicio de limpieza es criticado siempre. (ayer)**
6 **Siempre pierde las carreras. (el sábado pasado)**
7 **Pochita juega todos los domingos. (ayer y anteayer)**
8 **Leonardo no come en casa. (anoche)**
9 **El líder sindical organiza una reunión de trabajadores todos los meses. (el viernes pasado)**
10 **Steven viaja los lunes. (hace dos horas)**

Exercise 2

Match the phrases 1 to 10 with the phrases (a) to (j).

1 **El Código Alimentario establece . . .**
2 **En la foto de grupo . . .**
3 **La jueza . . .**
4 **Un coche-bomba . . .**
5 **Parecen iguales, . . .**
6 **Lo que necesitan los estudiantes . . .**
7 **El multimillonario pagó . . .**
8 **Hay un automóvil . . .**
9 **La comida que preparó Karina . . .**
10 **Ha bajado . . .**

(a) **cuatro kilos.**
(b) **denunció al ministro.**
(c) **pero no lo son.**
(d) **que hay tres clases de agua para el consumo humano.**
(e) **fue deliciosa.**
(f) **explotó en el museo.**
(g) **como primer premio.**
(h) **aparece junto a sus compañeros de escuela.**
(i) **para sus trabajos de investigación.**
(j) **muchos millones de dólares por el cuadro del pintor holandés.**

¿Vas a ir al teatro? 🔲

While reading the dialogue below, see if you can find answers to these questions:

Do both want to go to the same place?
Why does Estela refuse Germán's invitation to go to the movies?

Estela and Germán are talking about going to the theater or movies

ESTELA: ¿Vas a ir al teatro?
GERMÁN: No. No me gusta la obra. Creo que iré al cine.
ESTELA: Pero tú dijiste que querías ir al teatro.
GERMÁN: No dije cuándo. Hoy no puedo. Quizás el próximo fin de semana.
ESTELA: Quizás yo no pueda el próximo fin de semana.
GERMÁN: ¿Por qué no vas al cine conmigo?
ESTELA: ¿Esta noche?
GERMÁN: Sí. Esta noche. Es una película francesa.
ESTELA: Creo que no. Va a venir Irene y creo que ella también quiere ir al teatro. Iremos juntas.
GERMÁN: Bueno. Nos vemos luego.
ESTELA: Chao.

ESTELA: *Are you going to go to the theater?*
GERMÁN: *No. I don't like the play. I think I'll go to the movies.*
ESTELA: *But you said you wanted to go to the theater.*
GERMÁN: *I didn't say when. I can't today. Perhaps next week.*
ESTELA: *I may not be able to go next weekend.*
GERMÁN: *Why don't you come to the movies with me?*
ESTELA: *Tonight?*

GERMÁN:	*Yes, tonight. It's a French film.*
ESTELA:	*I don't think so. Irene is coming and I think she also wants to go to the theater. We'll go together.*
GERMÁN:	*All right. See you later.*
ESTELA:	*Bye.*

Exercise 3

Match the phrases in 1 to 5 with the phrases (a) to (e).

1 **Voy a llegar tarde a la reunión.**
2 **Estaremos en el centro mañana.**
3 **Ayer compramos un nuevo juego de muebles.**
4 **Se ha dislocado el brazo.**
5 **Hace frío.**

(a) **Hay que llevarla al hospital.**
(b) **Ponte una chaqueta.**
(c) **No hay problema. Se ha postergado para mañana.**
(d) **¿Es de roble o caoba?**
(e) **Yo también. Tengo que hacer compras.**

Exercise 4

Give Spanish equivalents for the following sentences:

1 I wish you had not brought that book.
2 Let's hope Sharon has brought the same one.
3 If I were you I would send the money tomorrow.
4 If I were Sharon I would go there tonight.
5 If only I had enough time to visit all the museums and exhibitions in this city.

Exercise 5

Choose the correct form of the verb in brackets.

1 **Es posible que (vendrá/venga) mañana.**
2 **Le han recomendado que (viva/vive) en el campo.**
3 **¿Le (guste/gustaría) ir al cine esta noche o preferiría (quedarse/quedará) en casa?**
4 **Es importante que (coma/comería) fruta.**
5 **Me parece que no (tiene/tenga) plata para comprar el helado.**
6 **El televisor (no funciona/no funcione).**

7 **No creo que (coman/comen) en un restaurante de mariscos porque son vegetarianos.**
8 **Ojalá (llega/llegue) pronto.**
9 **Si (viene/venga) dale este dinero.**
10 **El médico le ha recomendado que (viajará/viaje) al campo.**

Exercise 6

Choose the correct form of the verb in brackets.

1 **Si (estaba/estuviera) en Cancún (estaría/estaré) en la playa y no en la cocina preparando la comida.**
2 **Mañana (estaremos/estuviéramos) en Río de Janeiro. Parece un sueño.**
3 **Ojalá (haya traído/trajo) el programa de actividades.**
4 **Caroline (trajo/trajese) el manual ayer, pero no sé dónde lo dejó.**
5 **Si la tienda (estuvo/estuviese) en el centro iríamos a pie en vez de ir en carro.**
6 **Quisiera (ser/fuese) diplomático para conocer varios países.**
7 **Quisiera que (ser/fuese) sábado, no lunes entonces no tendría que ir a trabajar.**
8 **Le dije que no podía continuar con el trabajo, a menos que (comiera/comerá) algo primero.**
9 **Esteban no (saldrá/saliera) al extranjero este mes porque tiene mucho que hacer en la empresa. Quizás (saliera/salga) el mes que viene.**
10 **Si (podría/pudiera) te visitaría.**

Exercise 7

Choose the phrase in the group (a) to (j) that best completes the sentence started in the group 1 to 10.

1 **Ralph tiene un suéter ...**
2 **La revista dedica ...**
3 **Muchos padres invierten ...**
4 **La década del 90 ...**
5 **El secretario se llama ...**
6 **Los colegios no dicen ...**
7 **El próximo mes ...**
8 **Yo ... es todo.**

9 Estas son las obras . . .
10 Hay mucha preocupación . . .

(a) . . . tiempo y dinero en la educación de sus hijos.
(b) . . . de teatro más vistas este año.
(c) . . . tejido de lana de alpaca.
(d) . . . sus páginas al automovilismo.
(e) . . . Antonio Suárez.
(f) . . . por el medio ambiente.
(g) . . . creo que saldremos de vacaciones.
(h) . . . creo que eso
(i) . . . cuándo empezará el año escolar.
(j) . . . es la última de este siglo.

Exercise 8

Complete the sentence with a preposition from the list, if it is necessary.

desde	a	para	de	en
por	hasta	abajo de/debajo de	durante	

1 Se casaron _____ el mes pasado.
2 Hoy estamos a 21 _____ septiembre.
3 Voy a la escuela _____ la mañana.
4 Caracas, 22 _____ enero _____ 1994.
5 La tienda abre _____ las diez _____ las siete.
6 Terminarán el edificio _____ fines de mes.
7 Faltan muchos días _____ el fin _____ año.
8 No estaba sobre la mesa sino _____ de ésta.
9 He trabajado _____ dos días seguidos y necesito un descanso.
10 Estaré con ustedes _____ verano.

Exercise 9

Rearrange the following words in three groups under the headings **fruta** (fruit), **viajes** (traveling) and **colores** (colors).

bicicleta	azul	negro
manzana	barco	amarillo
ciclomotor	plátano	sandía
verde	vuelo	carro
frutilla	piña	rojo

Exercise 10

Match each of the questions 1 to 5 with the most suitable reply (a) to (e).

1 **¿Adónde vas tan apurada?**
2 **¿Quién es esa persona que te dio la llave?**
3 **¿Cómo piensas ir a la universidad esta tarde?**
4 **¿No te parece que ya es demasiado tarde para ir al teatro?**
5 **¿Cuándo llegan tus padres?**

(a) **Creo que Marcelo va a llevarme en su auto; de lo contrario iré en el metro.**
(b) **La Sra Taboada. Ella es la dueña del hotel. Es un negocio de familia.**
(c) **Hay dos posibilidades: una es a fines de este mes. Otra, a mediados del próximo.**
(d) **Esta noche la función empieza media hora más tarde que de costumbre, así que llegaremos a tiempo.**
(e) **Al colegio a recoger a los chicos.**

Reading

Read the following text from an advertisement for a private ambulance service.

MEDIC-MOVIL

Medic es un servicio de atención médica especializada. Sus unidades móviles cuentan con equipos de atención y resucitación que operan en toda la capital.

Si usted o uno de sus trabajadores sufre una emergencia médica, llame a nuestro teléfono y de inmediato un operador u operadora con conocimientos médicos se pondrá en comunicación por radio a la unidad móvil más cercana al lugar donde se encuentre el paciente.

Si está interesado llámenos por teléfono y nuestro representante lo visitará a la brevedad posible para darle mayor información.

Informes: 442255

Exercise 11

Based on the reading text above, say if the following statements are **verdadero** (true) or **falso** (false).

1 Medic es un servicio de ambulancias que opera en todo el país.
2 El servicio es sólo para ejecutivos.
3 Los operadores se comunican por radio con las unidades móviles.
4 Los operadores tratan de ubicar la unidad móvil más cercana al paciente.
5 Para mayor información hay que ir personalmente a Médic-móvil.

Exercise 12

Complete the sentences with the correct form of **ser** or **estar**.

1 El taller _____ en la calle Emancipación.
2 _____ abogado (yo).
3 La niña _____ molesta.
4 ¿_____ (ustedes) en la casa de mi hermana?
5 Estela y Lucrecia _____ obreras.
6 Guayaquil _____ en Ecuador.
7 El autor del libro _____ en Colombia.
8 El banco _____ cerrado.
9 No _____ representantes sino distribuidores (nosotros).
10 No _____ en su despacho (ella).

Exercise 13

Change these commands to the negative.

Example:

Compren frutillas.
No compren frutillas.

1 Vayan a la reunión.
2 Llama por teléfono a tu jefe.
3 Trata de vender tu carro.
4 Abra el archivo para ver.
5 Copien el documento en diskette.
6 Pide diez cuadernos.

7 **Ven con tu novio.**
8 **Tome fotos.**
9 **Prepare el plato que le recomendé.**
10 **Instala la antena.**

Exercise 14

Rewrite these sentences in the imperative. Follow the examples.

Examples:

Ustedes deben venir mañana.
Vengan mañana.

Tienes que decir cuál es el problema.
Di cuál es el problema.

1 **Ustedes deben comprar una nueva máquina.**
2 **Tienes que oir lo que dice este señor.**
3 **Tiene que venir el próximo sábado.**
4 **Usted debe mandar el paquete por correo.**
5 **Debes escribir pronto.**
6 **Tienes que comer menos grasas.**
7 **Ustedes deben estudiar este contrato.**
8 **Tienes que hacer esto.**
9 **Usted debe ser más paciente.**
10 **Tienes que subir al tercer piso.**

Reading 📼

Read the information about Maribel Hernández and then fill in the form which follows.

Maribel Hernández tiene 39 años. Está separada de su esposo. Es profesora en una escuela primaria en las afueras de Quito. Maribel tiene dos hijos que se llaman Alberto y Estela. Alberto tiene 11 años y Estela tiene 8 años. Viven en un departamento en la calle Iglesias 341 – C. El departamento tiene dos dormitorios. Uno es de Maribel, los niños comparten el otro. Alberto y Estela ayudan a su mami en las tareas de la casa.

Nombre:
Edad:
Estado civil:

Ocupación:
Nº de hijos:
Nombre de los hijos:
Edad de los hijos:
Domicilio:

Exercise 15

Based on the passage above, say if the following statements are **verdadero** (true) or **falso** (false).

1 **Estela no tiene hermanos.**
2 **Los niños no ayudan a Maribel en las tareas de la casa.**
3 **Estela es menor que Alberto.**
4 **Viven en el centro de la capital ecuatoriana.**
5 **Tienen un departamento de dos dormitorios.**

HORIZONTAL

  1 Primer nivel de educación.
  6 Aplicación de las ciencias prácticas o mecánicas en la industria y el comercio.
  8 País latinoamericano.
  9 Uno diferente. Uno más.

VERTICAL

  1 Fruta.
  2 Lo contrario de activo.
  3 Lo contrario de bajo.
  4 Hay muchos en las calles, carreteras y autopistas.
  5 País latinoamericano de la zona andina.
  6 Normalmente hay mucha en el centro de una ciudad.

Grammar summary

The Spanish alphabet

a	a	**n**	ene
b	be (alta, grande)	**ñ**	eñe
c	ce	**o**	o
ch	che	**p**	pe
d	de	**q**	cu
e	e	**r**	erre
f	efe	**s**	ese
g	ge	**t**	te
h	hache	**u**	u
i	i (latina)	**v**	ve (corta, chica)
j	jota	**w**	ve doble
k	ka	**x**	equis
l	ele	**y**	y griega
ll	elle	**z**	zeta
m	eme		

Stress and written accent

If the word ends in a vowel, **-n** or **-s** the stress is on the penultimate syllable, i.e. the syllable before the last one.

tra*ba*jo
es*cri*bes
dele*ga*do
***Car*men**

If the word ends in a consonant, except **-n** or **-s**, the stress is on the final syllable.

pa*pel*
co*lor*
ciu*dad*

When there is a deviation from these rules an acute accent is written on the vowel of the stressed syllable.

acá
latón
pacífico

Word order

Word order (position of the subject in relation to the object of a sentence) is not as rigid in Spanish as it is in English. The most common patterns are:

subject + verb + object
Mariela vendió la casa.

object + verb + subject
La casa la vendió Mariela.

object + subject + verb
La casa Mariela la vendió.

In most cases adjectives are placed after the noun they qualify. In negative sentences **no** always precedes the verb.

Nouns and gender

Nouns in Spanish are either masculine or feminine. Not only people and animals are included in this classification, but things as well.

masc.		*fem.*	
hombre	man	**mujer**	woman
gato	male cat	**gata**	female cat
sol	sun	**luna**	moon

Generally speaking, the ending of a noun tells you whether it is masculine or feminine. The following are the most common endings.

Masculine: **-o, -l, -r, -y**; e.g. **alumno, papel, actor, rey**.

Feminine: **-a**, **-ión**, **-dad**, **-tad**, **-tud**, **-itis**; e.g. **alumna**, **canción**, **ciudad**, **libertad**, **altitud**, **artritis**.

Usually when the masculine ends in **-o**, you form the feminine by changing it to **-a**.

alumno   **alumna**

Usually when the masculine ends in a consonant, you form the feminine by adding **-a**.

vendedor   **vendedora**

Some nouns are both masculine and feminine but with a difference in meaning, as in the following examples:

el capital   the capital (money)   **la capital**   the capital (city)

el policía   the police officer   **la policía**   the police

Plural of nouns

When a noun ends in an **unstressed vowel** or a stressed **-e**, an **-s** is added

Examples:

niña   niñas
café   cafés

When a noun ends in a **consonant**, **-y** or a **stressed vowel** (except **-e**), **-es** is added

Examples:

pared   pared**es**
cuy   cuy**es**
rubí   rubí**es**

Note: There are exceptions to this third case (stressed vowel, other than **-e**). The most common exceptions are: mamá–mamás; papá–papás

Nouns ending in **-z** change the -z to **-e**, before adding **-es**

Examples:

luz   luc**es**
cruz   cruc**es**

Articles

The definite article

	masc.	*fem.*	
sing.	**el**	**la**	the
pl.	**los**	**las**	the

The definite article agrees in gender and number with the noun it precedes.

el carro	the car	**los carros**	the cars
la casa	the house	**las casas**	the houses

Note: if the definite article precedes a singular feminine noun which starts with a stressed **a-** or **ha-**, then **el** is used instead of **la**.

el agua	the water
el haba	the broad bean

The indefinite article

	masc.	*fem.*	
sing.	**un**	**una**	a/an
pl.	**unos**	**unas**	some

The indefinite article agrees in gender and number with the noun it precedes.

un gato	a cat	**una gata**	a jack
unos libros	some books	**unas libras**	some pounds

The neuter article

The neuter article **lo** never precedes a noun. Its main use is to form abstract nouns. In this case it is followed by an adjective or a past participle.

lo interesante	what is interesting
lo dicho	what has been said

Adjectives

Almost all adjectives agree in gender and number with the noun or pronoun they refer to.

When the adjective ends in **-o** the feminine is usually formed by changing the final letter to **-a**.

distribuidor exclusivo	sole distributor
moda exclusiva	exclusive fashion

Adjectives ending in a consonant usually add **-a**.

activador	**activadora**	activating
francés	**francesa**	French

Although the usual position of the adjective in a sentence is after the noun, it can appear before it.

una casa nueva	**una nueva casa**	a new house

Plural of adjectives

When an adjective ends in a vowel you add **-s** to form the plural, unless the final vowel is stressed, in which case you add **-es**.
When it ends in a consonant you add **-es**.

un médico peruano	a Peruvian doctor
médicos peruanos	Peruvian doctors
una palabra guaraní	a Guarani word
dos palabras guaraníes	two Guarani words
una solución fácil	an easy solution
soluciones fáciles	easy solutions

Demonstrative adjectives

These adjectives agree in number and in gender with the noun and usually precede it.

	masc.	*fem.*	
sing.	**este**	**esta**	this
	ese	**esa**	that
	aquel	**aquella**	that (distant)

pl.	estos	estas	these
	esos	esas	those
	aquellos	aquellas	those (distant)

Possessive adjectives

Possessive adjectives agree in number with the noun which they precede. Only **nuestro** (our) has a feminine form, **nuestra**, which agrees in number and gender with the noun.

mi	my
tu	your (sing.)
su	his, her, its, your (formal)
nuestro	our (masc.)
nuestra	our (fem.)
su	your (pl.)
su	their

Examples:

mi cuaderno de ejercicios	my exercise book
su diccionario bilingüe	her bilingual dictionary

If the noun possessed is in the plural you add an **-s** to the possessive adjective.

Mis amigos no han llegado.	My friends haven't arrived.
Nuestras empresas firmaron el contrato.	Our companies signed the contract.

Personal pronouns

These pronouns are used far less than their equivalents in English. Sometimes they are used for emphasis or to avoid confusion.

Singular		*Plural*	
yo	I	**nosotros**	we (masc.)
tú	you (informal)	**nosotras**	we (fem.)
usted	you (formal)	**ustedes**	you
él	he	**ellos**	they (masc.)
ella	she	**ellas**	they (fem.)

Adverbs

These are usually formed by adding the ending -**mente** to the feminine adjective. Note that adjectives ending in -**e** have the same form in the masculine and the feminine.

lento	**lentamente**	slowly
sincero	**sinceramente**	sincerely
urgente	**urgentemente**	urgently

When an adverb appears with a verb in the same sentence, it usually follows the verb. It can precede the verb for emphasis.

Se dirigieron a la escuela lentamente.	They made their way to school slowly.
Lentamente pasaron uno por uno.	They slowly went past one by one.

Prepositions

These link parts of a sentence and usually express manner, time or place:

a	to, at	**ante**	before
en	in, on, at	**bajo**	under
de	of, from	**delante de**	in front of
desde	from	**detrás de**	behind
hacia	towards	**encima**	over
por	for, by, through	**entre**	between
para	for	**sobre**	on

Verbs

The infinitive

The infinitive is the form of a verb given in a dictionary. It is also the form that you will find in the glossary of this book. According to the ending of the infinitive there are three types of verbs in Spanish:

verbs ending in -**ar**	also called verbs of the first conjugation
verbs ending in -**er**	also called verbs of the second conjugation
verbs ending in -**ir**	also called verbs of the third conjugation

Examples:

-ar	**comprar**	to buy
	trabajar	to work
	estudiar	to study
-er	**comer**	to eat
	vender	to sell
	comprender	to understand
-ir	**vivir**	to live
	escribir	to write
	subir	to go up

The present tense indicative

The present tense indicative is used with actions which are habitual or timeless.

Examples:

Siempre voy en tren.	I always go by train.
Martha es peruana.	Martha is Peruvian.

Here are three examples of regular verbs in the present tense indicative: **trabajar** (to work), **comer** (to eat) and **escribir** (to write).

trabajo	I work
trabajas	you work (informal)
trabaja	you work (formal); he/she works
trabajamos	we work
trabajan	you work (formal and informal)
trabajan	they work

como	**comemos**	**escribo**	**escribimos**
comes	**comen**	**escribes**	**escriben**
come	**comen**	**escribe**	**escriben**

Irregular verbs

Some verbs do not follow the pattern or rule of regular verbs. For that reason they are called *irregular*. Here is one example: **tener**.

tengo	I have
tienes	you have (informal)

tiene	you have (formal); he/she/it has
tenemos	we have
tienen	you have
tienen	they have

Forming questions

Both regular and irregular verbs form questions by adding question marks to affirmative and negative statements. When speaking you sound as if you are asking a question. Unlike English, you do not need an auxiliary word like 'do'.

Trabajan mucho.	They work hard.
¿Trabajan mucho?	Do they work hard?
No tienes tiempo.	You do not have time.
¿No tienes tiempo?	Don't you have time?

Radical changing verbs

These are verbs in Spanish which undergo a change of the stem vowel (i.e. the vowel in the part of the verb that remains the same when it is conjugated) when you conjugate them. In these verbs the vowel -**e**- in the stem becomes -**ie**-, and the vowel -**o**- becomes -**ue**-. The exception is the first person plural.

Examples:

-**e**- → -**ie**-	-**o**- → -**ue**-
preferir	**dormir**
prefiero	**duermo**
prefieres	**duermes**
prefiere	**duerme**
preferimos	**dormimos**
prefieren	**duermen**
prefieren	**duermen**

The present continuous tense

The present continuous tense is formed by using **estar** + the gerund form of the verb. The gerund ends in -**ando** or -**iendo** (-**ando** for -**ar** verbs; **-iendo** for **-er** and **-ir** verbs.) The forms correspond to the English ending '-ing', as in 'eating', 'running', etc.

estoy estudiando	I am studying
estás estudiando	you are studying (informal)
está estudiando	you are studying (formal); he/she is studying
estamos estudiando	we are studying
están estudiando	you are studying (formal and informal)
están estudiando	they are studying

The present continuous refers to an action which is in progress at the time of speaking.

The present perfect tense

The present perfect tense is formed by the auxiliary verb **haber** and the past participle of the main verb of the sentence.

Example:

He perdido mi maletín.   I have lost my briefcase.

The forms of **haber** are:

he	I have
has	you have (informal)
ha	you have (formal); he/she has
hemos	we have
han	you have (plural)
han	they have

You form the past participle of a verb by replacing the infinitive ending **-ar** by the ending **-ado**, and the endings **-er** and **-ir** by **-ido**.

trabajar	**trabajado**
comer	**comido**
vivir	**vivido**

The most common irregular past participles are:

abrir (to open)	**abierto**
decir (to say)	**dicho**
escribir (to write)	**escrito**
hacer (to do, to make)	**hecho**
morir (to die)	**muerto**

poner (to put)	**puesto**
romper (to break)	**roto**
ver (to see)	**visto**
volver (to return)	**vuelto**

The present perfect is used to indicate that an event has happened in a period of time in the past but which includes the present or whose effects still bear on the present.

The present perfect continuous

This tense is used to indicate that an action has been in progress over a period of time and continues to be in progress at the time of speaking. It is formed by using **haber** plus the past participle plus the gerund, i.e. the verb showing action in progress, (e.g. **escribiendo** 'writing', **viajando** 'traveling'.

Example:

Hemos estado trabajando todo el día en este asunto.   We have been working on this matter all day.

ir a *+ infinitive*

One way of expressing the future is by using the present tense of the verb **ir** (to go) followed by **a** plus the infinitive expressing the intended action. This is similar to the English structure 'to be going to + infinitive'.

Example:

Vamos a visitar el museo.   We are going to visit the museum.

Here are all the forms of the verb **ir + a**:

voy a	I am going to
vas a	you are going to (informal)
va a	you are going to (formal) he/she/it is going to
vamos a	we are going to
van a	you are going to
van a	they are going to

The past tense or preterite

The past tense, or preterite, is used to express an action in the past already complete at the time of speaking.

Example:

Ayer comimos en un restaurante.	Yesterday we went to a restaurant for a meal.

The past tense of regular verbs is formed as follows:
-ar verbs: **terminar** (to finish)

terminé	I finished
terminaste	you finished (informal)
terminó	you finished (formal); he/she/it finished
terminamos	we finished
terminaron	you finished
terminaron	they finished

-er verbs: **comer**

comí	**comimos**
comiste	**comieron**
comió	**comieron**

-ir verbs: **vivir**

viví	**vivimos**
viviste	**vivieron**
vivió	**vivieron**

Here are some examples of irregular verbs in the past:

hacer	ir	tener	dar
hice	**fui**	**tuve**	**di**
hiciste	**fuiste**	**tuviste**	**diste**
hizo	**fue**	**tuvo**	**dio**
hicimos	**fuimos**	**tuvimos**	**dimos**
hicieron	**fueron**	**tuvieron**	**dieron**
hicieron	**fueron**	**tuvieron**	**dieron**

The future tense

To form the future of regular verbs you add the same endings to the infinitive of all **-ar**, **-er** or **-ir** verbs.

trabajar	comer	vivir
trabajaré	comeré	viviré
trabajarás	comerás	vivirás
trabajará	comerá	vivirá
trabajaremos	comeremos	viviremos
trabajarán	comerán	vivirán
trabajarán	comerán	vivirán

The future tense is used mainly in written language. In conversation the future tense is less common than its equivalent in English. Spanish speakers tend to prefer the '**ir + a** + verb' structure to express ideas in the future.

Here are some irregular verbs in the future:

decir	hacer	salir	venir
diré	haré	saldré	vendré
dirás	harás	saldrás	vendrás
dirá	hará	saldré	vendrá
diremos	haremos	saldremos	vendremos
dirán	harán	saldrán	vendrán
dirán	harán	saldrán	vendrán

The imperfect indicative tense

The imperfect tense is used to indicate a habitual or repeated action in the past. It is the equivalent of verbs with 'used to' or 'was' in English.

Example:

**Los fines de semana nos   We used to gather in groups at the
   reuníamos en grupos.**   weekends.

It is also used to describe characteristics in the past when such characteristics continued to exist for a period of time.

Example:

**La gata se llamaba   The cat used to be called/was
   Magdalena.**   called Magdalena.

Regular verbs have their forms in the imperfect indicative as follows:

comprar	vender	vivir
compraba	vendía	vivía
comprabas	vendías	vivías
compraba	vendía	vivía
comprábamos	vendíamos	vivíamos
compraban	vendían	vivían
compraban	vendían	vivían

There are only three verbs which are irregular in the imperfect indicative:

ir	ser	ver
iba	era	veía
ibas	eras	veías
iba	era	veía
íbamos	éramos	veíamos
iban	eran	veían
iban	eran	veían

The imperfect continuous tense

This tense is used to refer to an action already in progress in the past when something else happened, interrupting the first action.

Example:

Estaba escuchando música   I was listening to music when the
cuando sonó el timbre.   bell rang.

In the imperfect continuous you use the verb **estar** in the imperfect indicative together with the continuous form of the main verb.

trabajar

estaba trabajando	I was working
estabas trabajando	you were working (informal)
estaba trabajando	you were working (formal); he/she was working
estábamos trabajando	we were working

estaban trabajando	you were working (formal and informal)
estaban trabajando	they were working

The present subjunctive

The subjunctive is a verb form used in Spanish to express attitude, such as wishing, hoping, doubting, etc., and to indicate actions which are only hypothetical or a possibility in the future, at the moment of speaking. It is little used in English.

Examples:

Espero que puedas venir a la fiesta.	I hope you can make it to the party.
Quisiera que ayudes a Isabel.	I would like you to help Isabel.

The present subjunctive of regular verbs is formed as follows:

trabajar	**comer**	**vivir**
trabaje	**coma**	**viva**
trabajes	**comas**	**vivas**
trabaje	**coma**	**viva**
trabajemos	**comamos**	**vivamos**
trabajen	**coman**	**vivan**
trabajen	**coman**	**vivan**

The conditional tense

The conditional tense (in English 'I would go', etc.) is formed by adding the following endings to the infinitive: **-ía, -ías, -ía, -íamos, -ían**. The same endings are used with the three conjugations.

trabajar	**comer**	**vivir**
trabajaría	**comería**	**viviría**
trabajarías	**comerías**	**vivirías**
trabajaría	**comería**	**viviría**
trabajaríamos	**comeríamos**	**viviríamos**
trabajarían	**comerían**	**vivirían**
trabajarían	**comerían**	**vivirían**

Here is a list of the main irregular verbs in the conditional tense:

decir	haber	hacer
diría	habría	haría
dirías	habrías	harías
diría	habría	haría
diríamos	habríamos	haríamos
dirían	habrían	harían
dirían	habrían	harían

poder	poner	querer
podría	pondría	querría
podrías	pondrías	querrías
podría	pondría	querría
podríamos	pondríamos	querríamos
podrían	pondrían	querrían
podrían	pondrían	querrían

salir	tener	venir
saldría	tendría	vendría
saldrías	tendrías	vendrías
saldría	tendría	vendría
saldríamos	tendríamos	vendríamos
saldrían	tendrían	vendrían
saldrían	tendrían	vendrían

The imperative

The imperative form is used to give commands, orders or instructions.

Examples:

Prepare un informe para mañana. (usted)   Prepare a report for tomorrow.

Toma estas pastillas. (tú)   Take these tablets.

The imperative for the second person singular informal (**tú**) is the same as the form for the third person singular in the present indicative, in the case of regular verbs.

preparar	prepar*a*
comer	com*e*
subir	sub*e*

The most frequently used irregular verbs in the imperative for the second person informal (**tú**) are:

decir	di	**salir**	sal
estar	está	**ser**	sé
hacer	haz	**tener**	ten
ir	ve	**venir**	ven
oír	oye		

The imperative for the second person singular formal (**usted**) is the same as the present subjunctive for **usted**, **él** or **ella**.

preparar	prepar*e*
comer	com*a*
subir	sub*a*

The imperative for the second person plural (**ustedes**) is the same as the present subjunctive for **ustedes**, **ellos** or **ellas**.

preparar	prepar*en*
comer	com*an*
subir	sub*an*

The imperfect subjunctive

The imperfect subjunctive indicates actions which are hypothetical and also remote possibilities at the time of speaking. Compared to the present subjunctive, the action is less likely to take place. One use of the imperfect subjunctive is for sentences expressing hope. Another is in hypothetical conditional sentences.

Ojalá llamase.

The imperfect subjunctive has two alternative conjugations, which are interchangeable. Here is an example of a regular verb, **trabajar**, in the two forms of the imperfect subjunctive:

trabajara	trabajase
trabajaras	trabajases
trabajara	trabajase
trabajáramos	trabajásemos
trabajaran	trabajasen
trabajaran	trabajasen

The conditional perfect tense

The verb **haber** in the conditional tense (**habría, habrías,** etc.) together with the past participle of the main verb are used to form the conditional perfect tense. Here are the forms of **trabajar** in the conditional perfect:

habría trabajado	I would have worked
habrías trabajado	you would have worked (informal)
habría trabajado	you would have worked (formal); he/she would have worked
habríamos trabajado	we would have worked
habrían trabajado	you would have worked
habrían trabajado	they would have worked

The pluperfect subjunctive

To form the pluperfect subjunctive, you use the imperfect subjunctive of **haber** together with past participle of the verb. Here are the forms of **comprar** in the pluperfect subjunctive:

hubiera comprado	I would have bought
hubieras comprado	you would have bought (informal)
hubiera comprado	you would have bought (formal); he/she would have bought
hubiéramos comprado	we would have bought
hubieran comprado	you would have bought
hubieran comprado	they would have bought

As in the case of the imperfect subjunctive, it is possible to use the alternative form -**se**. They are interchangeable.

The passive voice

The verb **ser** is used with the past participle to form the passive voice. There is agreement in number and gender with the subject of the verb **ser**. The passive voice is used to put the emphasis on the action taking place rather than on the subject performing the action (as in sentences in the active voice).

Example:

Los expedientes han sido devueltos.　　The dossiers have been returned.

The following are examples of the passive voice in various tenses.

Present
soy llevado
eres llevado
es llevado
somos llevados
son llevados
son llevados

Imperfect
era llevado
eras llevado
era llevado
éramos llevados
eran llevados
eran llevados

Preterite
fui llevado
fuiste llevado
fue llevado
fuimos llevados
fueron llevados
fueron llevados

Future
seré llevado
serás llevado
será llevado
seremos llevados
serán llevados
serán llevados

Conditional
sería llevado
serías llevado
sería llevado
seríamos llevados
serían llevados
serían llevados

Present perfect
he sido llevado
has sido llevado
ha sido llevado
hemos sido llevados
han sido llevados
han sido llevados

Pluperfect
había sido llevado
habías sido llevado
había sido llevado
habíamos sido llevados
habían sido llevados
habían sido llevados

Future perfect
habré sido llevado
habrás sido llevado
habrá sido llevado
habremos sido llevados
habrán sido llevados
habrán sido llevados

Conditional perfect
habría sido llevado
habrías sido llevado
habría sido llevado
habríamos sido llevados
habrían sido llevados
habrían sido llevados

The impersonal se

Se is used in spoken Spanish to replace the passive construction learned above, which is mainly used in written language.

Examples:

Se sabe que no funciona.	It is known that it doesn't work.
Se espera que compren nuestros productos.	It is expected that they will buy our products.

Key to exercises

Please note that with open-ended exercises, answers will not always appear in the Key.

Chapter 1

Exercise 1

(c)	1	(d)	34
(j)	7	(k)	62
(h)	12	(l)	79
(e)	13	(b)	93
(g)	15	(i)	94
(f)	27	(a)	100

Exercise 2

(a)	25	**veinticinco**	(d)	13	**trece**
(b)	68	**sesenta y ocho**	(e)	44	**cuarenta y cuatro**
(c)	76	**setenta y seis**			

Exercise 3

Carlos trece
Luisa dieciseis
Milagros cuarenta y ocho
Carolina veinte
Esteban noventa y uno
(N.B. These answers will, of course, vary according to the year it is.)

Exercise 4

(a) **Buenos días**
(b) **Buenas tardes**
(c) **Buenas tardes**

(d) **Buenas noches**
(e) **Buenos días**

Exercise 5

1 **Arturo tiene carro/auto.**
2 **Lupe trabaja en Méjico/México.**
3 **La agencia de viaje tiene fax.**
4 **¿Trabajas? ¿Trabaja (ud.)?**

Exercise 6

1 **tengo ... tiene**
2 **tenemos**
3 **tienen**

4 **tiene**
5 **tienen**

Chapter 2

Exercise 1

1 **viene**
2 **Salgo**
3 **va**

4 **hace**
5 **decimos**

Exercise 2

¿A qué hora sale el avión a Caracas?
Sale a las trece cuarenta y cinco.

¿A qué hora sale el avión a Lima?
Sale a las nueve veinte.

¿A qué hora sale el avión a Quito?
Sale a las seis (horas).

¿A qué hora llega el avión de Madrid?
Llega a las once cuarenta y cinco.

¿A qué hora llega el avión de Santiago?
Llega a las once cincuenta.

¿A qué hora llega el avión de México D.F.?
Llega a las diez veinte.

Exercise 3

Camisas	treinta y seis
Blusas	veintiocho
Abrigos	noventa y cuatro, cinco
Pañuelos	cinco, cuarenta
Pantalones	treinta y ocho, cuarenta
Camisetas	diez, ochenta

Exercise 4

Hombres	Mujeres	Ambos
corbata	medias	zapatos
calzoncillo	lápiz labial	suéter
	aretes	pañuelo
	blusa	camisa
	falda	
	vestido	

Exercise 5

1
3
4

Exercise 6

Páguese a Viajes El Sol la suma de dos mil cuatrocientos veinticinco soles.

Chapter 3

Exercise 1

1 **los**
2 **la**
3 **el**
4 **los**
5 **el/la**

6 **el**
7 **la**
8 **el/la**
9 **los**
10 **el**

Exercise 2

1 (h)	5 (e)
2 (d)	6 (f)
3 (b)	7 (c)
4 (a)	8 (g)

Exercise 4

VENTAJAS

piscina
aire acondicionado
caja fuerte individual

DESVENTAJAS

céntrico
desayuno incluido
calefacción central
cambio de moneda
restaurante
teléfono en la habitación

Exercise 5

Mi plan para el martes es leer una guía turística.
Mi plan para el miércoles es buscar información.
Mi plan para el jueves es estudiar el informe.
Mi plan para el viernes es preparar documentos y hacer las maletas.
Mi plan para el sábado el llegar al aeropuerto a las 2.30 y comprar una
 novela.
Mi plan para el domingo es descansar.

Exercise 6

1 Hasta el lunes
2 Hasta el sábado
3 Hasta el domingo
4 Hasta el martes
5 Hasta mañana

Exercise 7

1 25 de diciembre
3 1 de enero

Exercise 8

1 **individual con baño**
2 **el viernes**

Exercise 9

TELEFAX
Dirigido a Señora Urrutia
Hotel Embajador

Estimada señora:
Le ruego reservar una habitación doble con baño y teléfono para 3 noches a partir del sábado próximo.

Atentamente

Chapter 4

Exercise 2

1 (e)	4 (c)
2 (d)	5 (a)
3 (b)	

Exercise 3

1 **soy**	4 **es**
2 **son**	5 **son**
3 **somos**	

Exercise 4

1 (f)	9 (e)
2 (l)	10 (c)
3 (k)	11 (n)
4 (b)	12 (o)
5 (g)	13 (h)
6 (i)	14 (m)
7 (d)	15 (a)
8 (j)	

Exercise 5

1 está	6 está
2 soy	7 es
3 está	8 está
4 Estamos	9 Somos
5 son	10 está

Exercise 6

(a)
¿Dónde está la librería?
La librería está a la izquierda.

¿Dónde está la comisaría?
La comisaría está a la izquierda.

¿Dónde está el cine?
El cine está a la izquierda.

¿Dónde está el hotel?
El hotel está a la derecha.

¿Dónde está el banco?
El banco está a la derecha.

¿Dónde está el supermercado?
El supermercado está a la derecha.

¿Dónde está la panadería?
La panadería está a la derecha.

(b)
¿Dónde está la librería?
La librería está a la izquierda, enfrente del banco.

¿Dónde está la comisaría?
La comisaría está a la izquierda, enfrente del supermercado.

¿Dónde está el cine?
El cine está a la izquierda, enfrente de la panadería.

¿Dónde está el hotel?
El hotel está a la derecha, enfrente del bar.

¿Dónde está el banco?
El banco está a la derecha, enfrente de la librería.

¿Dónde está el supermercado?
El supermercado está a la derecha, enfrente de la comisaría.

¿Dónde está la panadería?
La panadería está a la derecha, enfrente del cine.

(c)
¿Dónde está la librería?
La librería está a la izquierda, enfrente del banco, al lado del bar/al lado de la comisaría.

¿Dónde está la comisaría?
La comisaría está a la izquierda, enfrente del supermercado, al lado de la librería/del cine.

¿Dónde está el cine?
El cine está a la izquierda, enfrente de la panadería, al lado de la comisaría.

¿Dónde está el hotel?
El hotel está a la derecha, enfrente del bar, al lado del banco.

¿Dónde está el banco?
El banco está a la derecha, enfrente de la librería, al lado del hotel/del supermercado.

¿Dónde está el supermercado?
El supermercado está a la derecha, enfrente de la comisaría, al lado del banco/de la panadería.

¿Dónde está la panadería?
La panadería está a la derecha, enfrente del cine, al lado del supermercado.

Exercise 7

1 (b)	5 (a)
2 (c)	6 (f), (g)
3 (b), (e)	7 (h)
4 (d)	8 (f), (h)

Exercise 8

1 V	4 V
2 F	5 V
3 F	

Chapter 5

Exercise 1

(Answers may vary according to individual choice)

1 **diario**	4 **mensual**
2 **anual**	5 **semanal**
3 **trimestral**	

Exercise 2

(Answers may vary according to individual choice)

1 **una vez por semana.**
2 **todos los días.**
3 **tres veces por semana.**
4 **dos veces por año.**
5 **una o dos veces por año.**

Exercise 3

(Answers may vary according to individual choice)

1 **Hago las compras**
2 **Voy de vacaciones**
3 **Limpio las ventanas**
4 **Desayuno**
5 **Voy a la iglesia**

Exercise 5

1 **Quisiera comprar un periódico.**
2 **Quisiéramos visitar el museo.**
3 **Quisiéramos dos habitaciones individuales.**
4 **Quisiera un libro nuevo.**
5 **Quisiera ir a Uruguay.**

Exercise 6

(a) **Por/en la mañana**
(b) **En la madrugada**
(c) **Por/en la noche**

(d) **En/por la tarde**
(e) **En/por la noche**

Exercise 7

(Answers may vary according to individual choice)

POR LA MAÑANA	POR LA TARDE	POR LA NOCHE
despertarse: 7.00 a.m.	**trabajar**: 2.00 p.m.	**cenar**: 9.00 p.m.
desayunar: 7.45	**jugar al tenis**: 4.00 p.m.	**mirar la tele**: 22.00
vestirse: 8.15	**conversar/platicar**: 5.30 p.m.	**acostarse**: 23.45

Exercise 8

1 **lejos**
2 **allá**
3 **barato**

4 **rápido**
5 **subir**

Exercise 9

1 V
2 F
3 F

4 V
5 F

Chapter 6

Exercise 1

1 **empieza**
2 **recuerdo**
3 **cerramos**

4 **mueren**
5 **recuerda**

Exercise 2

1 F
2 F
3 F

4 F
5 V

Exercise 3

1 **La chica más inteligente en el/del grupo.**
2 **Es la peor película del festival.**
3 **Los modelos más funcionales están acá/aquí.**
4 **Me gustaría el producto más barato.**
5 **Es el problema más difícil.**

Exercise 4

1 **puedo**	4	**puede**
2 **Podemos**	5	**puedo**
3 **Puede**		

Chapter 7

Exercise 1

1 Está estudiando.
2 Están escribiendo.
3 Estoy trabajando en la oficina.
4 Estamos arreglando el jardín.
5 Están practicando el baile.

Exercise 2

1 The telephone company apologizes for the inconvenience.
2 They are installing new telephone lines.

Exercise 3

1 We are interviewing candidates for two positions.
2 The group is making inroads into the international market.
3 The economic recovery is beginning.
4 I am looking for an alternative to this product.
5 Genaro is working on a new project.

Exercise 4

1 **Sus**	4	**Mi**
2 **Su**	5	**Su**
3 **Su**		

Exercise 5

A: **haciendo**
M: **preparando**
A: **haciendo**
M: **escribiendo**

Exercise 6

1 **Estoy**   4 **está**
2 **está**   5 **está**
3 **están**

Exercise 7

1 **Maribel**
2 **Asunción y Genaro**
3 **Usted . . . tú**
4 **Yo**
5 **La radio**

Chapter 8

Exercise 1

(Answers may vary according to individual choice)

1 **En el trabajo tengo que abrir la correspondencia.**
2 **En el trabajo tengo que enviar faxes.**
3 **En el trabajo tengo que escribir cartas.**
4 **En el trabajo tengo que supervisar la producción.**
5 **En el trabajo tengo que trabajar hasta tarde.**
6 **En el trabajo tengo que presentar informes.**
7 **En el trabajo tengo que llamar por teléfono.**
8 **En el trabajo tengo que tratar con el público.**
9 **En el trabajo tengo que utilizar la computadora.**

1 **En casa tengo que preparar la comida.**
2 **En casa tengo que limpiar.**
3 **En casa tengo que pasar la aspiradora.**
4 **En casa tengo que planchar.**
5 **En casa tengo que ayudar a los niños con sus tareas.**
6 **En casa tengo que contestar el teléfono.**

7 **En casa tengo que atender el jardín.**
8 **En casa tengo que hacer reparaciones.**

Exercise 2

1 **en contra**
2 **en favor**
3 **en contra**

Exercise 3

(Answers may vary according to individual choice)

Primero tiene que preparar un informe, después tiene que visitar la fábrica. Entonces tiene que ver muestras y probar el producto. Más tarde tiene que discutir precios. Por último tiene que estudiar el contrato.

Exercise 5

1 (b)		3 (c)	
2 (d)		4 (a)	

Exercise 6

1 (e)		5 (c)	
2 (d)		6 (f)	
3 (b)		7 (a)	
4 (g)			

Exercise 8

1 **Quiero ir contigo.**
2 **La Sra Rosas vive en una casita/casa chica con ellas.**
3 **Ven conmigo.**
4 **Quieren una reunión contigo.**
5 **Siempre llega con ellos.**

Chapter 9

Exercise 1

1 **He terminado mi trabajo.**
2 **He estado escribiendo esta carta desde hace 2 horas.**

3 Elena y yo hemos escrito una carta al periódico.
4 Roger está en Cali desde hace una semana.
5 Carlos Fuentes ha publicado un libro nuevo/otro libro.
6 Has/ha vivido en Paraguay desde hace mucho tiempo.
7 El banco ha abierto una sucursal nueva.
8 No hemos visto a Lorena desde esta mañana.
9 Han llegado.
10 ¿No has/ha terminado?

Exercise 3

1 para   4 por
2 Por   5 por
3 para

Chapter 10

Exercise 1

1 (c)   4 (f)
2 (b)   5 (d)
3 (e)   6 (a)

Exercise 2

El martes voy a asistir a la reunión y también voy a comer en un restaurante
    céntrico.
El miércoles voy a estudiar el reglamento y también voy a escribir cartas.
El jueves voy a probar el equipo nuevo y también voy a entrevistar al posi-
    ble jefe de ventas.
El viernes voy a recoger la nueva impresora láser y también voy a compar
    'compact discs'.
El sábado voy a descansar.
El domingo también voy a descansar.

Exercise 4

1 Sí es posible.
2 No es posible.
3 No es posible.
4 Sí es posible.
5 Sí es posible.

Exercise 5

1 V
2 F
3 F
4 V
5 F

Exercise 6

1 (c)
2 (d)
3 (a)
4 (b)
5 (e)

Exercise 7

Clásico

Chapter 11

Exercise 1

1 **Se abre temprano.**
2 **Se fabrican carros aquí.**
3 **Se arreglan computadoras.**
4 **Se prepara un informe cada día.**
5 **Se dice que está muy enfermo.**

Exercise 2

Hotel	Nº de noches	desayuno	piscina	pasaje	asistencia médica
Amsterdam	7	sí	sí	sí	sí
Central	5	sí	no	sí	sí
Apartamento	7	no	no	sí	sí

Exercise 4

1 **Graciela no vive tan cerca como Carlos.**
2 **Carolina es tan alta como José.**
3 **La rosa es tan linda como el clavel.**
4 **Mi televisor no es tan grande como el (televisor) de mi novia.**
5 **Esta impresora no es tan rápida como la otra (impresora).**

Exercise 5

1 (c)
2 (b)
3 (a)

4 (d)
5 (e)

Exercise 6

1 **más de**
2 **más de**
3 **menos de**

4 **menos de**
5 **más de**

Exercise 7

1 F
2 F
3 V
4 V
5 F

6 V
7 F
8 V
9 V
10 F

Exercise 8

1 F
2 F
3 V

4 V
5 F

Chapter 12

Exercise 1

(Other answers are possible depending on what you 'chose to do'.)

Compré la revista Quehacer y después visité la exposición de pintura en la galería Forum. Luego llamé por teléfono a una amiga y más tarde bailamos en la discoteca.

Exercise 2

1 (e)
2 (a)
3 (c)

4 (d)
5 (b)

Exercise 3

1 fui	6 llegó
2 Vimos	7 Aprendí
3 visitaron	8 estuvimos
4 Compré	9 Vimos
5 Visitaste	10 Escribió

Exercise 4

En la primera semana estudió el sistema operativo. Escribió texto y fórmulas. Imprimió la hoja de trabajo, diseñó pantallas y alimentó datos. En la segunda semana analizó economía empresarial y preparó estrategias financieras. Entonces, aplicó estadísticas y probabilidades. Por fin, desarrolló métodos de valuación de proyectos.

Exercise 5

1 Anoche escuchó un programa de radio.
2 El año pasado Marcelo y Estela diseñaron ropa para una firma extranjera.
3 El sábado pasado Carlos imitó a Elvis Presley en la tele.
4 Ayer salió la revista 'Decoración'.
5 Ayer fue criticado el servicio médico.
6 El sábado pasado ganó las carreras.
7 Ayer y anteayer entrenó Pochita.
8 Anoche Leonardo comió en casa.
9 El viernes pasado el jefe organizó una reunión de ejecutivos.
10 Hace dos horas (que) volvió Steven.

Chapter 13

Exercise 1

1 Comeremos juntos.
2 Marcelo preparará la comida mañana.
3 Esteban y yo escribiremos el informe.
4 Esperaremos hasta que llegue la nueva computadora.
5 Abrirán a las 9.30 en vez de las 10.00.
6 Vendrás mañana temprano, ¿no?
7 Se llevarán todo.

8 Elena empezará a trabajar el lunes.
9 La reunión será en mi despacho.
10 Dejaré a mi hija en la escuela.

Exercise 2

1 Ann y yo iremos a la agencia de viajes el martes próximo/que viene.
2 Viajaré a Guatemala y Nicaragua el año que viene/próximo.
3 Discutiremos precios en nuestra próxima reunión.
4 La compañía crecerá en los próximos años.
5 Se anunciarán nuevos precios para el gas la semana que viene.

Exercise 3

1 La semana que viene saldremos de paseo al campo.
2 El lunes que viene firmaremos el contrato.
3 El semestre que viene será decisivo para la empresa.
4 El mes que viene terminamos el proyecto.
5 La entrevista que viene será con el Director.

Exercise 4

El lunes irá/va a ir a la feria de informática. Comprará/va a comprar un nuevo equipo.
El martes visitará/va a visitar la tienda de repuestos.
El miércoles enviará/va a enviar fax a las sucursales. Informará/va a informar sobre cambios en el horario.
El jueves terminará/va a terminar el informe anual.
El viernes empezará/va a empezar las negociaciones con el nuevo socio.

Exercise 5

1 V   4 F
2 V   5 V
3 F

Exercise 6

1 vendrán   6 celebrará
2 empezará   7 aparecerá
3 regresaremos   8 presentará
4 pondrá   9 hablará
5 establecerán   10 veremos

Exercise 7

1 (c)	4 (a)
2 (e)	5 (b)
3 (d)	

Exercise 8

1 F	4 F
2 V	5 V
3 V	

Chapter 14

Exercise 1

1 trabajaba	6 fueron ... volvieron
2 iba	7 compró
3 llegó	8 tenía
4 costaba	9 tenía
5 llamé	10 volvió

Exercise 2

1 Iris was working/worked/used to work in a travel agency.
2 We used to study in the evening.
3 We were watching television when Rosana arrived.
4 Every Sunday he used to come and visit his grandparents.
5 The computers were available to the students.

Exercise 3

1 ¿Qué estabas haciendo cuando sonó el teléfono?
2 El avión estaba aterrizando cuando oímos la explosión.
3 Viajaba mucho.
4 La comida era barata en esos días.
5 La oficina estaba en la segunda planta.

Exercise 4

1 **Se llamaba Colegio San Antonio.**
2 **Estaba en Avenida de la Montaña 2759.**
3 **Tenía un laboratorio de idiomas.**
4 **Hacían viajes estudiantiles a Brasil, EE. UU, Canadá, Inglaterra, España y Japón.**
5 **Aconsejaban a los alumnos con orientación personal.**
6 **Practicaban atletismo, tenis y natación.**
7 **Sí, era grande.**
8 **Ofrecía también bachillerato internacional.**
9 **Había 4 canchas.**
10 **Sí, había pista de atletismo.**

Exercise 5

1 Nobody has anything.
2 He/she never buys any presents.
3 Estela does not eat meat or eggs.
4 Nobody learns a language in one day.
5 The museum is very near.

Chapter 15

Exercise 1

1 I do not believe he will finish everything.
2 How interesting that he is including this in his book.
3 It is probable that he is going out tonight.
4 I want you to go to the doctor.
5 I am asking you to continue in your job.
6 It does not seem to them that it offers possibilities.
7 It annoys us that she does not arrive early.
8 It is important that we eat vegetables and fruit.
9 We doubt that she will write from Ecuador.
10 I am sorry that you cannot come to the meeting.

Exercise 2

1 **Es necesario que comas menos.**
2 **Es interesante que responda en español.**

3 **Busco algo que ayude a todos.**
4 **(Te) aconsejamos que lo hagas.**
5 **Piden que contestes pronto.**

Exercise 3

1	vendrá	6	esté
2	venga	7	encuentre
3	prepare	8	sea
4	trajo	9	escuchará . . . hable
5	compre	10	empezarán

Exercise 4

1 **Quiero que tenga capacidad para cinco pasajeros.**
2 **Quiero que sea económico con el combustible.**
3 **Quiero que sea de tamaño mediano.**
4 **Quiero que incluya cierre electrónico de puertas.**
5 **Quiero que cuente con motor de 1300 o 1400 centímetros cúbicos.**
6 **Quiero que venga con caja de cambios de cinco velocidades.**
7 **Quiero que sea de un precio razonable.**
8 **Quiero que funcione con gasolina sin plomo.**
9 **Quiero que ofrezca fiabilidad.**
10 **Quiero que esté entre los líderes del mercado.**

Exercise 5

1	(b)	6	(g)
2	(e)	7	(a)
3	(j)	8	(f)
4	(c)	9	(h)
5	(i)	10	(d)

Exercise 6

1	tengas	6	devuelvas
2	sea	7	llegará
3	tiene	8	traigan
4	dice	9	ayuden
5	prepare	10	será

Chapter 16

Exercise 2

1 (f)	6 (d)
2 (g)	7 (a)
3 (i)	8 (c)
4 (h)	9 (e)
5 (j)	10 (b)

Exercise 3

1 **No vengan a la fiesta.**
2 **No llames a tu novia.**
3 **No compres cigarillos.**
4 **No abras la ventana.**
5 **No copien el documento en diskette.**
6 **No pidas diez cuadernos.**
7 **No vengas con tu novio.**
8 **No tomes fotos.**
9 **No prepare el plato que le recomendé.**
10 **No instales la antena.**

Exercise 4

1 **Bajen al primer piso.**
2 **Sean más eficientes.**
3 **Toma esto.**
4 **Revisen este contrato.**
5 **Regresa pronto.**
6 **Come más proteínas.**
7 **Envíe el paquete por vía aérea.**
8 **Vaya el próximo domingo.**
9 **Haz lo que dice esta señorita.**
10 **Vendan la máquina.**

Chapter 17

Exercise 2

1 If I could I would travel more.
2 If Marcelo was better organized, he would have better results.
3 Since you are coming by car, you will arrive before Alberto.
4 If you are writing a check, spell the name correctly.
5 If they gave me the opportunity, I would work in Uruguay.
6 I would visit the capital if I had more time, but I will only be here for two days.
7 I would bring it on floppy disk, if it was compatible.
8 If the figures indicated the opposite, we would have to carry out an investigation.
9 If the novel was shorter, I would have more success.
10 If you know the answer, why don't you say it?

Exercise 3

1 **Si hay un problema te envío un fax.**
2 **No creo que Helen vaya al trabajo/a trabajar mañana.**
3 **Si tuviese la oportunidad, ¿volvería/regresaría?**
4 **Como tiene/tienes sólo uno, llévese/llévate estos otros dos.**
5 **Si llama, le damos los detalles.**

Exercise 4

1 (b), (c)   4 (e)
2 (c), (b)   5 (d)
3 (a)

Exercise 5

1 **Si tuviéramos/tuviésemos más personal podríamos obtener mejores resultados.**
2 **Necesitamos pedir ayuda a una consultoría.**
3 **Nuestra empresa se ampliaría a mercados extranjeros si tuviéramos/tuviésemos una mejor política de exportación.**
4 **Su enfoque no es muy profesional.**
5 **Creo/Pienso que no es muy buena idea.**

Exercise 6

1 V		6 V
2 F		7 F
3 F		8 F
4 V		9 F
5 F		10 V

Chapter 18

Exercise 1

1 Si hubiera tenido tiempo habría terminado la pintura.
2 Si hubiéramos tenido las entradas habríamos ido al teatro.
3 Si hubieras tenido suficiente dinero habrías comprado el regalo.
4 Si hubieran tenido una invitación habrían venido a la fiesta.
5 Si hubiera tenido los datos necesarios habría preparado el informe.

Exercise 2

1 (b)		6 (a)
2 (i)		7 (e)
3 (j)		8 (h)
4 (d)		9 (g)
5 (c)		10 (f)

Exercise 3

1 Aunque no tenía licencia de conducir, manejó el auto.
2 Aunque tenía tarjetas de crédito, pagó al contado.
3 Aunque el supermercado está cerca, compro en una tiendecita.
4 Aunque no se afeita, le regaló una loción para después de afeitarse.
5 Aunque recibió su carta, no contestó.
6 Aunque llegaba de madrugada, organizó una reunión para la mañana siguiente.
7 Aunque la computadora es nueva, no es compatible con las demás de la oficina.
8 Aunque es latinoamericano, no le gusta la comida picante.
9 Aunque es el archivo más grande del país, no tiene sistema computarizado.
10 Aunque estuvo a dieta todo el año pasado, no bajó de peso.

Exercise 4

1 Hay demasiados estudiantes en esta sala/aula/habitación.
2 Todo es demasiado caliente.
3 La temperatura es demasiado fría para esta época del año.
4 Está demasiado alto. No puede alcanzar.
5 Puse demasiadas monedas en la máquina. No funciona.

Exercise 5

1 Even though he did not have any money, he ordered expensive food.
2 We finished, even though the conditions were negative.
3 In spite of his complaints, he is not receiving help.
4 He visits his grandchildren very often, in spite of being very old.
5 In spite of the opportunities that he had, he never triumphed/succeeded.
6 In spite of having a great cast, this film is not good.
7 In spite of problems with his health, he carries on playing football.
8 He does not go out, even though the doctor advised it.
9 In spite of the rain, they walked all afternoon.
10 In spite of having a very high salary, he always asks for loans.

Exercise 6

1 He will not answer the questions, even if he is tortured.
2 She will wait for her son, even if he arrives very late.
3 We will go, even if it rains all night.
4 We would tell you, even if it is very late.
5 In my case, I would have rung you, even if it had been Sunday.

Chapter 19

Exercise 1

1 La nueva autopista fue construida.
2 La multa fue aplicada por la municipalidad.
3 El presupuesto fue aprobado por el gobierno.
4 Los precios fueron rebajados por la tienda.
5 La obra fue terminada.
6 La obra habría sido publicada por la casa editorial.
7 Todos serían llevados a la comisaría.
8 Todos habrán sido interrogados por el juez.

9 Hemos sido engañados.
10 El libro sería leído por un gran número de personas.

Exercise 2

1 Se ha decidido que representarás a la empresa en la feria.
2 Se dice que los competidores están desmoralizados.
3 Se explica en el folleto.
4 Al final se aceptó.
5 Se ha repetido por tercera vez.
6 Se sabe que el producto afecta la piel.
7 Se manda/envía por correo.
8 Se ofrece a los socios de la organización.
9 Se dan por adelantado.
10 Se devolverán el próximo día/al día siguiente.

Exercise 3

1 It is thought that there will not be an increase in salaries.
2 It is known that they will not arrive until tomorrow.
3 I believe that the idea is understood now.
4 The session has finished.
5 First, the product is placed inside the machine.
6 It was agreed upon during the last meeting.
7 Procedures for paying export taxes could/would be simplified.
8 The loan will not be invested in public services.
9 A new system of classification will be introduced.
10 The new prices of industrial gas will be published next week.

Exercise 4

1 La exposición sobre comercio exterior fue inaugurada por la Directora.
2 Una nueva revista será publicada por los comerciantes del centro.
3 La máquina será reemplazada por el distribuidor.
4 Más de cien kilómetros de la carretera al norte serán reconstruidos por el Ministerio de Transportes.
5 Una nueva gama de productos será introducida por la Compañía de Teléfonos.
6 La nueva tarjeta de identificación ha sido distribuida por el Ministerio del Interior.
7 El delincuente fue detenido por la policía.
8 El donativo fue entregado por las empresas extranjeras.

9 Una computadora fue donada por el dueño de la tienda.
10 El entrenador fue llevado en hombros por los hinchas.

Exercise 5

1 The book was destined to be a success.
2 The book was destined for the external market.
3 Julián was punished for not finishing his homework.
4 Julián was punished by his mother.
5 This material is processed on a very modern machine.
6 The food was already processed.
7 The soldiers were instructed every morning.
8 The flowers were cut carefully by the women working there.
9 The flowers were cut.
10 The capital was attacked by foreign troops.

Exercise 6

1 No quiero queso, sino quiero jamón.
2 No tiene una casa ahora, pero quizás tenga una el año próximo.
3 No tienen (un) gato, sino (un) perro.
4 No queremos un boleto de ida, sino uno de ida y vuelta.
5 Ha ido a México, pero no sé cuando vuelve.

Exercise 7

1 F	4 F
2 V	5 V
3 F	

Chapter 20

Exercise 1

1 Anoche vi un programa de televisión.
2 El año pasado Marcelo y Estela diseñaron interiores para una firma conocida.
3 El sábado pasado Cecilia imitó a varios peronajes en la tele.
4 Ayer se transmitió la telenovela 'Adoración'.
5 Ayer criticaron al servicio de limpieza.
6 El sábado pasado perdió las carreras.

7 **Ayer y anteayer jugó Pochita.**
8 **Anoche Leonardo no comió en casa.**
9 **El viernes pasado el líder sindical organizó una reunión de traba-**
   jadores.
10 **Hace dos horas (que) viajó Steven.**

Exercise 2

1	(d)	6	(i)
2	(h)	7	(j)
3	(b)	8	(g)
4	(f)	9	(e)
5	(c)	10	(a)

Exercise 3

1	(c)	4	(a)
2	(e)	5	(b)
3	(d)		

Exercise 4

1 **Ojalá no hubieras/hubieses traído ese libro.**
2 **Ojalá Sharon haya traído el mismo.**
3 **Yo que tú, mandaría el dinero/la plata mañana.**
4 **Yo que Sharon, iría allá esta noche.**
5 **Ojalá tuviera/tuviese tiempo para visitar todos los museos y exposiciones**
   en esta ciudad.

Exercise 5

1	**venga**	6	**no funciona**
2	**viva**	7	**coman**
3	**gustaría . . . quedarse**	8	**llegue**
4	**coma**	9	**viene**
5	**tiene**	10	**viaje**

Exercise 6

1	**estuviera . . . estaría**	6	**ser**
2	**estaremos**	7	**fuese**
3	**haya traído**	8	**comiera**

4 trajo

5 estuviese

9 saldrá. . . . salga

10 pudiera

Exercise 7

1 (c)	6 (i)
2 (d)	7 (g)
3 (a)	8 (h)
4 (j)	9 (b)
5 (e)	10 (f)

Exercise 8

1 –	6 a
2 de	7 para . . . de
3 en/por	8 abajo de/debajo de
4 de . . . de	9 durante
5 desde . . . hasta	10 en

Exercise 9

FRUTA	VIAJES	COLORES
manzana	bicicleta	verde
frutilla	ciclomotor	azul
plátano	barco	negro
piña	vuelo	amarillo
sandía	carro	rojo

Exercise 10

1 (e)	4 (d)
2 (b)	5 (c)
3 (a)	

Exercise 11

1 F	4 V
2 F	5 F
3 V	

Exercise 12

1 está
2 Soy
3 está
4 están
5 son

6 está
7 está
8 está
9 somos
10 está

Exercise 13

1 No vayan a la reunión.
2 No llames por teléfono a tu jefe.
3 No trates de vender tu carro.
4 No abra el archivo para ver.
5 No copien el documento en diskette.
6 No pida diez cuadernos.
7 No vengas con tu novio.
8 No tome fotos.
9 No prepare el plato que le recomendé.
10 No instales la antena.

Exercise 14

1 Compren una nueva máquina.
2 Oiga lo que dice este señor.
3 Venga el próximo sábado.
4 Mande el paquete por correo.
5 Escribe pronto.
6 Come menos grasas.
7 Estudien este contrato.
8 Haz esto.
9 Sea más paciente.
10 Sube al tercer piso.

Exercise 15

1 F
2 F
3 V

4 F
5 V

CRUCIGRAMA

Spanish–English glossary

Abbreviations

(adj.)	adjective
(Ar.)	Argentina
(aux.)	auxiliary
(Bo.)	Bolivia
(Ch.)	Chile
(Col.)	Colombia
(conj.)	conjunction
(Ec.)	Ecuador
(f.)	feminine noun
(for.)	formal
(inf.)	informal
(m.)	masculine noun
(Méx.)	Mexico
(Pe.)	Peru
(pl.)	plural
(prep.)	preposition
(pron.)	pronoun
(sing.)	singular
(Sp.)	equivalent in Spain
(Uru.)	Uruguay

a	to; at
a continuación	now follows
a fin de	in order to
a menos que	unless
a partir de	from, as from
a pesar de	despite
a pie	on foot
a tiempo completo	full-time
a tiempo parcial	part-time
a veces	sometimes
a vuelta de correo	by return of post
abajo de (Sp. **debajo de**)	under
abierto	open
abrasivo	abrasive
abrigo (m.)	coat
abril (m.)	April
abrir	to open
abuela (f.)	grandmother
abuelo (m.)	grandfather
abuelos (m. pl.)	grandparents
acá (Sp. **aquí**)	here
acabar	to finish
académico	academic
acceso (m.)	access
aceite (m.)	oil
aceituna (f.)	olive
aceleradamente	fast
aceptable	acceptable
aceptar	to accept
acerca de	about
acercarse	to get near
acero (m.)	steel
acompañar	to go with
aconsejar	to advise
acordar	to agree
acordarse	to remember
acostarse	to go to bed
actividad (f.)	activity
acto (m.)	act; ceremony; event

actor (m.)	actor	**ahí**	there
actriz (f.)	actress	**ahora**	now
actual	present, current	**ahorita**	straight away
actualidad (f.)	current affairs	(Sp. **enseguida**)	
actualizado	updated	**ahorros** (m. pl.)	savings
actualizar	to update	**aire** (m.)	air
actualmente	at present	**aire**	air conditioning
acuerdo (m.)	agreement	**acondicionado**	
acusado (m.)	accused, defendant	(m.)	
adelgazar	to slim	**ajustar**	to adjust
además	besides	**al aire libre**	in the open air
adentro	inside	**al contrario**	on the contrary
(Sp. **dentro**)		**al día**	up to date
adiós (for.)	goodbye	**al final**	in the end
(Sp. for.		**al lado de**	next to
and inf.)		**alberca** (m.)	swimming pool
adjuntar	to enclose	**alcalde** (m.)	mayor
adolescente	teenager	**alcanzar**	to reach
(m., f.)		**alegre**	cheerful, glad
adonde, adónde	where (to)	**alfabeto** (m.)	alphabet, literate
adorno (m.)	ornament	**algo**	something
aeróbicos	aerobics	**algodón** (m.)	cotton
(m. pl.)		**alguien**	somebody
aeropuerto (m.)	airport	**alguno**	some; someone
afectar	to affect	**alimentación** (f.)	feeding
afeitarse	to shave	**alimentar**	to feed
África (f.)	Africa	**alimento** (m.)	food
afueras (f. pl.)	outskirts	**aliviar**	to relieve
agarrar	to take	**almorzar**	to have lunch
(Sp. **coger**)		**aló** (Sp. **dígame**)	hello (answering
agencia de	travel agent		the phone)
viajes (f.)		**alta resolución**	high resolution
agenda (f.)	diary	(f.)	
agosto (m.)	August	**alternativa** (f.)	alternative
agradable	pleasant	**alto**	tall, high
agradecer	to thank	**altura** (f.)	height
agregar	to add	**alumno** (m.)	pupil
(Sp. **añadir**)		**allá**	there
agua (f.)	water	**allí**	there
aguacate (m.)	avocado	**amar**	to love
aguaitar (Sp.	to watch	**amarillo**	yellow
acechar, mirar)		**amarrar** (Sp. **atar**)	to tie, to tie up

ambiente (m.)	atmosphere	**apagar**	to blow out; to
ambos	both		turn off
amenazar	to threaten	**apartado de**	PO box
América (f.)	the Americas	**correos** (m.)	
América Central	Central America	**aparte**	apart
(f.)		**aparte de**	apart from
América Latina	Latin America	**apellido** (m.)	surname
(f.)		**aplicar**	to apply
americano	Latin American;	**aportar**	to afford
	American	**apoyar**	to support
amigo (m.)	friend	**apoyo** (m.)	support
ampliar	to extend	**aprender**	to learn
amplio	ample, large	**aprendizaje** (m.)	learning
analfabeto (m.)	illiterate	**aprobar**	to approve
analizar	to analyze	**apropiado**	appropriate,
andar	to walk		suitable
ándele, ándale	come on!	**apuntes** (m. pl.)	notes
(Méx.)		**apurado** (m. pl.)	rushed
(Sp. **venga**)		(Sp. **apresurado**)	
angosto	narrow	**apurarse** (Sp.	to hurry up
(Sp. **estrecho**)		**darse prisa**)	
animal (m.)	animal	**aquel, aquellos**	that, those
animal doméstico	pet	**aquél, aquéllos**	that one, those
(m.)			ones
anoche	last night	**aquella, aquellas**	that, those
anteayer	the day before	**aquélla, aquéllas**	that one, those
	yesterday		ones
antena (f.)	aerial	**aquí**	here
anteojos (m.)	glasses,	**árbol** (m.)	tree
(Sp. **gafas**)	spectacles	**archivo** (m.)	archive(s)
antepasado (m.)	ancestor	**aretes** (m. pl.)	earrings
anterior	previous	(Sp. **pendientes**)	
antes	before	**Argentina** (f.)	Argentina
anticuado	old-fashioned	**argentino**	Argentinian
antiguo	old	**aroma** (f.)	smell
antojitos (m. pl.)	snacks	**arquitecto** (m.)	architect
(Sp. **tapas**)		**arquitectura** (f.)	architecture
anual	yearly	**arrancar**	to start up
anunciar	to announce	**arreglar**	to tidy up
anuncio (m.)	advertisement	**arroz** (m.)	rice
año (m.)	year	**arte** (m.)	art
Año Nuevo (m.)	New Year	**artesanía** (f.)	handicraft

artículo (m.) article
artículos de toiletries
  tocador (m. pl.)
artículos para household goods
  el hogar (m. pl.)
artificial artificial, man-made
asado roasted
ascensor (m.) lift
así even if; so, thus
asiento (m.) seat
asistencia medical
  médica (f.) assistance
asistir to be present, to
  attend
aspiradora (f.) vacuum cleaner
astronomía (f.) astronomy
asunto (m.) matter
atacar to attack
ataque (m.) attack
ataúd (m.) coffin
atender to attend to
atentamente sincerely
  (end of letter)
atento attentive
aterrizar to land
atletismo (m.) athletics
atracción (f.) attraction
atractivo attractive
atraer to attract
atrás de behind
  (Sp. **detrás de**)
auditorio (m.) auditorium
aula (f.) classroom
aumentar to increase
aumento (m.) increase
aunque although
ausencia (f.) absence
Australia (f.) Australia
australiano australian
auténtico authentic
auto, automóvil car, motorcar
  (m.)

autopista (f.) motorway
autor (m.) author
autoridad (f.) authority
autorizar to authorize
aventura (f.) adventure
averiguar to find out
avión (m.) aeroplane
avisar to warn, to advise
ayer yesterday
aymara (m.) indigenous
  language
  spoken in Peru
  and Bolivia
ayuda (f.) assistance, help
ayudante (m., f.) assistant, helper
ayudar to help
azafata (f.) air hostess
azafate (m.) tray
  (Sp. **bandeja**)
azúcar (f.) sugar
  (Sp. m.)
azul blue
azul marino navy blue
bachillerato baccalaureate,
  internacional school-leaving
  (m.) examination
bailar to dance
bailarina (f.) ballerina
baile (m.) dance
bajar to go down
bajar de peso to lose weight
bajo short (height)
balcón (m.) balcony
banco (m.) bank
bandera (f.) flag
banqueta (f.) pavement
  (Méx.)
  (Sp. **acera**)
baño (m.) bath; bathroom;
  (Sp. **servicio**, toilet
  aseo = toilet)
bar (m.) bar

barato	cheap	**bolsa** (f.)	bag
barba (f.)	beard	**bolsa de dormir**	sleeping bag
barco (m.)	ship	(f.) (Sp. **saco**	
barrio (m.)	neighborhood;	**de dormi**r)	
	residential area	**bombero** (m.)	firefighter
base (f.)	base	**bonito**	nice
base de datos (f.)	database	**botar** (Sp. **tirar**)	to throw away
básico	basic	**botella** (f.)	bottle
bastante	fairly	**Brasil** (m.)	Brazil
batería (f.)	battery (for a	**brasileño**	Brazilian
	car)	**brazo** (m.)	arm
beber	to drink	**brillo** (m.)	brightness
bebida (f.)	drink	**brindar**	to drink a toast
bebida gaseosa	soft drink		to
(f.)		**británico**	British
beneficio (m.)	benefit	**broqueta** (f.)	brochette
berenjena (f.)	aubergine	**bucear**	to dive
biblioteca (f.)	library	**buceo** (m.)	diving
bicicleta (f.)	bicycle	**budín** (m.)	bread pudding
bien	well	**buen**	good
bienvenida (f.)	welcome	**buenas**	short for **buenos**
bienvenido	(to be)		**días**
	welcome	**buenas noches**	good evening;
bigote (m.)	moustache		good night
bilingüe	bilingual	**buenas tardes**	good afternoon
billete (m.)	banknote	**bueno**	good
billetera (f.)	wallet	**buenos días**	good morning
bizcochuelo (m.)	cake	**buscar**	to look for
blanco	white	**buzón** (m.)	postbox
blanco y negro	black and white	**caballero** (m.)	gentleman
blando	soft	**caballeros** (m. pl.)	gentlemen (sign
blusa (f.)	blouse		on toilets)
bocaditos	snacks	**cabeza** (f.)	head
(m. pl.)		**cacao** (m.)	cacao
boletería (f.)	ticket office	**cada**	each; every
(Sp. **taquilla**)		**café** (m.)	coffee
boleto (m.)	ticket	**cafetería** (f.)	café
(Sp. **billete**)		**caja** (f.)	box
boleto de avión	air ticket	**caja de cambios**	gear box
(m.)		(f.)	
Bolivia (f.)	Bolivia	**caja fuerte** (f.)	safe
boliviano	Bolivian	**cajero** (m.)	cashier

calato naked
(Sp. **desnudo**)
calavera (f.) skull
calefacción (f.) heating
calefacción central heating
central (f.)
calentar to warm up
calidad (f.) quality
cálido hot (climate)
caliente hot
calor (m.) heat
caloría (f.) calorie
calzado (m.) footwear
calzón (m.) knickers
calzoncillo (m.) men's under-
pants
calle (f.) street
calle principal (f.) main street
cama (f.) bed
cámara (f.) camera
cambiar to change, to
exchange
cambio (m.) change; exchange
caminar to walk
camino (m.) way, road
camión (m.) lorry
camión (m.) bus
(Méx.)
(Sp. **autobús**)
camioneta (f.) light van; station
wagon
camisa (f.) shirt
camiseta (f.) vest, T-shirt
campamentismo camping
(m.)
campeón (m.) champion
campeonato (m.) championship
campesino (m.) peasant
camping (m.) campsite
campo (m.) field
campo de sports field
deportes (m.)

canadiense Canadian
cáncer (m.) cancer
cancha (f.) sports court *or*
field
canción (f.) song
canillita (Sp. news-vendor
vendedor de
periódicos)
cansado tired
cantante (m., f.) singer
cantar to sing
cantidad (f.) quantity
cantina (f.) bar
(Sp. **taberna**)
caña de azúcar sugar cane
(f.)
caoba (f.) mahogany
capacidad (f.) capacity
capital (m., f.) capital (m. = sum
of money)
(f. = city)
capitalista capitalist
capítulo (m.) chapter
cara (f.) face
característica (f.) characteristic
carapulcra (f.) Peruvian dish
made with
dried potatoes
cargo (m.) position (job)
cariño (m.) affection
carne (f.) meat
carnicería (f.) butcher's
caro expensive
carpeta (f.) desk
(Sp. **pupitre**)
carrera (f.) career; run; race;
avenue (Col.)
carretera (f.) road
carro (Sp. **coche**) car
carta (f.) letter
cartelera (f.) list of cinemas
and theaters

cartera (f.)	purse, handbag, wallet
cartero (m.)	postman, mailman
cartón (m.)	cardboard
casa (f.)	house, home
casa editorial (f.)	publishing house
casado	married
casarse	to get married
casi	almost
casona (f.)	large old house
cassette (m.)	cassette
castellano (Sp. **español**)	Spanish (language)
castigado	punished
castigar	to punish
castigo (m.)	punishment
catedral (f.)	cathedral
categoría (f.)	category
católico	catholic
causar	to cause
cebiche (m.)	dish made with raw fish marinated in lemon
celebración (f.)	celebration
celebrar	to celebrate
cena (f.)	evening meal, supper
cenar	to have an evening meal, to have supper
centígrado (m.)	centigrade
céntrico	central
centro (m.)	center
Centroamérica (f.)	Central America
centro comercial (m.)	shopping center
cerca	near
cercano	nearby
cerdo (m.)	pig
cerebro (m.)	brain
cerrado	closed
cerrar	to close
cerveza (f.)	beer
ciclomotor (m.)	moped
cielo (m.)	sky, heaven
ciencia (f.)	science
cierre (m.)	locking device
cierto	certain
cifra (f.)	figure
cigarrillo (m.)	cigarette
cine, cinema (m.)	cinema
cine de estreno (m.)	cinema which shows new films
cinta (f.)	tape, ribbon
círculo (m.)	circle
cita (f.)	date
ciudad (f.)	city
ciudadano (m.)	citizen
clase (f.)	lesson, class
clasificación (f.)	classification
clausurar	to bring to a close
clavel (m.)	carnation
cliente (m.)	client, customer
clima (m.)	climate
climatizado	air-conditioned
clínica (f.)	private hospital
club (m.)	club
cobrar	to charge (money)
cobre (m.)	copper
cocina (f.)	kitchen
coctel (m.)	cocktail
coche-bomba (m.)	car bomb
coger	to take (in Ar., Méx., Uru. it has sexual connotations)
colegio (m.)	school
colgar	to hang up (phone)
colocar	to place
colocarse	to place oneself

Colombia (f.)	Colombia	**comprobar**	to check
colombiano (m.)	Colombian	**compromiso** (m.)	commitment
colonia (f.)	residential	**computador** (m.),	computer
(Ch., Méx.)	suburb	**computadora**	
(Sp. **barrio,**		(f.) (Sp.	
urbanización)		**ordenador**)	
colonia proletaria	shanty town	**comunicación**	communication
(f.) (Méx.)		(f.)	
(Sp. **chabolas**)		**comunista**	communist
color (m.)	color	**con**	with
combinación (f.)	combination	**con tal que**	provided that
combustible (m.)	fuel	**concejo** (m.)	council
comedor (m.)	dining room	**concierto** (m.)	concert
comenzar	to start, to begin	**concurrido**	well attended,
comer	to eat		busy
comercial	commercial	**concursante**	contestant
comerciante	trader,	(m., f.)	
(m., f.)	shopkeeper	**concurso** (m.)	contest,
comercio (m.)	commerce		competition
cómico	comic(al)	**condición** (f.)	condition
comida (f.)	meal	**conducir**	to drive
comisaría (f.)	police station	**conferencia** (f.)	conference
comisión (f.)	committee,	**confianza** (f.)	confidence
	commission	**confirmación** (f.)	confirmation
cómo	how	**confirmar**	to confirm
cómodo	comfortable	**confundir**	to confuse
como siempre	as always	**congreso** (m.)	congress,
compañero (m.)	classmate,		conference
	workmate	**conmigo**	with me
compañía (f.)	company	**conocer**	to know
comparación (f.)	comparison	**conseguir**	to obtain
compatible	compatible	**consejo** (m.)	advice
competencia (f.)	competititon	**conservación** (f.)	conservation
competidor (m.)	competitor	**conservar**	to preserve
competitivo	competitive	**construcción** (f.)	construction
completo	complete,	**construir**	to build
	comprehensive	**cónsul** (m., f.)	consul
complicado	complicated	**consulado** (m.)	consulate
compra (f.);	purchase;	**consultar**	to consult
compras (f. pl.)	shopping	**consultor** (m.)	consultant
comprar	to buy	**consultoría** (f.)	consultancy
comprender	to understand	**consumidor** (m.)	consumer

consumir	to consume	**creer**	to believe
consumo (m.)	consumption	**criollo** (m.)	creole
contabilidad (f.)	accountancy	**criticar**	to criticize
contacto (m.)	contact	**cruzar**	to cross
contador (m.)	accountant	**cuaderno** (m.)	exercise book,
(Sp. **contable**)			notebook
contaminación	contamination,	**cuadra** (f.)	block (of houses)
(f.)	pollution	(Sp. **manzana**)	
contaminante	polluting	**cuadrado**	square
contar	to count; to tell	**cuadro** (m.)	frame, painting,
contar con	to have		chart
contento	contented, happy	**cuadro**	statistics chart
contestar	to answer	**estadístico** (m.)	
contigo	with you	**cuál**	which
continuar	to continue	**cualquiera**	any, anyone,
contra	against		whichever
contrario	opposite	**cuándo, cuando**	when
contrato (m.)	contract	**cuánto, cuánta**	how much
convencer	to convince	**cuántos, cuántas**	how many
convenio (m.)	agreement	**cuarto** (m.)	fourth; bedroom
corazón (m.)	heart	**Cuba** (f.)	Cuba
corbata (f.)	tie	**cubano** (m.)	Cuban
corregir	to correct	**cubiertos** (m. pl.)	cutlery
correo (m.)	post office	**cuchara** (f.)	spoon
correr	to run	**cucharada** (f.)	spoonful
correspondencia	correspondence;	**cucharita** (f.)	teaspoon
(f.)	post	**cuenta** (f.)	check
corresponsal	correspondent	**cuenta corriente**	current account
(m., f.)		(f.)	
corte (f.)	cut; court	**cuento**	short story
corto	short	**cuero** (m.)	leather
cosa (f.)	thing	**cuidado** (m.)	care; be careful!
costa(f.)	coast	**cuidadosamente**	carefully
Costa Rica (f.)	Costa Rica	**cuidar**	to look after
costar	to cost	**cultivar**	to cultivate
costarricense,	Costa Rican	**cultivo** (m.)	cultivation
costariqueño		**cultural**	cultural
costo (m.)	cost	**cumpleaños** (m.)	birthday
(Sp. **coste**)		**cuota mensual**	monthly
costumbre (f.)	custom	(f.)	payment
crecer	to grow	**cupón** (m.)	coupon, voucher
crédito (m.)	credit	**curso** (m.)	course

champiñón (m.) mushroom
chancho (m.) pig, pork
  (Sp. **cerdo**)
chao, chau (inf.) bye
chaqueta (f.) jacket
charla (f.) talk
che (Ar., Uru.) hey!
  (Sp. **oiga, oye**)
cheque (m.) check
  (Sp. **talón**)
cheque de traveler's check
  viaje/viajero
  (m.)
chica (f.) girl
chicano (m.) Mexican working
  in the USA
chico (m.); (adj.) boy; small
  (Sp. **pequeño**)
Chile (m.) Chile
chileno Chilean
chipa (f.) Paraguayan dish
  made with corn
chiste (m.) joke
chistoso funny
chocolate (m.) chocolate
chompa (f.) (Pe.) jumper; sweater;
  (Sp. **jersey**) cardigan
dama (f.) lady
damas (f. pl.) ladies (sign on
  toilets)
danza (f.) dance
dañino harmful
dar to give
datos (m. pl.) information, data
de of; from; than
  de acuerdo agreed!, I agree!
  de lo contrario otherwise
  de nada you're welcome
Debajo debajo underneath
deber (m.) duty
deberes (m. pl.) homework
débil weak

década (f.) decade
decidir to decide
décimo (m.) tenth
decir to say
decisión (f.) decision
decisivo decisive
declarar to declare
decorar to decorate
dedicarse to devote oneself
  to
defecto (m.) defect
defender to defend
dejar to leave
delante de in front of
deletrear to spell
delgado thin
delicado delicate
delicioso delicious
delincuente delinquent,
  (m., f.) criminal
demasiado too much/many;
  too
democracia (f.) democracy
democrático democratic
demorar to take (time)
  (Sp. **tardar**)
denunciar to denounce
dentro de inside
depender to depend
deporte (m.) sport
deportivo sporty
derecha right
derecho (m.) law; right
derechos human rights
  humanos
  (m. pl.)
derroche (m.) waste (of money)
desacuerdo (m.) disagreement
desaparecer to disappear
desarrollar to develop
desastre (m.) disaster
desayunar to have breakfast

desayuno (m.)	breakfast	**dietético**	healthy (food)
descansar	to rest	**diferencia** (f.)	difference
descanso (m.)	rest	**diferente**	different
descartable	disposable	**difícil**	difficult
descolgar	to take the phone off the hook	**dificultad** (f.)	difficulty
		dinero (m.)	money
descuento (m.)	discount	**diputado** (m.)	deputy (in Parliament)
desde	from; since	**dirección** (f.)	address; direction
desear	to want, to wish		
desempleo (m.) (Sp. **paro**)	unemployment	**dirigido**	planned, directed
		disco (m.)	record (music)
desgraciada- mente	unfortunately	**disco compacto** (m.)	compact disc
desilusión (f.)	disappointment	**disco duro** (m.)	hard disk
desilusionado	disappointed	**discoteca** (f.)	discoteque
desmoralizado	demoralized	**disculpar**	to excuse
despacio	slowly	**disculparse**	to apologize
despacho (m.)	office	**discurso** (m.)	speech
despedida (f.)	farewell	**discusión** (f.)	discussion
despedirse	to say goodbye	**discutir**	to discuss
despertador (m.)	alarm clock	**diseño** (m.)	design
despertarse	to wake up	**diskette** (m.)	diskette, data disk
después	afterwards		
destinar	to destine, to assign	**dislocar**	to dislocate
		disminuir	to reduce, to go down
destruir	to destroy		
desventaja (f.)	disadvantage	**disponible**	available
desvestir (Sp. **desnudar**)	to undress	**distinción** (f.)	distinction
		distinguido	distinguished
detalle (m.)	detail	**distinto**	different
detrás de	behind	**distribuidor** (m.)	distributor
devolver	to give back	**Distrito Federal** (m.)	Federal District (Méx.)
día (m.)	day		
diálogo (m.)	dialogue	**diurno**	daytime (adj.)
diario, diariamente	daily	**diversión** (f.)	entertainment
		diverso	diverse
dibujos animados (m. pl.)	cartoons	**divertido**	entertaining, funny
diccionario (m.)	dictionary	**divertirse**	to have a good time
diciembre (m.)	December		
dictadura (f.)	dictatorship	**divisa** (f.)	foreign currency

divorciado	divorced	**efectivizar**	to implement
divorcio (m.)	divorce	**efectivo** (m.)	cash
doblar	to turn	**ejecutivo** (m.)	executive
doble	double	**ejército** (m.)	army
docena (f.)	dozen	**el; él**	the (m. sing.); he
doctor (m.)	doctor	**el otro día**	the other day
documental (m.)	documentary	**El Salvador**	El Salvador
documento (m.)	document	(m.)	
dólar (m.)	dollar	**elaborar**	to make
doler	to hurt	**elección** (f.)	election
dolor (m.)	pain	**electo**	elected
domicilio (m.)	address	(Sp. **elegido**)	
domingo (m.)	Sunday	**electricidad** (f.)	electricity
dominicano	Dominican	**eléctrico**	electric
donativo (m.)	donation	**electrónico**	electronic
dónde; donde	where	**elegante**	elegant
dormido	asleep	**elegido**	elected
dormir	to sleep	**elegir**	to elect
dormitorio (m.)	bedroom	**ella**	she
dudar	to doubt	**ellas**	they (f.)
dueño (m.)	owner	**ellos**	they (m.)
dulce (m.; adj.)	sweet	**embajada** (f.)	embassy
duplicado (m.)	duplicate	**embajador** (m.)	ambassador
durable	durable	**embarcar**	to board
duración (f.)	duration	**embarque** (m.)	boarding
durante	during	**emigrar**	to emigrate
durar	to last	**empanada** (f.)	pasty
duro	hard	**empatar**	to draw
e	and (only before	**empezar**	to start
	words begin-	**empleado** (m.)	employee
	ning with **i**-)	**empresa** (f.)	firm, company
ecológico	ecological, 'green'	**empresario** (m.)	businessman
economía (f.)	economy	**empujar**	to push
económico	economical	**en**	in, on, at
ecuador (m.)	equator	**enamorado** (m.);	boyfriend;
Ecuador (m.)	Ecuador	**enamorada** (f.)	girlfriend
ecuatoriano	Ecuadorean	**encantado**	pleased to meet
edad (f.)	age		you
edición (f.)	edition	**encargado** (m.)	person in charge
edificio (m.)	building	**en cartelera**	on at the theater
educación (f.)	education		or at the
educativo	educational		cinema

encender	to light, to turn on	**error** (m.)	mistake, error
encima	over	**esa, esas**	that, those (f.)
encontrar	to find	**ésa, ésas**	that one, those ones (f.)
encuesta (f.)	survey		
enero (m.)	January	**escalera** (f.)	stairs, ladder
enfermera (f.)	nurse	**escaso**	scarce
enfermo	ill	**escocés**	Scottish
enfrente de	opposite	**Escocia** (f.)	Scotland
engañar	to deceive	**escoger**	to choose
engaño (m.)	deception	**esconder**	to hide
en peligro	endangered	**escribir**	to write
ensalada (f.)	salad	**escrito**	written
enseguida	straight away	**escritor** (m.)	writer
enseñar	to show; to teach	**escritorio** (m.)	desk
entender	to understand	**escritura**	hieroglyphic
entonces	then	**jeroglífica** (f.)	writing
entorno (m.)	environment	**escuchar**	to listen
entrada (f.)	admission ticket; entrance	**escuela** (f.)	school (primary)
		ese, esos	that, those (m.)
entrar	to enter	**ése, ésos**	that one, those ones (m.)
entre	between, among		
entrega (f.)	delivery	**espacio** (m.)	space
entregado	handed over	**espalda** (f.)	back (part of the body)
entregar	to give, to deliver		
		España (f.)	Spain
entrenador (m.)	coach, manager (of a sports team)	**español** (m.)	Spanish (person and language)
		especial	special
entrenar	to train	**especializada**	specialized
entretener	to entertain	**especie** (f.)	species
entrevista (f.)	interview	**especificaciones** (f. pl.)	specification
entrevistar	to interview		
envase	packet, container	**espectador** (m.)	spectator
en vez de	instead of	**esperar**	to wait
enviar	to send	**espinaca** (f.)	spinach
época de lluvias (f.)	rainy season	**esposo** (m.); **esposa** (f.)	husband; wife
época del año (f.)	time of the year	**esquí** (m.)	ski
equipaje (m.)	luggage	**esquina** (f.)	corner
equipo (m.)	team	**esta, estas**	this, these (f.)
equivalente	equivalent	**ésta, éstas**	this one, these ones (f.)
equivocarse	to be mistaken		

establecer	to establish
estación (f.)	station, season
estacionamiento (m.)	car parking
estacionar	to park
estadía (f.) (Sp. estancia)	stay
estadio (m.)	stadium
estadística (f.)	statistics
estado (m.)	state
estado civil (m.)	marital status
Estados Unidos (m. pl.)	United States
estadounidense	from the United States
estampilla (f.) (Sp. sello)	stamp (postage)
estante (m.)	shelf
estantería (f.)	shelving
estar	to be
estatura (f.)	height (of a person)
estatuto (m.)	statute
este	east
este, estos	this, these (m.)
éste, éstos	this one, these ones (m.)
estéreo	stereo
estilo (m.)	style
estimado	dear (in a letter)
estómago (m.)	stomach
estrategia (f.)	strategy
estratégica	strategic
estudiante (m., f.)	student
estudiar	to study
estudios (m. pl.)	studies
etiqueta (f.)	label
Europa (f.)	Europe
europeo (m.)	European
evento (m.)	event
evitar	to avoid
exacto	exact

examen (m.)	exam
examinar	to examine
excelente	excellent
exceso (m.)	excess
exclusivo	exclusive
excursión (f.)	excursion
exigir	to demand
éxito (m.)	success
expansión (f.)	expansion
expectativa (f.) (Sp. expectación)	expectation
expediente (m.)	dossier, process
experiencia (f.)	experience
experimentar	to experiment, to experience
explicación (f.)	explanation
explicar	to explain
explosión (f.)	explosion
explotar	to exploit
exportación (f.)	export
exportador (m.)	exporter
exportar	to export
exposición (f.)	exhibition
expresar	to express
exprimir	to extract
extranjero (m.)	foreign, foreigner; abroad
extrañar (Sp. echar de menos)	to miss (to feel the absence of)
fábrica (f.)	factory
fabricar	to manufacture
fácil	easy
facsímil (m.)	facsimile
factura (f.)	invoice
falda (f.)	skirt
falso	false
falta (f.)	lack
faltar	to lack
falla (f.) (Sp. fallo)	failure, fault

familia (f.)	family
familiares (m. pl.)	relatives
famoso	famous
farmacia (f.)	chemist's
fauna (f.)	fauna
favor (m.)	favor
febrero (m.)	February
fecha (f.)	date
felicitaciones	congratulations
(f. pl.) (Sp.	
enhorabuena)	
felicitar	to congratulate
feliz	happy
femenino	feminine; women's
feria (f.)	fair
festival (m.)	festival
fiabilidad (f.)	reliability
fibra (f.)	fiber
fibra de vidrio (f.)	glass fiber
fiebre (f.)	fever
fiesta (f.)	party, festival
fin (m.)	end
fin de semana	weekend
(m.)	
final (m.)	end
finalmente	finally, lastly
financiero	financial
fino	fine (quality)
firma (f.)	signature
firmar	to sign
flexible	flexible
flor (f.)	flower
folklórico (m.)	folk
folleto (m.)	leaflet
fondo (m.)	bottom
formar	to form
fórmula (f.)	formula
formulario (m.)	form
Forum	well-known art gallery in Lima
fósforo (m.)	match
(Sp. **cerilla**)	

foto(grafía) (f.)	photo(graph)
fracasar	to fail
fracaso (m.)	failure
francés	French
Francia (f.)	France
frazada (f.)	blanket
(Sp. **manta**)	
frecuente	frequent
freir	to fry
frío	cold
frito	fried
frontera (f.)	border, frontier
fruta (f.)	fruit
frutal	fruity
frutería (f.)	fruit shop
frutilla (f.)	strawberry
(Sp. **fresa**)	
fuente (f.)	source
fuente de divisas	source of foreign
(f.)	exchange
fuerte	strong
fumador (m.)	smoker
fumar	to smoke
función (f.)	show (in a cinema, theater)
funcional	functional
funcionar	to work
funcionario (m.)	official
fútbol (m.)	football
futuro (m.)	future
galería (f.)	gallery
Gales (m.)	Wales
galés	Welsh
gama (f.)	range
ganador (m.)	winner
ganar	to win
garaje (m.)	garage
garantía (f.)	guarantee
garantizar	to guarantee
garbanzo (m.)	chickpea
garganta (f.)	throat
garrafa (f.)	carafe

gas (m.)	gas (fuel)	**habla castellana** (f.)	Spanish speaking
gasolina (f.)	gas	**hablar**	to speak
gasolina sin plomo (f.)	lead-free gas	**hace**	ago
gastar	to spend (money)	**hacer; hace (frío/ viento**/etc.)	to do, to make; it's (cold/ windy/etc.)
gasto (m.)	expense	**hacia**	towards
gato (m.)	cat	**hallar**	to find
general (m.)	general	**hambre** (f.);	hunger; to be
generalmente	generally	**tener hambre**	hungry
gente (f.)	people	**hasta**	until
geografía (f.)	geography	**hasta luego**	see you later
gimnasio (m.)	gymnasium	**hay**	there is/are
gimnasio cubierto (m.)	indoor gymnasium	**hecho** (m.)	fact
gobierno (m.)	government	**helado** (m.)	ice cream
gordo	fat	**helicóptero** (m.)	helicopter
grabar	to record on tape	**hermano** (m.); **hermana** (f.)	brother; sister
gracias	thanks, thank you	**hervir**	to boil
grado (m.)	degree	**hielo** (m.)	ice
gráfico (m.)	graphic	**hijo** (m.), **hija** (f.)	son; daughter
grande	big, large	**hijos** (m. pl.)	children
grasa (f.)	fat	**hincha** (m.)	football fan
gratis	free	**historia** (f.)	history
gripe (f.)	influenza, cold	**historial** (m.)	record, history
grueso	thick	**hoja** (f.)	sheet
grupal	in groups	**hoja de cálculo** (f.)	spreadsheet
grupo (m.)	group		
guacamole (m.)	typical Mexican sauce or dip	**hoja de ruta** (f.)	route plan
		hola	hello
guaraní (m.)	language spoken in Paraguay	**hombre** (m.)	man
		hombro (m.)	shoulder
guardar	to keep	**Honduras** (f.)	Honduras
Guatemala (f.)	Guatemala	**hondureño**	Honduran
guatemalteco	Guatemalan	**hora** (f.)	hour
guerra (f.)	war	**horario** (m.)	opening hours
guía turística (f.)	tourist guide	**hornalla, hornilla** (f.)	burner (in a cooker)
gustar	to like		
haber	to have (aux.)	**hospital** (m.)	hospital
habitación (f.)	room	**hospitalidad** (f.)	hospitality
habitante (m.)	inhabitant	**hotel** (m.)	hotel

hoy	today	**indicar**	to indicate
huevo (m.)	egg	**índice de**	literacy rate
humano	human	**alfabetismo**	
húmedo	wet, damp	**indígena** (m., f.)	indigenous
ida (f.)	single (trip,		person
	journey)	**individual**	individual
ida y vuelta (f.)	return (trip,	**industria** (f.)	industry
	journey)	**industrial**	industrial
ideal	ideal	**infancia** (f.)	infancy
identificación (f.)	identification	**infantil**	children's
idioma (m.)	language	**inferior**	inferior
iglesia (f.)	church	**inflación** (f.)	inflation
igual	equal, the same	**información** (f.)	information
igualdad (f.)	equality	**informar**	to inform
ilegal	ilegal	**informática** (f.)	computing
iluminado	illuminated, lit	**informativo** (m.)	news
imagen (f.)	picture (TV)		program
impedir	to prevent	**informe** (m.)	report
imperfecto	imperfect	**ingeniero** (m.)	engineer
importación (f.)	import	**Inglaterra** (f.)	England
importador (m.)	importer	**inglés**	English
importante	important	**ingreso** (m.)	income
importar	to import	**iniciar**	to begin
imposible	impossible	**iniciativa** (f.)	initiative
imprenta (f.)	printing works	**inmediato**	immediate
impresora (f.)	printer	**inmenso**	huge
impresora	dot matrix	**inmigración** (f.)	immigration
matricial (f.)	printer	**inmigrante** (m., f.)	immigrant
imprimir	to print	**inmigrar**	immigrate
impuesto (m.)	tax	**inocente**	innocent
inauguración (f.)	opening,	**insistir**	to insist
	inauguration	**inspirar**	to inspire
inaugurar	to inaugurate	**instalar**	to install
incendio (m.)	fire	**instruir**	to instruct
incentivo (m.)	incentive	**instrumento** (m.)	instrument
incienso (m.)	incense	**inteligente**	intelligent
incluido	included	**intentar**	to attempt
incómodo	uncomfortable	**interés** (m.)	interest
inconveniente	inconvenient	**interesado**	interested
increible	incredible	**interesante**	interesting
incremento (m.)	increase	**internacional**	international
incursionar	to make inroads	**interno**	internal

interpretar	to sing; to interpret
intérprete (m., f.)	singer; interpreter
interrogar	to interrogate
interrumpir	to interrupt
interrupción (f.)	interruption
inversión (f.)	investment
invertir	to invest
investigación (f.)	investigation, research
invierno (m.)	winter
invitación (f.)	invitation
invitado (m.)	guest
ir	to go
ir de compras	to go shopping
Irlanda (f.)	Ireland
irlandés	Irish
isla (f.)	island
itinerario (m.)	itinerary
izquierda (f.)	left
jabón (m.)	soap
Jamaica (f.)	Jamaica
jamaiquino	Jamaican
jamás	never
jamón (m.)	ham
Japón (m.)	Japan
japonés	Japanese
jardín (m.)	garden
jefe (m.)	boss, head
jefe de ventas (m.)	head of sales
jenjibre (m.)	ginger
joven	young
juego (m.)	game
jueves (m.)	Thursday
juez (m.)	judge
jugar	to play (a game or sport)
jugo (m.)	juice
juguete (m.)	toy
julio (m.)	July
junio (m.)	June
junto a	next to
juntos	together
justo	fair, just
juventud (f.)	youth
kilo (m.)	kilo
kilómetro (m.)	kilometer
la, las	the (f. sing., f. pl.)
laboratorio de idiomas (m.)	language laboratory
lado (m.)	side
lago (m.)	lake
lágrima (f.)	tear
lamentablemente	regrettably
lamentar	to regret
lana (f.)	wool
langostino (m.)	prawn
lapicero (m.), **lapicera** (f.)	ball-point pen
lápiz labial (m.)	lipstick
largo	long
láser (f.)	laser
lástima (f.)	pity
lateral	lateral
Latinoamérica (f.)	Latin America
latinoamericano	Latin American
lavadora (f.)	washing machine
lavar	to wash
lavar en seco (Sp. **limpiar en seco**)	to dry clean
le ruego	would you please
lección (f.)	lesson
lectura (f.)	reading
leche (f.)	milk
lechuga (f.)	lettuce
leer	to read
legal	legal
legalizar	to legalize
lejos	far
lengua (f.)	tongue

lenguado (m.)	sole	**listo**	ready
lentes (m. pl.)	glasses, spectacles	**literatura** (f.)	literature
		liviano	light
lentes de contacto (m. pl.) (Sp. **lentillas**)	contact lenses	**lo**	it
		local (m.)	premises
		loción (f.)	lotion
lento	slow	**loco**	mad
letrero (m.)	sign	**lograr**	to achieve
levantacristales eléctrico (m.)	electric window winder (car)	**lomo** (m.)	beefsteak
		lona (f.)	canvas
levantar	to lift	**Londres** (m.)	London
levantarse	to get up	**longitud** (f.)	length
ley (f.)	law	**los**	the (m. pl.)
libertad (f.)	freedom	**lo siento**	I'm sorry
libertad de expresión (f.)	freedom of expresion	**luchar**	to fight
		luego	then, later
libertad de prensa (f.)	freedom of the press	**lugar** (m.)	place
		luna (f.)	moon
libra (f.)	pound	**lunes** (m.)	Monday
libra esterlina (f.)	pound sterling	**luz** (f.)	light
		llamada (f.)	call
libre	free	**llamar**	to call
librería (f.)	bookshop	**llamarse**	to be called
libro (m.)	book	**llave** (f.)	key
licencia de conducir (f.)	driving licence	**llavero** (m.)	key-ring
		llegada (f.)	arrival
licuado energético (m.)	isotonic drink	**llegar**	to arrive
		llenar	to fill
líder (m.)	leader	**lleno**	full
líder sindical (m.)	union leader	**llevar a cabo**	to take place, to carry out
ligero	light		
limitar con	to have borders with	**llover**	to rain
		lluvia (f.)	rain
limón (m.)	lemon	**lluviosa** (**imagen**)	snowy (TV picture)
limpiar	to clean		
limpieza (f.)	cleanliness	**lluvioso**	rainy
lindo (Sp. **bonito**, **majo**)	pretty	**macerar**	to marinate
		machucar	to mash (food)
línea (f.)	line	**madera** (f.)	wood
línea aérea (f.)	airline	**madre** (f.)	mother
linterna (f.)	torch	**madrugada** (f.)	early hours of the morning
lista (f.)	list		

mal	badly
malecón (m.)	promenade
maleta (f.)	suitcase
maletín (m.)	briefcase
malo	bad; poor
malla entera de baño (f.)	one-piece swimsuit
mandar	to send
¿mande? (Sp. ¿cómo?)	pardon?
manejar	to drive
manera (f.)	manner, way
mano (f.)	hand
mantener	to maintain
manualidades (f. pl.)	handicraft
manzana (f.)	apple
mañana (f.); (m.)	morning; tomorrow
mapa (m.)	map
máquina (f.)	machine
maquinaria (f.)	machinery
máquina de escribir (m.)	typewriter
mar (m.)	sea
marca (f.)	brand, make
marido (m.)	husband
marisco (m.)	seafood
mármol (m.)	marble
marrón	brown
martes (m.)	Tuesday
marzo (m.)	March
más	more
más adelante	later
más adentro	further inside
más tarde	later
matar	to kill
mate (m.)	infusion drunk mainly in Argentina
materia prima (f.)	raw material
material (m.)	material
máximo	maximum
mayo (m.)	May
mayor	elder; more
mayoría (f.)	majority
mecánica (f.)	mechanics
mecánico (m.)	mechanic
mediano	medium
medianoche (f.)	midnight
medias (f. pl.)	socks, stockings
medicina (f.)	medicine
médico (m.)	doctor
medida (f.)	measurement, measure
medio	half a
medio ambiente (m.)	environment
mediodía (m.)	midday
medios de transporte (m. pl.)	means of transport
medir	to measure
mejor	better; best
mejorar	to improve
melón (m.)	melon
memoria (f.)	memory
menor	younger; less
menos	less
mensaje (m.)	message
mensual	monthly
mentira (f.)	lie
menú (m.)	menu
mercado (m.)	market
mercado de cambios (m.)	currency market
mercado paralelo (m.)	free rate currency market
mes (m.)	month
mesa (f.)	table
mestizo (m.)	person who has one Spanish and one

	indigenous		bother
metal (m.)	parent	**molestia** (f.)	trouble,
metro (m.)	metal		inconvenience
mexicano,	subway; meter	**molesto**	annoyed,
mejicano	Mexican		bothered
México, Méjico		**momento** (m.)	moment
(m.)	Mexico	**moneda** (f.)	coin; currency
mezcla (f.)		**monitor** (m.)	monitor
mi, mis	mixture	**montaña** (f.)	mountain
mí	my	**montañismo** (m.)	mountaineering
	me (pron. after	**montañoso**	mountainous
	prep.)	**montar**	to ride
miedo (m.)	fear	**monumento** (m.)	monument
mientras	while	**morir**	to die
miércoles (m.)	Wednesday	**mostrar**	to show
mil	thousand	**motocicleta** (f.)	motorbike
milanesa (f.)	escalope	**mucho**	much
militar	military	**muchos**	many
millón (m.)	million	**muebles** (m. pl.)	furniture
mineral (m.)	mineral	**muela** (f.)	tooth
minería (f.)	mining	**muerte** (f.)	death
mínimo	minimum	**muerto**	dead
ministerio (m.)	ministry	**muestra** (f.)	sample
ministro (m.)	minister	**mujer** (f.)	woman; wife
minusválido (m.)	handicapped	**mulato** (m.)	mulatto (person
	person		with one white
minuto (m.)	minute		and one black
mirar	to look		parent)
mirar tiendas	to go window	**multa** (f.)	fine
	shopping	**mundo** (m.)	world
misa (f.)	mass (religion)	**municipalidad** (f.)	city/local council
mismo	same	(Sp. **ayunta-**	
mitad (f.)	half	**miento**)	
mochila (f.)	rucksack	**muñeco** (m.)	doll
moda (f.)	fashion	**museo** (m.)	museum
modales (m. pl.)	manners	**música** (f.)	music
modelo (m.)	model	**musical**	musical
moderar	to moderate	**muy**	very
moderno	modern	**nacer**	to be born
modo (m.)	manner, way	**nacimiento** (m.)	birth
módulo (m.)	module, unit	**nación** (f.)	nation
molestar	to annoy, to	**nacional**	national

nacionalidad (f.)	nationality
nada	nothing
nadar	to swim
nadie	nobody
naranja (f.)	orange
natación (f.)	swimming
natatorio (m.) (Ch., Ar. **piscina**)	swimming pool
natural	natural
Navidad (f.)	Christmas
necesario	necessary
necesidad (f.)	need, necessity
necesitar	to need
negar	to deny
negativo (m.)	negative
negociación (f.)	negotiation
negociar	to negotiate
negocio (m.)	business
negro	black
nervioso	nervous
neutro (m.)	neutral
nevar	to snow
ni	nor
Nicaragua (f.)	Nicaragua
nicaragüense	Nicaraguan
niebla (f.)	fog
nieto (m.); **nieta** (f.)	grandson; granddaughter
ninguno	no one
niño (m.); **niña** (f.)	boy; girl
niños (m. pl.)	children
ni siquiera	not even
nivel (m.)	level
nivel de precios (m.)	price range
no	no, not
nocturno	nocturnal, in the evening
noche (f.)	night
no fumador (m.)	non-smoker
nogal (m.)	walnut tree
no hay de qué	you're welcome
no importa	it doesn't matter
no más (Sp. **nada más**)	no more
nombre (m.)	name
no precisa/no responde	don't know (in a survey)
norma de calidad (f.)	quality standards
normal	normal
normalmente	normally
norte (m.)	north
norteamericano	North American; American
nosotros	we
nos vemos	see you (inf.)
nota (f.)	note; grade, mark
notar	to notice
noticia (f.)	news item
noticiero, noticiario (m.)	news bulletin
novela (f.)	novel
noveno	ninth
noviembre (m.)	November
novio (m.); **novia** (f.)	fiancé; fiancée
nube (f.)	cloud
nublado	cloudy
nuestro/a, nuestro/as	our
Nueva York (f.)	New York
nuevamente	again
nuevo	new
número (m.)	number
nunca	never
nutrición (f.)	nutrition
o	or
objetivo (m.)	target
objeto (m.)	object
obligación (f.)	obligation

obligar	to force, to oblige	**oportunidad** (f.)	opportunity
obligatorio	obligatory, compulsory	**óptimo**	optimum
		oreja (f.)	ear
obra cómica (f.)	comedy	**organización** (f.)	organization
obra de teatro (f.)	play (theater)	**organizar**	to organize
obras públicas (f. pl.)	public works	**orientación** (f.)	guidance, counselling
obrero (m.)	manual worker	**oro** (m.)	gold
obtener	to obtain	**orquesta** (f.)	orchestra
Oceanía (f.)	Australasia	**otoño** (m.)	autumn
océano (m.)	ocean	**otra época** (f.)	bygone era
Océano Atlántico (m.)	Atlantic Ocean	**otro**	another, other
Océano Pacífico (m.)	Pacific Ocean	**paciente** (m., f.)	patient
		padre (m.); **padres** (m. pl.)	father; parents
octavo	eighth	**pagar**	to pay
octubre (m.)	October	**página** (f.)	page
ocupacíon (f.)	occupation	**pago** (m.)	payment
ocupado	busy	**páguese a**	payable to
ocupar	to occupy	**país** (m.)	country
ocurrir	to occur	**paisaje** (m.)	landscape
oeste (m.)	west	**palabra** (f.)	word
oferta (f.)	reduced merchandise	**palanca** (f.)	lever
		pan (m.)	bread
oficina (f.)	office	**panadería** (f.)	bread shop
ofrecer to	offer	**Panamá** (m.)	Panama
oído (m.)	hearing, inner ear	**panameño**	Panamanian
		panqueque (m.)	pancake
oír	to hear	**pantalón,** (m.) **pantalones** (m. pl.)	pants, (trousers)
ojalá	if only		
ojo (m.)	eye	**pantalla** (f.)	screen
ola (f.)	wave (in the sea)	**pañuelo** (m.)	handkerchief
olimpiadas estudiantiles (f. pl.)	school sports festival	**papa** (f.) (Sp. **patata**)	potato
		papel (m.)	paper
olvidar	to forget	**paquete** (m.)	parcel
omnibús (m.)	bus	**par** (m.)	pair
operación (f.)	operation	**para**	for; to; in order to
opinar	to give an opinion		
		para llevar	to take away
opinión (f.)	opinion	**parada** (f.)	stop (bus)

paradero (m.) (Col., Ec., Pe., Bo., Ch.)	stop (bus)
parado (Sp. **de pie**)	standing
Paraguay (m.)	Paraguay
paraguayo	Paraguayan
parar	to stop
pararse (Sp. **ponerse de pie**)	to stand up
parecer	to seem
parecerse	to resemble, to look alike
pared (f.)	wall
parientes (m. pl.)	relations
parque (m.)	park
parrillada (f.)	grilled meats
parte (f.)	part
participación (f.)	participation
participar	to take part
particular	private; particular
partido (m.)	match; party (political)
pasado	past; last
pasaje (f.)	fare
pasajero (m.)	passenger
pasaporte (m.)	passport
pasar	to pass
pasar la aspiradora	to vacuum
pasar las vacaciones	to spend your holiday
pasatiempo (m.)	pastime
pasear	to go for a walk
paseo (m.)	walk, stroll
pasillo (m.)	aisle, corridor
paso (m.)	step
paso a paso	step by step
pastel (m.)	pie, cake
pastelería (f.)	cake shop
pastilla (f.)	tablet
patio (m.)	yard, courtyard
patria (f.)	fatherland
paz (f.)	peace
pecho (m.)	breast, chest
pedido (m.)	order
pedir	to order (goods); to ask for
pelar	to peel
película (f.)	movie
película del oeste (f.)	western
peligro (m.)	danger
pelirrojo	red-haired
pelo (m.)	hair
peluquería (f.)	hairdresser's
pensar	to think
pensión (f.)	pension; boarding house
peor	worse
pequeño	little; small
pera (f.)	pear
perder	to lose
perderse	to get lost
¡perdón! (m.)	sorry!
perdonar	to forgive
perfecto	perfect
periódico (m.)	newspaper
periodista (m., f.)	journalist
período (m.)	period
permiso (m.)	permission
permitir	to allow
pero	but
perro (m.)	dog
perseguir	to pursue, to chase
persona (f.)	person
personaje (m.)	character (theater, novel, etc.)
personal (m.)	personnel, staff
personalidad (f.)	personality

Perú	Peru	**poco a poco**	little by little
peruano	Peruvian	**poder**	can
pesado	heavy	**poesía** (f.)	poetry
pesca (f.)	fishing	**poeta** (m.);	poet
pescado (m.)	fish	**poetisa** (f.)	
peso (m.)	weight	**policía** (f., m., f.)	police;
petróleo (m.)	oil; petroleum		policeman;
piano (m.)	piano		policewoman
picante	hot (spicy)	**policial**	police (adj.)
picar	to chop (food)	**política** (f.)	politics; policy
pie (m.)	foot	**polo** (m.) (Ch.,	T-shirt
piel (f.)	skin	Ar., Uru.	
pierna (f.)	leg	**polera**)	
pila (f.)	battery	**pollo** (m.)	chicken
pileta (f.)	swimming pool	**poner**	to put
pintar	to paint	**popular**	popular
pintor (m.)	painter	**por**	for; by; because
pintura (f.)	painting; paint		of
piña (f.)	pineapple	**por ahora**	for the time being
pionero (m.)	pioneer	**por ciento**	per cent
piscina (f.)	swimming pool	(Sp. **por cien**)	
pista (f.)	track	**porción** (f.)	portion, serving
plan (m.)	plan	**por correo**	by post
planchar	to iron	**por ejemplo**	for example
planta (f.)	plant; floor level	**por el momento**	for the time
	(in a building)		being
planta alta (f.)	upstairs	**por favor**	please
planta baja (f.)	downstairs	**por fin**	at last
plástico (m.)	plastic	**por otra parte**	on the other
plata (f.)	money		hand
(Sp. **dinero**)		**por qué**	why
plátano (m.)	banana	**por si acaso**	just in case
platicar	to talk	**por supuesto**	of course
plato (m.)	plate	**por todas partes**	everywhere
playa (f.)	beach	**por último**	lastly
plaza (f.)	square	**porque**	because
plegable	folding	**portugués**	Portuguese
población (f.)	population	**posibilidad** (f.)	possibility
poblado	populated	**posible**	possible
pobre	poor	**postal** (f.)	postcard
pobreza (f.)	poverty	**postergar**	to postpone
poco; pocos	little/few	(Sp. **aplazar**)	

postre (m.)	dessert	**prohibir**	to ban, to prohibit
potente	powerful		
practicar	to practise	**promedio**	average
precio (m.)	price	**promesa** (f.)	promise
preferir	to prefer	**prometer**	to promise
pregunta (f.)	question	**pronóstico del**	weather forecast
preguntar	to ask a question	**tiempo** (m.)	
premio (m.)	prize	**pronto**	soon
prensa (f.)	press	**pronunciación** (f.)	pronunciation
preocuparse	to worry	**pronunciado**	marked
preparar	to prepare	**pronunciar**	to pronounce
presentar	to present; to introduce	**propiedad** (f.)	property
		propietario (m.)	proprietor, owner
presidente (m.)	president		
presionar	to press	**propio**	own
preso (m.)	prisoner	**proponer**	to propose
préstamo (m.)	loan	**protestante**	protestant
prestar	to lend	**provincia** (f.)	province
presupuesto (m.)	budget	**próximo**	next
previo	prior, previous	**proyecto** (m.)	project
primaria (f.)	primary (education)	**publicación** (f.)	publication
		publicar	to publish
primavera (f.)	spring (season)	**publicidad** (f.)	advertising, publicity
primer/o	first		
principal	principal	**público** (m.)	public; audience
principio (m.)	beginning	**pueblo** (m.)	town, village; people (of a nation)
privado	private		
probabilidad (f.)	probability		
probable	probable	**puente** (m.)	bridge
probar	to try, to test	**puente aéreo** (m.)	shuttle service
problema (m.)	problem	**puerta** (f.)	door
procesamiento de texto (m.)	word processing	**puesto** (m.)	position (job); stall (market)
procesar	to process	**puesto de trabajo** (m.)	job
proceso (m.)	process		
procurar	to try	**puro**	pure
producción (f.)	production	**que**	that; than
producir	to produce	**qué**	what
producto (m.)	product	**¿qué pasa?**	what's happening, what's the matter?
profesor (m.)	teacher		
profundo	deep		
prohibición (f.)	ban, prohibition	**¡qué pena!**	what a pity!

que viene	next	**recoger**	to pick up
quechua (m.)	indigenous language spoken in the Andean countries	**recomendación** (f.)	recommendation
		recomendar	to recommend
		reconocer	to recognize
		reconstruir	to rebuild, to reconstruct
quedar	to stay; to be left		
queja (f.)	complaint	**recordar**	to remember
quejarse	to complain	**recorrer**	to go through, to travel
quemar	to burn		
quena (f.)	traditional Andean musical instrument	**recortar**	to cut back, to trim
		recreativo	leisure
		rector (m.)	vice-chancellor
querer	to want	**recuerdo** (m.)	souvenir
querido	dear (e.g. to start a letter)	**recuperación** (f.)	recovery
		recuperar	to recover
queso (m.)	cheese	**reducir**	to reduce
quien; quién	who	**reemplazar**	to replace
quinto	fifth	**refresco** (m.)	refreshing drink
quitar	to take away	**regalar**	to give (present), to give away
quizá, quizás	perhaps		
radio (m.)	radio	**regalo** (m.)	gift, present
ranura (f.)	slot	**región** (f.)	region
rápido	fast	**reglamento** (m.)	regulation
rato (m.)	while	**regresar**	to return
ratón (m.)	mouse	**regular**	regular; not too bad
rayo (m.)	lightning		
raza (f.)	race	**regular**	to adjust
razón (f.)	reason	**reir**	to laugh
razonable	reasonable	**religión** (f.)	religion
realidad (f.)	reality	**reloj** (m.)	watch; clock
realizar	to carry out	**reloj despertador** (m.)	alarm clock
rebajado	reduced		
rebajar	to reduce	**rellenar**	to fill in
recepción (f.)	reception	**remedio** (m.)	remedy
recepcionista (f.)	receptionist	**remuneración** (f.)	remuneration
recesión (f.)	recession	**renovar**	to renew
receta (f.)	receipt; prescription	**rentar**	to rent
		renunciar	to resign
recibir	to receive	**reparación** (f.)	repair
recibo (m.)	receipt	**reparar**	to repair

reparto (m.)	delivery	**romántico**	romantic
repetir	to repeat	**romper**	to break
representante (m.)	representative	**ron** (m.)	rum
		ropa (f.)	clothing
República Dominicana (f.)	Dominican Republic	**ropero** (m.)	wardrobe
		rosa (f.)	rose
		ruido (m.)	noise
repuesto (m.)	spare part	**rural**	rural
requisito (m.)	requirement	**ruta** (f.)	route
rescatar	to rescue	**sábado** (m.)	Saturday
reservación (f.)	reservation	**saber**	to know
reservar	reserve	**sabor** (m.)	flavor, taste
residente (m.)	resident	**sacar**	to take out
resolver	to solve	**sala** (f.)	living room; hall
respetar	to respect	**salario** (m.)	wage
respeto (m.)	respect	**salida** (f.)	departure
responder	to reply	**salir**	to leave; to go out
respuesta (f.)	reply		
restauración (f.)	restoration	**salsa** (f.)	sauce
restaurante (m.)	restaurant	**saltar**	to jump
restaurar	to restore	**salud** (f.)	health; cheers!
resto (m.)	rest, remainder	**saludable**	healthy
resultado (m.)	result	**saludar**	to greet
retrato (m.)	portrait	**saludo** (m.); **saludos**	greeting; regards (at the end of a letter)
reunión (f.)	meeting		
revelado (m.)	development (photographs)		
		salvado (m.)	bran
revelar	to reveal; to develop (a film)	**salvadoreño**	Salvadorian
		sandía (f.)	watermelon
		satisfecho	satisfied
revista (f.)	magazine	**se puede**	one can
revolución (f.)	revolution	**sección** (f.)	section
rezar	to pray	**seco**	dry
rico	tasty, delicious	**secretario** (m.), **secretaria** (f.)	secretary
río (m.)	river		
riqueza (f.)	wealth	**sector** (m.)	sector
rizado	curly	**sector informal** (m.)	the 'informal' sector (of the economy)
robar	to steal; to rob		
roble (m.)	oak		
robo (m.)	robbery, burglary	**secundaria** (f.)	secondary (education)
rojo	red	**sed** (f.)	thirst

seguido (Sp.	frequently	**sitio** (m.)	site, place
frecuentemente)		**situación** (f.)	situation,
seguir	to carry on		location
según	according to	**situar**	to locate
segundo	second	**sobre** (prep.);	on, over;
seguridad (f.)	safety	(m.)	envelope
seguro (m.)	insurance	**socialista**	socialist
selva (f.)	jungle	**sociedad** (f.)	society
semana (f.)	week	**socio** (m.)	member; partner
Semana Santa (f.)	Easter	**soldado** (m.)	soldier
semanal	weekly	**soledad** (f.)	loneliness
semestral	six-monthly	**solicitar**	to request, to
semestre (m.)	semester		apply for
senador (m.)	senator	**solidaridad** (f.)	solidarity
sentarse	to sit down	**sólido**	solid
sentimiento (m.)	feeling	**solo**	alone
sentir	to feel	**sólo**	only
señor	gentleman,	**solución** (f.)	solution
	mister	**somos**	we are
señora	lady, Mrs	**son**	you are (for. and
señorita	young lady, miss		inf.); they are
separado	separated	**sonido** (m.)	sound
ser	to be	**sonrisa** (f.)	smile
servicio (m.)	service	**soñar**	to dream
servir	to serve	**sorpresa** (f.)	surprise
sesión (f.)	session	**sorteo** (m.)	draw, raffle
setiembre,	September	**sortija** (f.)	ring
septiembre (m.)		**Sr**	Mr
sétimo, séptimo	seventh	**Sra**	Mrs
si	if	**Srta**	Miss
sí	yes	**su, sus**	your (for. sing.
siempre	always		and pl.); his; her
siglo (m.)	century	**suave**	soft
significar	to mean	**subcomisión**	subcommittee
silencio (m.)	silence	**subir**	to go up
silla (f.)	chair	**subsidio** (m.)	subsidy
simplificar	to simplify	**sucesor** (m.)	successor
sin	without	**sucio**	dirty
sindicato (m.)	trade union	**sucursal** (f.)	branch
sin duda	no doubt	**Sudamérica** (f.)	South America
sino	but	**sueldo** (m.)	salary
sistema (m.)	system	**suelto**	loose

suéter (m.)	sweater	**tener lugar**	to take place
suficiente	enough	**tener razón**	to be right
suma (f.)	amount, sum	**tener sed**	to be thirsty
supermercado (m.)	supermarket	**tener un aire de**	to have an air of
		tenis (m.)	tennis
supervisar	to supervise	**terminar**	to end, to finish
suponer	to suppose	**termo** (m.)	flask
sur	south	**terrible**	terrible
suyo	yours (for. sing. and pl.); his; hers;	**territorio** (m.)	territory
		terrorismo (m.)	terrorism
tabaco (m.)	tobacco	**texto** (m.)	text
talla (f.)	size (clothes)	**ti**	you (pron. after prep.)
tamaño (m.)	size		
también	also	**tía** (f.)	aunt
tampoco	neither	**tiempo** (m.)	time; weather
tan . . . como	as . . . as	**tienda** (f.)	shop
tapete (m.)	tapestry	**tierra** (m.)	earth; soil
tarde (f.)	afternoon; late	**timbre** (m.)	bell
tarea (f.)	homework	**timón** (m.) (Sp. **volante**) (Ch., Ar. **manurio**)	steering wheel
tarifa (f.)	tariff		
tarjeta (f.)	card		
tarta (f.)	pie		
taza (f.)	cup	**tinto** (m.)	red wine; black coffee (Col.)
té (m.)	tea		
teatro (m.)	theater	**tío** (m.)	uncle
teclado (m.)	keyboard	**tipo** (m.)	type
técnica (f.)	tecnique	**titular** (m.)	headline
técnico (m.)	technician	**tocar**	to play (a musical instrument)
tecnología (f.)	technology		
tela (f.)	fabric		
telefonear	to phone	**todavía**	still; yet
teléfono (m.)	telephone	**todo**	all; whole; every
telenovela (f.)	soap opera	**todo-terreno**	all-terrain
televisión (f.)	television	**todos**	all; everybody
Televisor (m.)	TV set	**tolerancia** (f.)	tolerance
tema (m.)	topic, theme, subject	**tomar**	to take; to eat; to drink
temperatura (f.)	temperature	**tomate** (m.)	tomato
templado	warm	**tonto** (m.)	silly, stupid
temprano	early	**tormenta** (f.)	storm
tener	to have	**torta** (f.) (Sp. **tarta**)	cake
tener hambre	to be hungry		

tortilla (f.)	omelette; maize pancake (Méx.)	**urgente**	urgent
		Uruguay (m.)	Uruguay
		uruguayo	Uruguayan
torturar	to torture	**usado**	used
trabajador (m.)	worker	**usar**	to use
trabajar	to work	**usted**	you (for.)
trabajo (m.)	work	**ustedes** (Sp. **vosotros** = inf.)	you (for. and inf.)
traducción (f.)	translation		
traer	to bring	**usuario** (m.)	user
trámites (m. pl.)	paperwork, red tape	**útil**	useful
		utilizar	to use
tranquilo	quiet	**vacaciones** (f. pl.)	holidays
transeunte (m.)	passer-by		
transmitir	to broadcast	**valer**	to be worth
transporte (m.)	transport	**válido**	valid
tranvía (m.)	tram	**valor** (m.)	value
trapo (m.)	cloth	**vamos**	let's go!
tratar con/sobre	deal with	**variada**	varied
tren (m.)	train	**varios** (pl.)	several
tribu (f.)	tribe	**vaso** (m.)	glass, tumbler
tribunal (m.)	court	**vecino** (m.)	neighbor
trimestral	quarterly	**vela** (f.)	candle
triste	sad	**velocidad** (f.)	speed
triunfar	to succeed	**vendedor** (m.)	seller; salesman
tropa (f.)	troop	**vendedor ambulante** (m.)	street seller
tropezar	to stumble		
tropical	tropical	**vender**	to sell
tu, tus	your (inf.)	**venezolano**	Venezuelan
tú	you (inf.)	**Venezuela** (f.)	Venezuela
turismo (m.)	tourism	**venir**	to come
turista (m., f.)	tourist	**venta** (f.)	sale
turno (m.)	turn	**ventaja** (f.)	advantage
u	or (only before words beginning with **o**-)	**ventana** (f.)	window
		ventanilla (f.)	window (at a bank)
ubicar (Sp. **localizar, situar**)	to locate		
		ver	to see; to watch
último	last; latest	**verano** (m.)	summer
un, uno, una	a; one	**verdad** (f.)	truth; right
único	unique; single	**verdadero**	true
unidad (f.)	unit	**verde**	green
universidad (f.)	university	**verdulería** (f.)	vegetable shop
		verdura (f.)	vegetable

vereda (f.)	pavement	**vivienda** (f.)	housing
(Sp. **acera**)		**vivir**	to live
vespertino	in the afternoon	**vocear**	to shout
vestido (m.)	dress; clothing	**vocero** (m.)	spokesperson
vestirse	to get dressed	**volar**	to fly
vez (f.)	time, occasion	**volver**	to return
viaje (m.)	trip	**voz** (f.)	voice
viajero (m.)	traveler	**vuelo** (m.)	flight
vida (f.)	life	**vuelta** (f.)	return
video (m.)	video	**y**	and
vidrio (m.)	glass	**ya**	already
viento (m.)	wind	**yo**	I
viernes (m.)	Friday	**zambo** (m.)	person with one
vino (m.)	wine		black and one
visa (f.)	visa		Indian parent
(Sp. **visado**)		**zapatilla** (f.)	sports shoe;
visita (f.)	visit		trainer
visitar	to visit	**zapato** (m.)	shoe
viuda (f.)	widow	**zona** (f.)	zone, area
viudo (m.)	widower		

English–Spanish glossary

a	**un, uno, una**	area	**zona** (f.)
able to, to be	**poder**	arm	**brazo** (m.)
abroad	**extranjero**	arrival	**llegada** (f.)
address	**dirección** (f.)	article	**artículo** (m.)
advise, to	**avisar**	artificial	**artificial**
airplane	**avión** (m.)	as	**como**
afternoon	**tarde** (f.)	at	**en**
afterwards	**después**	back (part of	**espalda** (f.)
against	**contra**	the body)	
age	**edad** (f.)	bad	**malo**
ago	**hace**	badly	**mal**
agreed, I agree	**de acuerdo**	ball-point pen	**lapicero** (m.);
aim	**fin** (m.)		**lapicera** (f.)
air	**aire** (m.)	bank	**banco** (m.)
air-conditioned	**climatizado**	banknote	**billete** (m.)
air ticket	**boleto de avión**	bar	**bar** (m.)
	(m.)	bath; bathroom	**baño** (m.)
all	**todo**	be, to	**ser; estar**
alone	**solo**	beach	**playa** (f.)
already	**ya**	beard	**barba** (f.)
also	**también**	because of	**por**
always	**siempre**	bed	**cama** (f.)
among	**entre**	beer	**cerveza** (f.)
ancestor	**antepasado** (m.)	begin, to	**comenzar**
and	**y**	behind	**atrás de**
animal	**animal** (m.)		(Sp. **detrás de**)
another	**otro**	better	**mejor**
answer, to	**contestar**	best	**el/la/lo mejor**
anyone	**cualquiera**	between	**entre**
apologize, to	**disculparse**	big	**grande**
apple	**manzana** (f.)	bill	**cuenta** (f.)

birthday	**cumpleaños** (m.)	chair	**silla** (f.)
blouse	**blusa** (f.)	change, to	**cambiar**
blow out, to	**apagar**	chapter	**capítulo** (m.)
blue	**azul**	cheap	**barato**
book	**libro** (m.)	cheers!	**salud**
bookshop	**librería** (f.)	cheese	**queso** (m.)
bottle	**botella** (f.)	chemist's	**farmacia** (f.)
box	**caja** (f.)	check	**cheque** (m.)
boy	**chico** (m.); **niño**		(Sp. **talón**)
	(m.)	chest	**pecho** (m.)
bread	**pan** (m.)	children	**hijos** (m. pl.);
breakfast	**desayuno** (m.)		**niños** (m. pl.)
breast	**pecho** (m.)	church	**iglesia** (f.)
bridge	**puente** (m.)	cinema	**cine, cinema**
bring, to	**traer**		(m.)
British	**británico**	city	**ciudad** (f.)
brother	**hermano** (m.)	classroom	**aula** (f.)
brown	**marrón**	clean, to	**limpiar**
building	**edificio** (m.)	climate	**clima** (m.)
burglary	**robo** (m.)	clock	**reloj** (m.)
bus	**omnibús** (m.),	close, to	**cerrar**
	camión (m.)	closed	**cerrado**
	(Méx.)	clothing	**vestido** (m.)
	(Sp. **autobús**)	coast	**costa** (f.)
businessman	**empresario** (m.)	coffee	**café** (m.)
but	**pero**	cold (illness)	**gripe** (f.)
buy, to	**comprar**	cold	**frío**
by	**por**	(temperature)	
café	**cafetería** (f.)	color	**color** (m.)
call, to	**llamar**	come, to	**venir**
car	**auto** (m.),	comfortable	**cómodo**
	automóvil (m.),	commerce	**comercio** (m.)
	carro (m.)	commercial	**comercial**
	(Sp. **coche**)	company	**compañía** (f.);
car parking	**estacionamiento**		**empresa** (f.)
	(m.)	computer	**computador**
cash	**efectivo** (m.)		(m.), **computa-**
cat	**gato** (m.)		**dora** (f.) (Sp.
cathedral	**catedral** (f.)		**ordenador**)
Central America	**Centroamérica**	condition	**condición** (f.)
	(f.)	confuse, to	**confundir**
center	**centro** (m.)	consulate	**consulado** (m.)

contact	**contacto** (m.)	drink (a)	**bebida** (f.)
contented	**contento**	drink, to	**beber; tomar**
continue, to	**continuar**	drive, to	**conducir;**
contract	**contrato** (m.)		**manejar**
cost	**costo** (m.)	each	**cada**
	(Sp. **coste**)	early	**temprano**
cost, to	**costar**	east	**este**
country	**país** (m.)	easy	**fácil**
court	**tribunal** (m.)	eat, to	**comer; tomar**
dance, to	**bailar**	electricity	**electricidad** (f.)
date	**fecha** (f.)	embassy	**embajada** (f.)
date	**cita** (f.)	end	**fin** (m.)
(appointment)		end, to	**terminar**
daughter	**hija** (f.)	England	**Inglaterra** (f.)
day	**día** (m.)	English	**inglés**
day before	**anteayer**	enough	**suficiente**
yesterday, the		enter, to	**entrar**
dear (in a letter)	**estimado**	error	**error** (m.)
December	**diciembre** (m.)	Europe	**Europa** (f.)
decision	**decisión** (f.)	European	**europeo** (m.)
declare, to	**declarar**	even if	**así**
deliver, to	**entregar**	every	**cada; todo**
departure	**salida** (f.)	exchange, to	**cambiar**
dessert	**postre** (m.)	exit	**salida** (f.)
dictionary	**diccionario** (m.)	expect, to	**esperar**
die, to	**morir**	expensive	**caro**
difference	**diferencia** (f.)	export, to	**exportar**
difficult	**difícil**	exporter	**exportador** (m.)
dining room	**comedor** (m.)	eye	**ojo** (m.)
direction	**dirección** (f.)	face	**cara** (f.)
dirty	**sucio**	fair	**justo**
discussion	**discusión** (f.)	family	**familia** (f.)
do, to	**hacer**	far	**lejos**
doctor	**médico** (m.);	fare	**pasaje** (f.)
	doctor (m.)	fast	**rápido**
document	**documento**	father	**padre** (m.)
	(m.)	February	**febrero** (m.)
dog	**perro** (m.)	fever	**fiebre** (f.)
dollar	**dólar** (m.)	film	**película** (f.)
door	**puerta** (f.)	find, to	**encontrar**
down, to go	**bajar**	fine	**multa** (f.)
dress	**vestido** (m.)	finish, to	**terminar**

fire (accidental)	**incendio** (m.)	have, to	**tener**
firm	**firma** (f.);	he	**él**
	empresa (f.)	head	**cabeza** (f.)
first	**primer/o**	health	**salud** (f.)
fish	**pescado** (m.)	hear, to	**oír**
flight	**vuelo** (m.)	hearing, inner ear	**oído** (m.)
food	**alimento** (m.)	heart	**corazón** (m.)
foot	**pie** (m.)	heat	**calor** (m.)
for	**para; por**	heating	**calefacción** (f.)
foreign, foreigner	**extranjero** (m.)	height (of a	**estatura** (f.)
forget, to	**olvidar**	person)	
form	**formulario** (m.)	hello (answering	**aló** (Sp. **dígame**)
free	**libre**	the phone)	
Friday	**viernes** (m.)	hello	**hola**
from	**desde; de**	help, to	**ayudar**
fruit	**fruta** (f.)	here	**acá, aquí**
fuel	**combustible** (m.)	high	**alto**
functional	**funcional**	holidays	**vacaciones**
gentleman	**señor**		**(f. pl.)**
gentlemen (sign	**caballeros**	home	**casa** (f.)
on toilets)	**(m. pl.)**	hope, to	**esperar**
get up, to	**levantarse**	hospital	**hospital** (m.)
girl	**chica** (f.); **niña**	hot	**caliente**
	(f.)	hotel	**hotel** (f.)
give, to	**dar; entregar**	hour	**hora** (f.)
go, to	**ir**	house	**casa** (f.)
go up, to	**subir**	how	**cómo**
good afternoon	**buenas tardes**	how many	**cuántos, cuántas**
good evening,	**buenas noches**	how much	**cuánto, cuánta**
good night		hunger	**hambre** (f.)
good morning	**buenos días**	hungry, to be	**tener hambre**
goodbye (inf.)	**chao, chau**	husband	**esposo** (m.);
granddaughter	**nieta** (f.)		**marido** (f.)
grandson	**nieto** (m.)	I	**yo**
green	**verde**	identification	**identificación** (f.)
hair	**pelo** (m.)	if	**si**
ham	**jamón** (m.)	ill	**enfermo**
hand	**mano** (f.)	import, to	**importar**
handbag	**cartera** (f.)	important	**importante**
handicraft	**artesanía** (f.)	in	**en**
handkerchief	**pañuelo** (m.)	in front of	**delante de**
happy	**contento**	in order to	**para**

industry	**industria** (f.)	light	**luz** (f.)
influenza	**gripe** (f.)	light, to	**encender**
information	**información** (f.)	like, to	**gustar**
innocent	**inocente**	listen, to	**escuchar**
insurance	**seguro** (m.)	little	**pequeño**
interesting	**interesante**	little by little	**poco a poco**
international	**internacional**	live, to	**vivir**
invest, to	**invertir**	London	**Londres** (m.)
investigation	**investigación** (f.)	long	**largo**
investment	**inversión** (f.)	look, to	**mirar**
invoice	**factura** (f.)	lorry	**camión** (m.)
Ireland	**Irlanda** (f.)	luggage	**equipaje** (m.)
Irish	**irlandés**	lunch, to have	**almorzar**
it's cold/windy/	**hace frío/viento/**	make, to	**hacer**
hot, etc.	**calor, etc.**	man	**hombre** (m.)
January	**enero** (m.)	man-made	**artificial**
July	**julio** (m.)	many	**muchos**
June	**junio** (m.)	map	**mapa** (m.)
just	**justo**	March	**marzo** (m.)
key	**llave** (f.)	market	**mercado** (m.)
kilo	**kilo** (m.)	married	**casado**
kilometer	**kilómetro** (m.)	mass (religion)	**misa** (f.)
kitchen	**cocina** (f.)	material	**material** (m.)
ladder	**escalera** (f.)	matter	**asunto** (m.)
ladies (sign on	**damas** (f. pl.)	matter, it doesn't	**no importa**
toilets)		meal	**comida** (f.)
language	**idioma** (m.)	meat	**carne** (f.)
large	**grande**	medium	**mediano**
last night	**anoche**	meeting	**reunión** (f.)
late	**tarde**	menu	**menú** (m.)
later	**luego**	meter	**metro** (m.)
Latin America	**Latinoamérica**	midday	**mediodía** (m.)
	(f.)	midnight	**medianoche**
Latin American	**latinoamericano**		(f.)
leaflet	**folleto** (m.)	milk	**leche** (f.)
learn, to	**aprender**	million	**millón** (m.)
left	**izquierda**	minute	**minuto** (m.)
leg	**pierna** (f.)	miss	**señorita**
less	**menos**	mistake	**error** (m.)
lesson, class	**clase** (f.)	Miss	**Srta**
letter	**carta** (f.)	moment	**momento** (m.)
lift	**ascensor** (m.)	Monday	**lunes** (m.)

money	**dinero** (m.); **plata** (f.) (Sp. **dinero**)	now	**ahora**
		number	**número** (m.)
		nurse	**enfermera** (f.)
month	**mes** (m.)	occasion	**vez** (f.), **ocasión** (f.)
more	**más**		
morning	**mañana** (f.)	occupation	**ocupación** (f.)
mother	**madre** (f.)	October	**octubre** (m.)
motorbike	**motocicleta** (f.)	of	**de**
mountain	**montaña** (f.)	office	**oficina** (f.)
mustache	**bigote** (m.)	on	**en**
movies	**cine**	one	**un, uno, una**
Mr	**Sr**	only	**sólo, solamente**
Mrs	**Sra**	opposite	**enfrente de**
much	**mucho**	or	**o**
museum	**museo** (m.)	orange	**naranja** (f.)
music	**música** (f.)	other	**otro**
my	**mi, mis**	over	**encima**
name	**nombre** (m.)	pain	**dolor** (m.)
navy blue	**azul marino**	pants	**pantalón** (m.) **pantalones** (m. pl.)
near	**cerca**		
necessary	**necesario**		
neither (conj.)	**tampoco**	paper	**papel** (m.)
never	**nunca**	paperwork	**trámite** (m.)
new	**nuevo**	parcel	**paquete** (m.)
news item	**noticia** (f.)	parents	**padres** (m.)
newspaper	**periódico** (m.)	park, to	**estacionar**
next	**próximo**	passenger	**pasajero** (m.)
next to	**junto a; al lado de**	passport	**pasaporte** (m.)
		pasty	**empanada** (f.)
nice	**bonito**	pay, to	**pagar**
no	**no**	pencil	**lápiz** (m.)
no one	**ninguno**	people	**gente** (f.)
no, not	**no**	people (of a nation)	**pueblo** (m.)
nobody	**nadie**		
noise	**ruido** (m.)	person	**persona** (f.)
non-smoker	**no fumador** (m.)	person in charge	**encargado** (m.)
normal	**normal**	petrol	**gasolina** (f.)
normally	**normalmente**	place	**lugar** (m.)
north	**norte**	place, to	**colocar**
North American, American	**norteamericano**	please	**por favor**
		pleased to meet you	**encantado**
November	**noviembre** (m.)		

police, policeman, policewoman	**policía** (f., m., f.)		**apresurado**)
		sad	**triste**
police station	**comisaría** (f.)	salad	**ensalada** (f.)
poor (in money)	**pobre;**	Saturday	**sábado** (m.)
poor (in quality)	**malo**	say, to	**decir**
possible	**posible**	school	**colegio** (m.)
post office	**correo** (m.)	sea	**mar** (m.)
postcard	**postal** (f.)	season	**estación** (f.)
potato	**papa** (f.) (Sp. **patata**)	seat	**asiento** (m.)
		second	**segundo**
poverty	**pobreza** (f.)	see, to	**ver**
prefer, to	**preferir**	see you later	**hasta luego**
price	**precio** (m.)	sell, to	**vender**
probable	**probable**	send, to	**mandar**
problem	**problema** (m.)	September	**setiembre,**
product	**producto** (m.)		**septiembre** (m.)
purse	**cartera** (f.)	seventh	**sétimo, séptimo**
put, to	**poner**	she	**ella**
question	**pregunta** (f.)	shirt	**camisa** (f.)
quiet	**tranquilo**	shoe	**zapato** (m.)
rain	**lluvia** (f.)	short (length)	**corto**
read, to	**leer**	short (height)	**bajo**
red tape	**trámite** (m.)	shoulder	**hombro** (m.)
refreshing drink	**refresco** (m.)	shuttle service	**puente aéreo**
relieve, to	**aliviar**		(m.)
repair, to	**reparar**	side	**lado** (m.)
repeat, to	**repetir**	sign, to	**firmar**
reply	**respuesta** (f.)	signature	**firma** (f.)
reply, to	**responder**	silver	**plata** (f.)
report	**informe** (m.)	since (as)	**como**
research	**investigación** (f.)	since (time)	**desde**
reservation	**reservación** (f.)	single (trip, journey)	**ida** (f.)
reserve	**reservar**		
restaurant	**restaurante** (m.)	sister	**hermana** (f.)
return (trip, journey)	**ida y vuelta** (f.)	size	**tamaño** (m.)
		size (clothes)	**talla** (fm.)
return, to	**volver**	skin	**piel** (f.)
right	**derecha; verdad** (f.)	skirt	**falda** (f.)
		sleep, to	**dormir**
robbery	**robo** (m.)	slow	**lento**
room	**habitación** (f.)	slowly	**despacio**
rushed	**apurado** (Sp.	small	**pequeño; chico**

so, thus	**así**	sweater	**suéter** (m.)
soap	**jabón** (m.)	swim, to	**nadar**
sock	**media** (f.)	swimming pool	**natatorio** (m.);
some	**alguien**		**piscina** (f.)
somebody	**alguien**	T-shirt	**camiseta** (f.)
someone	**alguno**	table	**mesa** (f.)
something	**algo**	take, to	**tomar**
son	**hijo** (m.)	tall	**alto**
soon	**pronto**	tax	**impuesto** (m.)
sorry!	**¡perdón!; lo**	tea	**té** (m.)
	siento	teacher	**profesor** (m.)
sort	**tipo** (m.)	telegram	**telegrama** (m.)
south	**sur** (m.)	telephone	**teléfono** (m.)
Spanish	**castellano**	television	**televisión** (f.)
(language)	(Sp. **español**)	temperature	**temperatura** (f.)
speak, to	**hablar**	than	**que**
spend, to	**gastar**	thanks, thank	**gracias**
(money)		you	
spring (season)	**primavera** (f.)	that (m.)	**aquel, ese**
square	**plaza** (f.)	that (f.)	**aquella, esa**
stairs	**escalera** (f.)	that one (m.)	**aquél, ése**
start, to	**comenzar;**	that one (f.)	**aquella, ésa**
	empezar	the	**el** (m. sing.), **la**
station	**estación** (f.)		(f. sing.), **las**
stay	**estadía** (f.)		(f. pl.), **los**
	(Sp. **estancia**)		(m. pl.)
stocking	**media** (f.)	then	**entonces**
stomach	**estómago** (m.)	then (later)	**luego**
stop, to	**parar**	there	**allá; ahí; allí**
street	**calle** (f.)	there is/are	**hay**
strong	**fuerte**	these (m.)	**estos**
student	**estudiante**	these ones (m.)	**éstos**
	(m., f.)	they	**ellos** (m.), **ellas**
study, to	**estudiar**		(f.)
subway	**metro**	thing	**cosa** (f.)
sugar	**azúcar** (m.)	thirst	**sed** (f.)
suitcase	**maleta** (f.)	thirsty, to be	**tener sed**
summer	**verano** (m.)	this (m.)	**este**
Sunday	**domingo** (m.)	this one (m.)	**éste**
supermarket	**supermercado**	those (m.)	**aquel, ese**
	(m.)	those (f.)	**aquellas, esas**
surname	**apellido** (m.)	those ones (m.)	**aquellos, ésos**

those ones (f.)	**aquellas, ésas**	until	**hasta**
thousand	**mil**	urgent	**urgente**
throat	**garganta** (f.)	vegetable	**verdura** (f.)
Thursday	**jueves** (m.)	very	**muy**
ticket	**boleto** (m.)	vest	**camiseta** (f.)
tie	**corbata** (f.)	village	**pueblo** (m.)
time	**tiempo** (m.)	visit, to	**visitar**
time (occasion)	**vez** (f.)	wait, to	**esperar**
tired	**cansado**	Wales	**Gales** (m.)
to	**para**	walk, to	**caminar; andar**
tobacco	**tabaco** (m.)	walk, to go for a	**pasear**
today	**hoy**	wallet	**billetera** (f.);
toilet	**baño** (m.) (Sp.		**cartera** (f.)
	servico, aseo)	want, to	**querer**
tomorrow	**mañana** (m.)	warm	**templado**
tongue	**lengua** (f.)	warn, to	**avisar**
too much/many;	**demasiado**	wash, to	**lavar**
too		watch	**reloj** (m.)
tooth	**muela** (f.)	watch, to	**ver**
tourist	**turista** (m., f.)	water	**agua** (f.)
town	**pueblo** (m.)	we	**nosotros**
train	**tren** (m.)	weather	**tiempo** (m.)
traveler's check	**cheque de**	weather forecast	**pronóstico del**
	viaje/viajero		**tiempo** (m.)
	(m.)	Wednesday	**miércoles** (m.)
trip	**viaje** (m.)	week	**semana** (f.)
trousers	**pantalón** (m.),	weekend	**fin de semana**
	pantalones		(m.)
	(m. pl.)	welcome	**bienvenido**
truth	**verdad** (f.)	well	**bien**
Tuesday	**martes** (m.)	Welsh	**galés**
turn off, to	**apagar**	west	**oeste** (m.)
turn on, to	**encender**	what?	**¿qué?**
type	**tipo** (m.)	what's happen-	**¿qué pasa?**
uncomfortable	**incómodo**	ing?, what's	
underground	**metro** (m.)	the matter?	
underneath	**debajo**	when?; when	**¿cuándo?;**
understand, to	**comprender**		**cuando**
United States	**Estados Unidos**	where?; where	**¿dónde?; donde**
(m. pl.)		which?; which	**¿cuál?; cuál**
(North)	**estadounidense**	whichever	**cualquiera**
American		white	**blanco**

who?; who	**¿quién?; quien**	write, to	**escribir**
whole	**todo**	year	**año** (m.)
wife	**esposa** (f.);	yellow	**amarillo**
	mujer (f.)	yes	**sí**
wind	**viento** (m.)	yesterday	**ayer**
window (at a bank)	**ventanilla** (f.)	you	**tú** (inf.), **usted** (for.), **ustedes** (for. and inf. pl.) (Sp. **vosotros** = inf.)
wine	**vino** (m.)		
winter	**invierno** (m.)		
with	**con**		
with me	**conmigo**	young	**joven**
with you	**contigo**	young lady	**señorita** (f.)
without	**sin**	your	**tu, tus** (inf.): **su** (for.)
woman	**mujer** (f.)		
wool	**lana** (f.)	you're welcome (in response to **gracias**)	**de nada**
word	**palabra** (f.)		
work, to	**trabajar**		
worth, to be	**valer**	zone	**zona** (f.)

Index of language points

The numbers refer to the lessons in the book.